DATE DUE

DEMCO 38-296

Gender and Development
in the Arab World

Gender and Development in the Arab World

Women's Economic Participation: Patterns and Policies

EDITED BY NABIL F. KHOURY
AND VALENTINE M. MOGHADAM

Published for the United Nations University
World Institute for Development Economics Research
(UNU/WIDER)

by

ZED BOOKS Ltd
London & New Jersey

and

UNITED NATIONS UNIVERSITY PRESS
Tokyo

*Gender and Development in the Arab World – Women's Economic Participation:
Patterns and Policies* was first published for the United Nations University
World Institute for Development Economics Research (UNU/WIDER),
Katajanokanlaituri 6B FIN-00160 Helsinki, Finland, by
Zed Books Ltd, 7 Cynthia Street, London N1 9JF, UK, and
165 First Avenue, Atlantic Highlands, New Jersey 07716, USA
and in Japan, China and Southeast Asia by the United Nations University Press,
53–70 Jingumae 5-chome, Shibuya-ku, Tokyo 150, Japan, in 1995.

Cover designed by Andrew Corbett
Typeset in Monotype Garamond by Lucy Morton, London SE12
Printed and bound in the United Kingdom
by Biddles Ltd, Guildford and King's Lynn

A catalogue record for this book is available from the British Library
US CIP data is available from the Library of Congress

ISBN 1 85649 365 2 Hb
ISBN 1 85649 366 0 Pb
UN ISBN 92 808 0915 6

About UNU/WIDER

The World Institute for Development Economics Research (UNU/WIDER)
was established by the United Nations University as its first research and
training centre, and started work in Helsinki, Finland, in 1985. The principal
purpose of the Institute is policy-oriented research on the main strategic issues of
development and international cooperation, as well as on the interaction between
domestic and global changes.

This volume was prepared with the assistance of the United Nations University
World Institute for Development Economics Research, and the Labour and
Population Team for the Middle East and Mediterranean Region of the
International Labour Organization.

Contents

List of Tables and Figures

Preface

Over the past decade considerable attention has been directed towards the questions related to the role and status of women. It is now widely recognized that social, political and economic changes have differential effects on men and women and that a conscious effort should be made to improve the role of women and their participation in the development process.

There is now a growing literature on the multiple dimensions of Arab women's issues in the context of human development which attempts to throw light on the legal, cultural, social and economic aspects. The primary focus of the present volume is on women and their share in employment and their contribution to national economic development. It documents the patterns and trends of female employment and highlights the determinants of labour-force participation in a number of countries.

Attention is drawn to systematic and cultural bias in underestimating women's real contribution to national product and family welfare. Various factors such as educational opportunities and attainments, prevalent social norms, and discriminating practices which limit the scope of women's employment and underlie the gap between the potential and the present performance are highlighted and analysed. This leads up to consideration of policy implications for improving Arab women's lot, especially in the world of work.

The volume includes an introduction, an analysis of the political economy of female employment, and an investigation into the real issue of women as mobilizers of human resources in the Arab World. The remaining part of the book deals with specific country case studies which cover a cross section of different profiles of socio-economic development and cultural values. The volume concludes with a statistical review of recent human development indicators for the Arab World.

The main conclusion to be drawn from the book is that Arab women are considered the unutilized human reserve which is capable of contributing towards the process of growth and development. It is therefore essential that this reserve be tapped to enhance women's contribution to national development and ensure the promotion and equality of opportunity and treatment for women in employment and their participation in decision-making at all levels.

Nabil F. Khoury
Valentine M. Moghadam

1

Introduction and Overview

Valentine M. Moghadam
and Nabil F. Khoury

Nearly a decade has passed since the publication of *Women, Employment, and Development in the Arab World* (Abu Nasr, Khoury and Azzam 1985), a study in which one of us was involved and through which one of us was inspired. The contributions in that book helped to fill the enormous gap that existed in the knowledge of women's economic roles in Arab countries, including barriers to women's integration into the development process. Since then, many important studies have been carried out, including *Modernizing Women: Gender and Social Change in the Middle East* (Moghadam 1993) which dealt with women's varied responses to, and involvement in, socio-political change, and *Education and Employment Issues of Women in Development in the Middle East* (Khoury and Doctor 1991) which analysed the patterns and trends in women's education and labour-force participation and identified possible measures to accelerate women's participation in the development process. However, there remains a relative paucity of research on gender and development issues, especially when compared with the state-of-the-art work in Latin America and the Caribbean, and in South and Southeast Asia. At the same time, conservative attitudes with respect to gender roles continue to hold sway in much of the region, and in some areas have resurfaced. The combination of a relative paucity of research and the persistence of conservative attitudes creates a situation in which policy-makers are unable to recognize or unwilling to acknowledge the positive relationship between women's socio-economic integration and overall development in the Arab world.

As a recent UN document states in its regional survey of changes in women's positions from 1970 to 1990: 'In northern Africa and western

Asia, women made gains in health and education. Fertility declined
slightly but remains very high – 5.5 children in northern Africa and 5.3
in western Asia. Women in these regions continue to lag far behind in
their economic participation and in social participation and decision-
making' (UN 1991: 1). It is unfortunate but true that, given the national
income levels of Arab countries (most are lower-middle income or upper-
middle income), women remain an under-endowed and under-utilized
human resource, and in many Arab countries the gaps between men
and women are unjustifiably large. As a result, in many parts of the
Arab world, the range of choices and life-options available to women is
limited, and there are many impediments to the full human development of women (see Tables A4, A5, A6 and A8 in the Appendix).

This has profound implications for the social and economic development of the Arab world. Educating girls and women has multiplier
effects. The World Fertility Survey of 1978–82 showed the causal
connection between women's increased education and lower fertility, the
links between a mother's education and a child's health, and the relationship between the rise in the age of first marriage and the expansion of
education (see International Statistical Institute 1984; Cleland and Scott
1987). Labour-force participation and involvement in gainful employment is not only an *effect* of economic development but a *contribution* to
it. Blumberg's work has gone the farthest in showing the positive effects
that women's educational attainment and economic participation have
had on 'the wealth of nations' (Blumberg 1989; see also contributions in
Blumberg et al. 1995). According to Tuma (1990), discriminatory and
exclusionary policies such as less education and training, restricted
specialization, lower participation in the labour force, lower capital
endowment, less access to land, restricted inheritance, and limited credit
facilities lead not only to lower private benefits for women and households but also to lower total output. Thus the under-endowment and
under-utilization of women is both discriminatory and economically
unsound.

Twenty-five years after the launching of the field of women in
development (WID), there is increasing consensus among theorists and
practitioners alike that gender is a 'key variable in the development
equation' (Blumberg 1989), is related to issues of *efficiency* as well as
equity (Palmer 1991), and must be taken into account at all levels of
programme formulation and policy-making (see, for example, Benería
and Feldman 1992; Blumberg et al., 1994; Commonwealth Secretariat
1989; Elson 1991; ESCAP 1992; Joekes 1989; Moghadam 1990). As a

result of these advances in our thinking about women in development, a number of European donor agencies now emphasize the gender dimension in their lending policies. There is also consensus around the need to improve statistics and to disaggregate statistics by gender. UN departments such as the UN Statistical Office, the Division for the Advancement of Women, and INSTRAW (the United Nations Research and Training Centre for the Advancement of Women), as well as research departments within the UNDP and ILO, have been taking the lead in improving measurement techniques so as to capture more fully the extent and types of economic activities performed by women, as well as to illustrate the most persistent gender inequalities that need to be addressed in social and economic policy (see, for example, UNDP 1993; UN 1990; INSTRAW 1993; UN 1988; INSTRAW 1990). As Reinharz has argued (in Young, Fort and Danner 1994: 61), quantitative research, vital to informing policy and programmes aimed at large groups, can help to identify differences among groups and show how a problem is distributed. This kind of research is most effective when based on gender-disaggregated statistics and grounded in sound theory.

Researchers of the Arab world face a number of interrelated challenges. One is to dispel widespread stereotypes regarding the position of Arab-Islamic women, and to draw attention to various structural features of the region that may explain women's labour-force participation rates and patterns. Quantitative research on micro-level determinants would also help to increase our knowledge of what the attitudes are and how decisions are made at the household or individual level. Another challenge is to improve the state of empirical research on women's economic participation, including the quality of measurement techniques and reliability of statistics and social indicators pertaining to women and work. In particular, labour-market researchers need to be encouraged and trained to carry out gender-specific analysis, with a view towards providing policy-makers with a more accurate representation of human resources and employment issues and problems. Yet another challenge is to make a strong case for the proper utilization of human resources, including and especially women, by showing the connection between investing in women and improving the welfare of children, households and communities. The ideas and goals of human development should be extended to women for reasons of gender equity and of societal development. What should be put to rest is the notion that enhancing women's positions is a zero-sum game.

The various contributions in this book take on these challenges. In

Chapter 2, Moghadam seeks to explain the relatively low levels of female employment in terms of macrostructural characteristics, including the depth, scope and type of industrialization that has so far obtained in the region. In Chapter 3, Zurayk and Saadeh argue that women are a crucial dimension of the human resource base in Arab countries, playing an especially important mobilizing role. In Chapter 4, Galal describes and explains variations in women and socio-economic development in the Maghreb, with a view toward improving policy options. In Chapter 5, Lackner draws attention to specificities of women and development in Yemen, with some comparisons of pre-unification North Yemen and South Yemen, where state policy and regime orientation made a difference to women's options. In Chapter 6, Boustani and Mufarrej examine the links between higher educational attainment of women and labour-force participation, focusing on Lebanon. In Chapter 7, Shakhatreh examines the determinants of female labour-force participation in Jordan, and finds that education has the strongest influence, leading him to make a number of important policy recommendations. In Chapter 8, Anker and Anker report on a method of improving data-collection on labour-force activity, which was applied to Egypt.

It is perhaps fitting that the publication of this book should coincide with the United Nations Conference on Population and Development (Cairo, September 1994), the World Summit for Social Development (Copenhagen, March 1995) and the Fourth World Conference on Women (Beijing, September 1995). Human resource development, productive employment, and gender equality are themes and goals that are as relevant to the Arab world as they are to any region of the world.

References

Abu Nasr, Julinda, Nabil F. Khoury, and Henry T. Azzam, eds. 1985. *Women, Employment, and Development in the Arab World*. Berlin, New York, Amsterdam: Mouton Publishers.

Benería, Lourdes, and Shelley Feldman, eds. 1992. *Unequal Burden: Economic Crises, Persistent Poverty, and Women's Work*. Boulder, CO: Westview Press.

Blumberg, Rae Lesser. 1989. 'Making a Case for the Gender Variable'. Washington DC: Women-in-Development Office of the U.S. Agency for International Development.

Blumberg, Rae Lesser, Cathy Rakowski, Irene Tinker and Michael Monteon, eds. 1995. *Engendering Wealth and Well-being*. Boulder, CO: Westview Press.

Cleland, John, and Chris Scott, eds. 1987. *The World Fertility Survey: An Assessment*. New York: International Statistical Institute and Oxford University Press.

Commonwealth Secretariat. 1989. *Engendering Adjustment for the 1990s*. London:

Commonwealth Secretariat.

Elson, Diane, ed. 1991. *Male Bias in the Development Process.* London: Macmillan.

ESCAP (UN Economic and Social Commission for Asia and the Pacific). 1992. *Integration of Women's Concerns into Development Planning in Asia and the Pacific.* New York: United Nations.

INSTRAW. 1990. *Methods of Collecting and Analyzing Statistics on Women in the Informal Sector and their Contribution to National Product* (Report on the Regional Workshop in Zambia). Santo Domingo: INSTRAW.

——— 1993. *Gender Training Portfolio.* Santo Domingo: INSTRAW.

International Statistical Institute. 1984. *The World Fertility Survey: Major Findings and Implications.* Voorburg, Netherlands: International Statistical Institute.

Joekes, Susan. 1989. 'Gender and Macroeconomic Policy'. Washington DC: Association for Women and Development, Occasional paper no. 4 (September).

Khoury, Nabil F., and Kailas C. Doctor, eds. 1991. *Education and Employment Issues of Women in Development in the Middle East.* Nicosia: Imprinta Publishers.

Moghadam, Valentine M. 1990. 'Gender, Development, and Policy: Toward Equity and Empowerment. WIDER Research for Action Series (November).

——— 1993. *Modernizing Women: Gender and Social Change in the Middle East.* Boulder, CO: Lynne Rienner Publishers.

Palmer, Ingrid. 1991. *Gender and Population in the Adjustment of African Economies: Planning for Change.* Geneva: International Labour Office.

UNDP (United Nations Development Programme). 1993. *Human Development Report 1993.* New York: Oxford University Press.

UN (United Nations). 1988. *Improving Statistics and Indicators on Women Using Households Surveys.* New York: United Nations.

——— 1990. *Methods of Measuring Women's Participation and Production in the Informal Sector.* New York: United Nations.

——— 1991. *The World's Women: Trends and Statistics 1970–1990.* New York: United Nations.

Young, Gay, Lucia Fort and Mona Danner. 1994. 'Moving from "The Status of Women" to "Gender Inequality": Conceptualisation, Social Indicators and an Empirical Application'. *International Sociology*, vol. 9, no. 1 (March), pp. 55–86.

2

The Political Economy of Female Employment in the Arab Region

Valentine M. Moghadam

Labour-force structure is an important indicator of national development patterns, social-production relations, and a country's position in the world economy. Many studies within the development literature show that the structure of the labour force and the pattern of industrialization are linked. Within the field of women in development, studies of female labour-force participation have described gender-based inequalities within national labour markets, or have made the case that women's work in its broadest sense deserves recognition as an important contribution to national development. The Arab region has not figured prominently in either of the two sets of literature. This chapter seeks to fill that gap by analysing patterns of female employment in the Middle East and North Africa in terms of national development strategies within the region and in terms of the region's location within the world-system.

Industrialization, Employment and Gender

Cross-national and comparative studies within the sociology of development, particularly within the dependency and world-systems perspectives, have frequently examined the effects of the world economy on labour-force structure in developing countries. Fiala (1992) identifies three development patterns within this literature. The first, that of *classic primary export dependence*, hinders development of a well-balanced domestic economy by failing to establish substantial links to the production of manufactured goods and capital equipment. This would hinder industrial expansion, concentrate economic activity in a few areas, and restrict expansion of secondary employment. A second pattern has been identified as *dependent development*, characterized by state collaboration with multinational capital and sections of the domestic bourgeoisie in an effort to increase economic growth (Evans 1979). Dependent development allows for greater industrialization and economic output partly through import-substitution industrialization (ISI), where machinery is imported to run local industries producing consumer goods. However, its capital-intensive nature leaves out broad segments of the population and is accompanied by substantial inequality. In a third pattern of development characteristic of the East Asian economies, *export-led industrialization*, labour-intensive techniques increase secondary employment (Deyo 1987; Gereffi and Wyman 1990).

The identification of distinct development strategies and their impact on the employment structure is crucial to our analysis of female employment in the Middle East. However, and as mentioned above, the literature does not examine the gender dimension of these development patterns. It has been within the field of women in development that increasingly sophisticated analyses of the relationship between paths of industrialization and women's employment – or the gender-specific effects of development strategies – are being conducted.

The field of women in development (WID) was launched with the publication in 1970 of the landmark study by the Danish economist Ester Boserup, *Women's Role in Economic Development*, in which she argued that the process of economic development marginalized women producers. Since then, debates have raged over the impact of industrialization on women's work and lives. Analyses have tended to be sharply critical of the spread of manufacturing, arguing at different points that women were being marginalized from the production process or were being super-exploited within world market factories or export-processing zones. During the 1970s and 1980s, many studies argued that the new or changing international division of labour was predicated upon the globalization of production and the search for cheap labour, and that the growth of female labour, especially in textiles and electronics, was the latest strategy of international capital. A major debate revolved around whether this new utilization of female labour reduced or improved women's economic status. Most of the case studies in the literature came from Latin America, especially Mexico, and from Southeast Asia, particularly South Korea and Malaysia (Elson and Pearson 1980; Ward 1984; Heyzer 1986; Sen and Grown 1987).[1]

A recent review by Ruth Pearson (1992) of the debates and the evidence on industrialization and women is useful for our analysis of women's employment in the Middle East. She describes and critically assesses what she calls 'the first consensus', which maintained that women were marginalized from industrial development. This consensus arose from focusing on early experiences of import substitution, especially in Latin America, which were associated with capital-intensive production and male employment generation. The 'second consensus' suggested that industrialization was based on the increasing employment of women. This view focused on the export-oriented industrialization since the 1970s which has used labour-intensive techniques, particularly in textiles, garments and electronics production, and where women have formed the majority of the labour force. Pearson argues that neither consensus has an adequate explanation of the relationship between industrialization and women's employment. Women are excluded at certain points and targeted at others, she argues, because industrialization is a *dynamic* rather than linear or uniform process. Similarly, the nature of the labour force itself is shaped by different skill requirements, production technologies, specialization, and social and political contexts. Both the industrialization process and the labour market include informal as well as formal sectors, homeworking and permanent waged employment. Pearson's essay is an eloquent and persuasive argument for a gender-based analysis of industrialization. What is only implicit in her essay, however, is that the diversity of the industrialization process around the world and the different modes of incorporation of female labour is a world-systemic feature. I will return to this presently.

The Middle East has not figured prominently in the development literature.[2] It is even more conspicuously absent from the WID literature, partly because of the difficulty of obtaining data, and partly because of a common view that in the Arab world cultural and religious factors influence women's lives more than do economic factors. In a recent essay, Ester Boserup states that when development is rapid, it is inevitable that these changes create tensions between sexes and generations and that pressure groups appear that seek to preserve or reintroduce the traditional, hierarchical cultural pattern. She cites the 'oil rich countries in the Arab world, which have attempted to preserve the family system of domesticated and secluded women by mass importation of foreign male labour, and in which mass movements of Muslim revival pursue the same aim.' (Boserup 1990: 24). A UN survey on women's employment concluded that 'the level of women's work [is] consistently low in countries with a predominantly Muslim population, such as Bangladesh, Egypt, Jordan, Pakistan, and the Syrian Arab Republic,

Table 2.1   Employment profile, cross-regional comparison, 1990–92

	Sub-Saharan Africa	Middle East and North Africa	South Asia	East and South-east Asia	Latin America and the Caribbean
Labour force	39	28	38	54	41
Women in labour force	37	19	28	42	34

Source: UNDP, *Human Development Report 1994* (New York: Oxford University Press, 1994), p. 210, Table 51.

where cultural restrictions that discourage women from doing most types of work are common' (cited in Blumberg 1989: 91). Note that only 'culture' is provided as an explanation.[3]

Cross-regional aggregate data on labour-force size and structure do show a smaller measured labour force and female labour force for the Middle East (see Table 2.1). The average female share of the labour force was 19 in 1992 in the Middle East and North Africa, much lower than in other regions. How is this to be explained? As an alternative approach to the study of female employment and as an explanation for the patterns of female employment that obtain, I would like to make the following propositions:

1. There is variation in female employment and occupational patterns across countries in the Middle East; some of these patterns are consistent with global patterns of female employment.

2. Women's employment patterns are largely shaped by the political economy of the region, and women's industrial employment in particular has been constrained by overall limited industrialization.

3. A useful framework for examining and explaining patterns of female employment rests on the concepts of gender, class, state policy, development strategy, and the world-system.

In the section below, I shall address my third point first, to clarify and elaborate the concepts. In subsequent sections I will demonstrate the variability of women's labour force participation, especially in industrial employment, in terms of the region's development strategies.

A Framework for Analysis

Gender

The concept of gender is analogous to class in that it refers to a structural relationship of inequality. With respect to class, that relationship derives from differential control over the means of production, and is expressed in the capital–labour contention; with respect to gender, that relationship derives from women's childbearing function and is expressed in the sexual division of labour. As Papanek (1990: 163) puts it, 'Gender differences, based on the social construction of biological sex distinctions, are one of the great "fault lines" of societies – those marks of difference among categories of persons that govern the allocation of power, authority, and resources.'

Gender asymmetry is universal, but the degree of inequality and the forms that gender take over time and space are intimately interconnected with political and economic factors, including social structure and the nature of the state. That is to say, gender relations are differently constructed in kinship-ordered, agrarian, developing, and advanced industrialized settings. Type of political regime and state ideology has a further influence on the gender system. States that are Marxist (for example, the former German Democratic Republic), theocratic (Saudi Arabia), conservative democratic (the USA), or social democratic (the Nordic countries) have quite different laws about women and policies on the family.[4] Contemporary gender systems are often designed by ideologues and inscribed in law, justified by custom and enforced by policy. Gender hierarchies are sustained by processes of socialization and reinforced through distinct institutions, including the labour market. Research in the sociology of work and the sociology of gender has sought to explain occupational sex segregation in terms of gender inequality (Reskin 1988, 1991).

The concept of gender is more useful than 'culture' because it is easier to operationalize and is more amenable to comparisons. Throughout the world there are gender systems in which women are as a group disadvantaged. The degree of disadvantage, however, is variable.

Class

Class constitutes a basic unit of social life and thus of social research. Class is here understood in the Marxian sense as determined by ownership or control of the means of production; social classes also have differential access to political power and the state. At the level of culture and ideology, class location shapes cultural practices, patterns of consumption, lifestyle, reproduction, and even 'world-view'. Class divisions 'find expression in terms of power, income, wealth, responsibility, "life chances", style and quality of life, and everything else that makes up the texture of existence' (Miliband 1989: 25).

Gender is elaborated by class. In the highly stratified societies of the Arab world, social class location, in addition to state action and the level and pace of economic development, act upon and modify gender relations and women's social positions. Although state-sponsored education has resulted in a certain amount of social mobility and has increased the numbers of women willing and able to fill the administrative and welfare jobs in the ever-expanding state systems as well as in the private sector, women's access to resources, including education, is largely determined by their class location. When relatively few women participate in the paid, non-agricultural labour force, those who do tend to be well-educated and from urban backgrounds, a point that is relevant to the large percentages of urban employed women in many Arab countries who are in professional positions.[5]

As in other Third World countries where social disparities are great, upper- and upper-middle-class urban women can exercise a greater number of choices (certainly vis-à-vis lower-middle-class, working-class, urban poor or peasant women) and thus become much more 'emancipated'. Professional and marital roles become compatible because of the availability of cheap domestic labour and because of the extended family network. As with their role in production and work generally, class also shapes women's choices and practices in reproduction; educated middle-class and upper-class women in the professions tend to have fewer children, while peasant or poor women may require children as labour inputs or for old-age security. To put it simply, the fertility behaviour and needs of peasant, proletarian, poor and professional women differ, for reasons having to do with their relationship to the means of production and their place within the distribution nexus.

The state: state policies and state managers

In developing countries, the state plays a major role in the formulation of social policies, development strategies and legislation that shape the opportunity structure for women. Family law, affirmative action, provisions for or restrictions on working mothers, policies on education, health, population and other components of social policy designed by state managers crucially affect women's status and gender arrangements. Strong states with the capacity to enforce laws may undermine customary discrimination and patriarchal structures – or they may reinforce them. The state can act as a facilitator or an obstacle in the integration of female citizens in public life. As Jean Pyle (1990) has found for the Republic of Ireland, state policy can have contradictory goals: development of the economy and expansion of services, and the maintenance of the 'traditional family'. Such contradictory goals could create role conflicts for women, who find themselves torn between the economic need or desire to work and the gender ideology that stresses family roles for women. Conversely, economic development and state-sponsored education could have unintended consequences, such as the growth of a stratum of educated women who actively pursue employment and political participation in defiance of cultural norms or the ambivalence of state managers.

In the Arab world, state managers are torn between the imperatives of national development and the desire to preserve the traditional family unit, including the family attachment of women. Some states have had explicitly pro-natalist policies (such as Saudi Arabia and Algeria under Boumedienne), resulting in the non-availability of effective contraception, a factor which inhibits female labour-force attachment. However, and notwithstanding the ambivalence of neo-patriarchal state managers, the expansion of state-sponsored schooling and higher tertiary enrolments for women have increased women's employment capacities. The positive relationship between female education and non-agricultural employment is marked throughout the Arab world, as discussed in this volume by Shakhatreh for Jordan (Chapter 7), and Boustani and Mufarrej for Lebanon (Chapter 6). Women's education seems to increase the aspirations of women in certain sectors of society for higher income and better standards of living. In turn, women have found job opportunities in public services and in some industrial branches.

The impact of state-directed legal measures, public campaigns, educational programmes, and investment decisions on women's legal and economic status has been considerable, but what needs to be stressed is that there are variations in state policies in the region, particularly with regard to the mobilization of female labour and women's integration into the formal structure of the economy and in public life. In some cases, a regime's search for political legitimacy, a larger labour force, or an expanded social base has led it to construct health, education and welfare services conducive to greater work participation by women, and to encourage female activity in the public sphere. Examples are the Iraqi Baathists during the 1960s and 1970s, Egypt under Nasser and Sadat, Tunisia under the late President Bourguiba, and the former People's Democratic Republic of Yemen (see Lackner, Chapter 5, this volume). In other cases, state managers remain wedded to the ideology of domesticity and refrain from encouraging female participation in the paid labour force. Examples are Saudi Arabia, Algeria and Jordan.

Economic development and development strategies

The study of women's employment cannot be separated from that of economic development and specific development strategies adopted by states.

The Middle East is a major oil-producing region, and in some countries oil revenues provide the bulk of the nation's foreign-exchange and government revenue. Thus many oil economies conform to the development pattern of classic primary export dependence. There is some debate as to the macroeconomic effects of oil production and export.[6] For now, we need only note that for about ten years after the oil price increases of the early 1970s, a massive investment programme by the oil-producing countries affected the structure of the labour force not only within the relevant countries, but throughout the region, as a result of labour migration, creating a regional oil economy. During this period, most of the large Arab countries such as Egypt, Tunisia, Syria and Algeria embarked on the development strategy of ISI, which involved central planning and a large public sector. Oil revenues and ISI changed the structure of the labour force in Arab countries, leading to the expansion of non-agricultural employment. The urban areas began to see the growth of the female labour force, as women occupied paid positions in factories and offices, as workers, administrators and professionals.

WID specialists have noted that during the period of ISI in Latin America and Southeast Asia, the bulk of the workforce, particularly in capital-intensive sectors such as steel, shipbuilding and heavy industry, was male (Pearson 1992: 223). The significant rise in female employment occurred with the shift from ISI to export-led industrialization (ELI) – a pattern of industrialization that allowed Third World economies to compete in Western consumer-goods markets, and that was largely based on the availability of productive labour at cheap cost. The expansion of export-oriented, labour-intensive manufacturing industry has been located primarily in Mexico, Brazil, the East and Southeast Asian countries of Hong Kong, Singapore, Taiwan, and South Korea, and subsequently in Malaysia, Indonesia, and other parts of the Third World such as the Caribbean and Mauritius (Pearson 1992: 229–30). The most important areas of activity for foreign investors in the export manufacturing sector in developing countries has been the textiles and clothing and electronics industries. Over the years, a majority of jobs created in the export manufacturing sector has gone to women. One study stresses 'the disproportionate access that women have to export manufacturing employment and their overwhelming importance as suppliers for the export manufacturing sector' (Joekes and Moayedi 1987: 21).[7]

It is important to note that due to the predominance of the oil economy, neither export manufacturing nor female involvement in manufacturing has been significant in Arab countries, at least until recently.

The world-system

Economic development and development strategies do not operate in a vacuum; rather, they are part of a global division of labour. Worldsystem theory holds that a capitalist world-economy exists which has integrated a geographically vast set of production processes, and whose driving force is capital accumulation. The economic organization of the world-system consists of a single, worldwide division of labour across the economic zones of core, periphery and semi-periphery that unifies the multiple cultural systems of the world's people into a single, integrated economic system (Wallerstein 1979, 1989; Berquist 1984; Shannon 1989). What is currently called 'globalization' is thus an extension or intensification of a pre-existing pattern of integrated markets through trade in commodities and services, technological diffusion and labour/capital flows. Among world-system theorists there is some debate as to which countries in the contemporary world-system are part of the semi-periphery, but what is agreed is that semi-peripheral states enjoy a greater degree of independence from the core than do those of the periphery, and that the semi-periphery experienced significant industrialization after 1960. The most successful semi-peripheral countries, the East Asian NICs, have created rapidly growing, increasingly diversified industrial sectors with manufacturing for export.[8]

Semi-peripheral and peripheral Arab countries alike are part of the regional oil economy, whose function within the world-system thus far has been to guarantee a steady supply of oil for foreign, especially core-country, markets, and to import industrial goods, especially armaments, mainly from core countries. One result has been limited industrialization and manufacturing for export. Another result has been limited employment opportunities for women in the formal industrial sector, as capital-intensive industries and technologies tend to favour male labour.

In the 1980s the world-economy began to experience an economic crisis that also affected the Arab region. The global oil market became very unstable, leading to fluctuating and declining prices. The near-collapse of prices in 1986 (from $28 per barrel to $7 per barrel) had repercussions throughout the Arab region: austerity measures were introduced, availability of development aid decreased, and major development projects were re-evaluated or suspended. In the 1980s, Arab countries experienced low or negative economic growth rates, declining state revenues, and high levels of indebtedness to foreign creditors. The most indebted Arab countries – Algeria, Egypt, Jordan, Morocco, Syria, Tunisia – had to impose austerities on their populations as a result of World Bank and IMF structural adjustment policy packages, and several experienced 'IMF riots' (see Niblock 1993; Seddon 1993; El-Naggar 1989). Tough economic reforms, along with poverty, unemployment, and debt servicing – as well as political repression – have served to delegitimize 'Western-style' systems and revive questions of cultural identity, including renewed calls for greater control over female mobility. It is in this context of economic failures and political delegitimation that Islamist movements are presenting themselves as alternatives, with their attendant pressures on women.

With this framework in mind, let us examine some comparative data on the size of the labour force, including the female labour force, in various Arab countries (Table 2.2). Data on the evolution of labour-force participation, not shown here, reveal steady increases for women in all Arab countries. Activity rates are highest at the youngest years, with a tendency for women to drop out of the labour force upon childbirth or to take early retirement.

I have suggested a conceptual framework for the study of female employment which rests on the macro-level structural determinants of gender, class, the state, development strategy, and the world-system. In the section below, we will analyse the development strategies in the region, and in particular the depth and scope of industrialization, to explore their relationship to women's employment.

Table 2.2   Characteristics of the economically active population of various Arab countries, 1980s, 1990s

Country	Year	Total population	Total EAP	Male Activity Rate (%)	Female Activity Rate (%)
Algeria	1987	23,038,942	5,341,102	42.4	4.4
Bahrain	1991	508,037	226,448	63.5	18.5
Egypt	1989	52,289,700	16,033,600	42.8	18.0
Iraq	1977	12,000,477	3,133,939	41.9	9.4
	1987	16,335,199	3,956,345	–	–
Jordan	1979	2,100,019	446,316	38.0	3.3
Kuwait	1988	1,878,000	729,915	53.5	21.0
Morocco	1987	21,979,641	3,895,126	48.6	16.8
Qatar	1986	369,079	201,182	73.2	16.2
Syria	1981	9,870,800	2,356,000	42.2	4.1
	1991	12,529,000	485,368	44.6	10.2
Tunisia	1989	7,909,500	2,360,600	46.5	12.7
UAE	1980	1,042,099	559,960	73.9	8.8

Note: For comparative purposes, it may be useful to note that in Mexico and Venezuela, both oil-producing Latin American countries, female activity rates were 13.6 per cent and 21.0 per cent, respectively, in 1990.

Sources: ILO, *Yearbook of Labour Statistics 1993*, Table 1; ILO, *Retrospective Edition on Population Censuses 1945–89*, Table 1; On Algeria: *Recensement Général de la Population et de l'Habitat 1987*; Donnés Sythétiques, Algeria, 1989.

The Political Economy of the Arab Region

In the political-economy literature of Middle East studies, I have come across three complementary typologies of the region. In their study of labour, Birks, Seccombe and Sinclair (1988) divide the Arab countries into capital-rich and capital-poor, and point out that economic activity rates are higher in the capital-poor countries (Egypt, Jordan, Lebanon, Morocco, Sudan, Syria, Tunisia, Yemen) than in the capital-rich countries (Algeria, Bahrain, Iraq, Kuwait, Libya, Oman, Qatar, Saudi Arabia, UAE). A second classification is provided by Mabro (1988), in the context of a discussion of industrialization in the Middle East (Arab and non-Arab):

A. Oil economies poor in other resources, including very small populations (United Arab Emirates [UAE], Saudi Arabia, Oman, Qatar, Kuwait, Libya);

B. Mixed oil economies (Algeria, Tunisia, Syria, Iraq, Iran, Egypt);

C. Non-oil economies (Israel, Turkey, Jordan, Morocco, Sudan, the Yemens).

In their analysis of the development prospects of Middle Eastern countries, Richards and Waterbury (1990) offer a third taxonomy (of Arab and non-Arab economies):

1. 'The Coupon Clippers': Libya, Kuwait, Oman, UAE, Bahrain, Qatar. These states have much oil, and little of anything else, including people. They have been, and will continue to be, almost entirely dependent upon oil and any money earned from overseas investments.

2. 'The Oil Industrializers': Iraq, Iran, Algeria, and Saudi Arabia. The first three states share the main features of the large oil exports, a substantial population, other natural resources, and a chance to create industrial and agricultural sectors that will be sustainable over the long run. Saudi Arabia lacks the other resources of the first three countries.

3. 'The Watchmakers': Israel, Jordan, Tunisia, and Syria. These four small countries have limited natural resources and must therefore concentrate on investing in human capital and on exporting skill-intensive manufactures. Manufactured goods now account for 84 per cent of Israeli, 52 per cent of Jordanian, and 42 per cent of Tunisian exports.

4. 'The NICS': Turkey, Egypt and Morocco. These countries have relatively large populations, relatively good agricultural land or potential, and a long experience with industrial production.

5. 'The Agro-Poor': Sudan and the Yemens. These are the poorest countries of the region and ones where the agricultural-development-led industrialization growth strategy seems to offer the best hope.

These classifications, quite useful for an understanding of the political economy of the Middle East, including labour flows, have not been utilized towards an understanding of patterns of female employment. But it is plausible to propose that patterns of women's employment may be explained in part by the given political economy. Mabro, as well as Richards and Waterbury, argue that overall, and unlike Latin America and Southeast Asia, industrialization has been fairly limited in the region. Concerted industrialization began in Latin America and Southeast Asia earlier than it did in the Middle East. In the case of South Korea, first the Japanese and then the Americans played a role in the expansion of agricultural and industrial production as well as education. In Brazil and Mexico, foreign investment played an important role in propelling industrialization. The success of the Southeast Asian countries in making a transition to export-led growth in the early 1960s contributed to their rapid economic growth, facilitated by the rapid expansion of world trade in the 1960s (Jenkins 1991). By contrast, in the Middle East the rate of industrial expansion remained slow until the mid-1950s. The industrialization drive gained momentum when revolutionary regimes took over in Egypt, Iraq and Syria, and decided to divert oil revenues to finance industrialization through ISI (Mabro 1988: 689; Richards and Waterbury 1990: 25–33). Foreign investment, however, was limited, and much of it was tied to military procurements.

In the same way that development theorists linked 'classic dependency' to limited employment, and just as WID specialists of Pearson's 'first consensus' argued that industrialization had marginalized women workers, Arab industrialization and the oil-financed ISI drive have constrained female employment in the Middle East, especially in terms of industrial employment. Those countries rich in oil and poor in other resources (Mabro's category A) chose an industrial strategy based on the transformation of hydrocarbon resources into petroleum products and petrochemicals. A strategy relying on oil, gas and finance, which is heavily capital-intensive and minimizes the use of labour, is not conducive to female employment. The industrialization of other countries (Mabro's groups B and C) followed a typical pattern of import-substitution, although Algeria, Iraq and Iran remained dependent on oil revenues for foreign exchange. Mabro notes that unlike Latin America, ISI in the Middle East did not evolve into manufacturing for export. Because of oil revenues, governments chose to extend the import-substitution process, moving into capital-intensive sectors involving sophisticated technology (Mabro 1988: 692). In both the oil and mixed oil economies the contribution of petroleum to the national income, both direct and indirect, is such as to make the apparent share of other sectors appear insignificant. What should be added is that investment in iron and steel plants, petrochemicals, car assembly plants, and similar industries, turned out to be not only costly and inefficient, but was not especially conducive to increased female employment.

The kinds of concentrations of female labour in TNCs that are characteristic of Southeast Asia and some Latin America and Caribbean countries are rarely found in the Middle East, in part because this kind of industrialization has not been pursued by all the countries of the region, and partly because of reliance on revenue and foreign exchange from oil exports. Industry in Middle Eastern countries has failed to make progress comparable to that achieved in India, Brazil or South Korea. Richards and Waterbury note that total manufacturing value-added (MVA) in the region is approximately equal to that of Brazil. This has implications for patterns of female employment. Lower levels of industrialization or manufacturing for export means less female proletarianization and activity in the productive sectors.

The non-oil economies, or those Arab countries without large petroleum reserves, have pursued development strategies of export-oriented manufacturing and agriculture. For example, although Tunisia exports oil, its oil share of exports is lower than that of OPEC countries (42 per cent in 1985 compared to Saudi Arabia's 97 per cent). What should be noted is that in the non-oil industrializing economies ('the watchmakers' and 'the NICs'), female labour-force participation is higher than elsewhere and in some places seems to be encouraged. Among Arab countries, Morocco and Tunisia are the countries in which manufacturing makes the largest relative contribution to GDP: 18 and 17 per cent, respectively, in 1991 (World Bank 1993: Table 3). They have also made the greatest advances in exports of manufactures and especially of clothing. Not surprisingly, they report the largest numbers of women in manufacturing employment (see Table 2.3).

An illustration of the convergence of the elements of our framework is provided by Algeria. Between 1967 and 1978, the Algerian government invested some 300 billion dinars, creating over a million jobs and bringing down unemployment from 25 per cent to 19 per cent of the active population. As a result of two national development plans, an industrial base was created which rested primarily on hydrocarbons, chemical and petrochemical industries, smelting industries, and construction and mechanical industries. Non-agricultural employment grew from 28 per cent to nearly 50 per cent of the active population. However, in spite of its size and importance, the industrial base created in the 1970s employed only about 150,000 people – that is, about 4 per cent of total employment or 11.6 per cent of the active population. In the words of

Table 2.3 Participation of women in manufacturing, some Arab countries and selected NICs

Country	Latest year	Total manufacturing workforce (A)	Number of women in manufacturing (B)	Number of B who are salaried (C)	Female share of total B/A (%)
Algeria	1977	261,706	18,187	16,479	6.9
	1985	595,000	40,632	35,790	6.8
Egypt	1989	1,958,700	344,600	125,200	17.6
Iraq	1977	284,395	48,618	27,217	17.1
	1986	386,809	44,680	−	11.6
Jordan	1989	32,438	4,040	4,038	12.5
Kuwait	1988	54,664	1,433	−	2.6
Morocco	1982	930,615	336,877	−	36.2
Syria	1991	456,162	34,600	24,099	7.6
Tunisia	1989	382,700	165,700	84,400	43.3
South Korea	1992	4,768,000	1,917,000	1,653,000	40.2
Mexico	1990	4,493,279	1,057,059	909,340	23.5
Malaysia	1988	987,300	449,200	352,500	45.5
Thailand	1990	3,132,500	1,563,700	1,089,700	49.9
Venezuela	1991	1,206,395	335,150	197,522	27.8

Sources: ILO, *Yearbook of Labour Statistics 1993*, Table 2A; ILO, *Retrospective Edition on Population Censuses 1945–1989*, Table 2A; ESCWA, 'Executive Summary, Participation of Women in Manufacturing Industries in Western Asia', mimeo.

one analyst, 'the planners opted for frontline technologies that are not large employers' (Addi 1992: 2). Nor are these technologies known to employ women in large numbers. The Algerian female labour force is small not only by international standards but is also among the smallest in the Arab world. There are hardly any women in manufacturing; those that are employed are mainly in public services.

In the 1980s, economic mismanagement – including ever growing importation of consumer goods – caught up with the Algerian government. The fall in the price of oil, from $30 a barrel in 1982 to $12 per barrel in 1988, led to a drastic reduction in state revenues, which were no longer large enough to service the debt and to import consumer goods and intermediate materials required by industry. One consequence was a sharp growth in unemployment – to an estimated 22 per cent of the active population in 1989 (Addi 1992). In this context, the government decided to shift from an administered to a market economy in line with World Bank and IMF prescriptions. This form of structural adjustment will without a doubt affect women's employment patterns and position within the labour market in Algeria, although exactly how remains to be seen. Much will of course depend upon the resolution of the present political crisis, as well as the volume and type of foreign and domestic investments.

Industrial Strategy and Female Employment

Table 2.3 provides data on women's participation in the manufacturing sector. For comparative purposes, data on Mexico, Malaysia and South Korea have been included. This table highlights the diversity in the region, from Algeria's very limited female participation in manufacturing to percentages in Tunisia and Morocco which are higher than Mexico and Venezuela, and closer to Malaysia and South Korea. 'Manufacturing employees' is a broad category that includes blue-collar and white-collar workers. In general, the female share of total manufacturing employees is lower in the Arab region than in Latin America, East Asia and Southeast Asia, but the countries that stand out for their high percentages are Morocco and Tunisia. Thus, among the countries of the region, Tunisia and Morocco depart from the pattern of low recorded female involvement in industry, and report figures of female participation in manufacturing which are similar to those of the East Asian NICs, for reasons that were explained above.

The data on salaried employment, however, show that in Tunisia, and probably in Morocco, a fairly high percentage of the measured manufacturing labour force is non-regular, that is, unpaid family workers or own-account workers, or informal-sector rather than formal-sector workers. There are probably many others engaged in homework who are not enumerated at all. By contrast, in South Korea and Mexico, most women manufacturing workers are salaried, indicating a high percentage working in the formal sector. The data for Tunisia show a decline in manufacturing employment by women, from a 55.5 per cent share in 1984 to a 43.5 per cent share in 1989. Could this be due to economic difficulties and the displacement of women by returning male migrants? Or has the decrease been caused by redundancies due to the loss of external markets? It should be noted that unstable employment is intrinsic to export-oriented industries, and the world market pits export industries against each other. Modern, competitive leather and textile firms in Asia have reduced the world market share controlled by Tunisian textile and leather firms, which are increasingly unable to compete with the modernized industries. According to one account, this caused a recession in the industries that eliminated 20,500 jobs held by women (Mehra et al. 1992: 31).

It is clear from the figures for Morocco and Tunisia that women's contribution to national industrial development and to exports certainly is considerable. What is unclear is whether these women are properly remunerated. In 1984, out of a reported 177,000 women in the manu-facturing sector in Tunisia, 61,000, or 35 per cent, were salaried. Some 52 per cent were 'employers and own-account workers', and 12.5 per cent were unpaid family workers. The 1989 Labour Force Sample Survey counted 165,700 women in manufacturing, and this time 50 per cent were said to be salaried. According to a Moroccan study, nearly half of the economically active women in the urban areas of Morocco are engaged in textiles and garments work, but much of this is homework (CERED 1989: 103–4).[9]

In terms of women's employment, the differences between the three Francophone North African countries are rather striking. (For other social indicators, see Galal, Chapter 4 in this volume.) The data for Algeria show huge male–female gaps in employment, in contrast to Morocco and Tunisia. We may attribute this to Algeria's chronically high unemployment, a conservative cultural stance on the part of the leadership, and the specific development strategy pursued by the state. Algeria's development strategy was one of heavy industrialization (partly on the assumption that it would eventually encourage mechanized ag-riculture). In the new, large-scale factories, such as steel works and petrochemicals, skilled workers were needed, and it was men who were trained for those jobs. The result was a very low female labour force participation in industry. Consequently, women are an under-utilized source of labour – with implications for fertility, population growth rates, and overall social development.

Is there a fit between the three typologies introduced earlier in this chapter, and patterns of female employment? Mabro's Group A (oil economies), Richards and Waterbury's coupon clippers, and the capital-rich countries identified by Birks et al. show a negligible female involve-ment in production work and among manufacturing employees. Among capital-poor countries, mixed oil economies, the watchmakers and the

NICs, there is a mixed picture, with generally low female involvement in production except for Tunisia and Morocco. In terms of women's involvement in manufacturing (and this would include various occupational categories), the countries that stand out are Morocco and especially Tunisia.

Given the importance of manufacturing to Jordan and to Syria, it is remarkable that the female share of production work and manufacturing is so low. In Syria, according to ILO data, women's employment in manufacturing increased steadily in the 1980s to a high of 49,000 women, or about 12 per cent of the manufacturing labour force, in 1989. It then decreased to 34,600 women, or 7.6 per cent of the total, in 1991. In contrast, men's employment in manufacturing has been steadily increasing throughout the 1980s.[10] In Jordan in 1991, out of a total of 38,200 paid manufacturing workers, only 4,300 were women.[11] Constructions of gender and the orientation of state managers, in addition to the composition of manufacturing exports, may provide an explanation.

The framework presented in this chapter has emphasized the role of the state as a structural determinant of women's access to employment. The relationship between economic development and women's employment is mediated by state policies which could serve to increase or reduce women's employment. In Jordan's case, out-migration of Jordanian male labour did not result in an increasing number of women being brought into the wage labour market. One may presume that women's activities in the informal sector and as unpaid family workers increased, although this is not reflected in the official statistics. Labour shortages due to migration led to labour importation, mainly of Egyptians, at all levels of skill, rather than the training of women in marketable skills to meet the shortages (Mujahid 1985: 105). Jordan's Five-Year Plan (1980–85) sought to further integrate women into the development process, and predicted a substantial increase of the total number of women in the working age bracket, excluding agricultural workers. But by 1988 the female participation rate was only 4.8 per cent, and the female share of the labour force was only 10 per cent, a 2 per cent increase over 1980. In his chapter on Jordan in this volume (Chapter 7), Shakhatreh explains the pattern of female labour-force participation in terms of household-level determinants. At a more structural level, Hijab (1988: 14) reports that in an untoward economic situation characterized by a large external debt, high male unemployment, and heavy dependence on foreign aid, there has been in fact an implicit government policy to discourage female employment. This is no doubt reinforced by legislation that bars women from 'nightwork', including the second shift in large and modern production units where women do indeed apply for jobs.[12]

The evidence from the Arab region would confirm the view in the development and WID literatures that in general ELI and female employment are positively related. Arab countries with export-led industrial strategies and higher levels of female labour-force participation are Morocco and Tunisia. Especially high are the female shares of manufacturing in Tunisia and Morocco. During the 1980s in Tunisia, 40 per cent of all employed women worked in the industrial sector, and in Morocco it was nearly 30 per cent. In her study of the Moroccan clothing industry, Joekes (1982) showed that the proportion of women workers was higher, both within and between firms, when the product was for foreign markets. The Arab region also provides evidence that oil-centred industrialization inhibits female employment. Among the large countries, Algeria has relied heavily on oil revenues, and reports a very small female labour force. According to the 1987 Census of Algeria, the employed population numbered 3.7 million men and a mere 365,000 women, or 9 per cent female share.[13]

Thus one cannot escape the conclusion that if, as Joekes has argued, industrialization in the Third World 'has been as much female-led as export-led' (Joekes 1987: 81), this must be qualified for the Middle East. And if, as Standing argues, 'women are being substituted for men in various occupational categories, including manufacturing and production work' (Standing 1989: 25), again, this is not quite (yet?) the case in the Middle East, where men predominate in the industrial sector. To be sure, in nearly all the large countries women are engaged in light manufacturing – clothing, woven goods, shoes, food processing, pharmaceuticals, confectioneries. But in the cities of the Arab region, most women are marginalized from production, and especially from the formal-sector productive process, and are concentrated in community, social and personal services. There does seem to be a widespread attitude that factory work is not suitable for women – although this may itself be a function of the limited demand for women's labour, given the current stage of industrialization and the high rates of male unemployment in the Arab region. Economic development has led to the creation of a female labour force, but that labour force is small in part because industrialization, an important stage of economic development, has been fairly limited in the region. From a world-system perspective, because the region is regarded first and foremost as a source of oil and petrodollars, international capital and Arab states alike have not aggressively pursued foreign investment in the kind of foreign industries likely to enhance female employment. As Mabro observes: 'The Arab countries, Iran, and, to a lesser extent, Turkey have still a long way to go on the road to industrialization' (Mabro 1988: 696).

Women in Public Services

In Arab countries, women have yet to participate in large numbers in the modern economy and become regular wage- and salary-earners. They are more visible in public services, and especially in the health and education sectors. Indeed, for many women, the government sector or public-service employment is a crucial source of women's livelihood and entry into public life. In this regard, Arab countries are not so different from other countries, for around the world the public sector and government employment have provided women with jobs and benefits that may elude them in the private sector.[14] Yet there are marked inequalities between men's and women's involvement in government employment. For example, in Algeria in 1990, 86 per cent of employed women (and 55 per cent of employed men) were engaged in the public sector. And yet Algerian women constituted a mere 11 per cent of the employees of ministries (Saadi 1991: 74; Institut National du Travail 1987).

In Tunisia, the female share of government employment in 1987 was, at 24.5 per cent, much higher than in Algeria. Tunisian women are also better distributed across the occupations and professions. Of the country's magistrates, 13.5 per cent were women; of medical personnel, 20.6 per cent were women; of para-medical personnel, 48 per cent were women; of the country's teachers, 31.5 per cent were female. Women's participation in formal politics matched the trends in employment. In 1981 there were seven female deputies in parliament; in 1983 there were 50,000 female members of the ruling social-democratic Neo-Destour Party and 57,000 members of the National Union of Tunisian Women; and in 1985 some 492 women were voted municipal councillors around the country (UNFPA/Ministère du Plan 1984; UNFT 1987). The distribution of the female labour force was more balanced in Tunisia than in many other countries; according to the 1989 Labour Force Sample Survey, about 20 per cent of the female labour force was in agriculture, 33 per cent in manufacturing, and 25 per cent in services.[15]

Table 2.4 Distribution of female labour force by occupation, major groups, 1980s (%)

Country (Year)	Group 1 (Prof.)	Group 2 (Admin. and mgt.)	Group 3 (Clerical)	Group 4 (Sales)	Group 5 (Service)	Group 6 (Agric.)	Group 7–9 (Prod.)	Not classified and unemployed
Algeria (1987)	33.5	0.7	15.0	1.0	13.2	1.7	7.3	27.2
Egypt (1984)	17.6	1.8	12.9	5.5	2.7	41.3	6.5	11.4
Kuwait (1985)	27.4	0.2	14.3	0.75	54.3	0.04	0.37	1.7
Morocco (1982)	6.6	5.4		1.4	13.7	32.5	33.2	6.8
Syria (1984)	26.0	0.9	8.2	1.2	2.6	44.0	10.4	6.7
Tunisia (1984)	2.2	0.4	13.2	0.18	6.5	22.0	28.2	27.0
Malaysia (1990)	9.4	0.6	14.1	11.4	14.1	28.1	22.3	0.0
Mexico (1980)	10.1	0.7	14.4	8.4	19.1	11.0	13.3	23.0
Venezuela (1989)	21.9	2.0	20.6	14.7	26.0	1.6	11.4	1.8

Group 1 = Professional, technical and related workers
Group 2 = Administrative and managerial workers
Group 3 = Clerical and related workers
Group 4 = Sales workers
Group 5 = Service workers
Group 6 = Agricultural, animal husbandry and forestry workers, fishermen and hunters
Groups 7–9 = Production/related workers, transport equipment operators and labourers

Source: ILO, *Yearbook of Labour Statistics 1988, 1991, 1993*; and Retrospective Edition on Population Censuses 1945–1989, Table 2B.

As seen in Table 2.4, Arab countries have minimal female presence in administrative and managerial occupations. There also appears to be a marked disinclination for women to enter sales work. Mujahid (1985: 115) explains this in terms of cultural norms, as it is an occupation in which the likelihood of indiscriminate contact with outsiders is highest. Clearly it is an extension of a long-standing pattern in which the merchant class has been typically male, and the traditional urban markets – bazaars and souks – have been the province of men. This table also shows that only in Morocco and Tunisia is the female labour force not overrepresented in professional, technical and related occupations.

How does this compare with global patterns of female occupational distribution? According to one cross-national study of 25 industrial countries, 'on the average, women are over-represented in professional, clerical, sales, and service occupations, and substantially under-represented in managerial and production jobs' (Charles 1992: 490). There are some exceptions among Western countries to the pattern of female overparticipation in sales work: women are 'grossly underrepresented in the sales occupation' in Italy (Charles 1992: 492). Indeed, men dominate sales occupations in several Western countries.

Global patterns of women's employment may be gleaned from data in the ILO's *Yearbook of Labour Statistics*, for various years. Only a handful of countries report large percentages of women in the agricultural workforce: Malawi, Haiti, Indonesia, Pakistan, Sri Lanka, Thailand and Turkey. Among European countries, only Greece has more women in agriculture than in any other sector. The manufacturing sector claims over 25 per cent of the female labour force only in the East Asian NICs and in the former socialist countries, and among Middle Eastern countries, in Tunisia and Morocco. In many countries, 25 per cent or more of the female workforce is in wholesale, retail trade, restaurants and hotels. These are not occupations in which Arab women are found in such large percentages. For example, in Tunisia in 1989, 5 per cent of the measured female labour force (26,700 out of 494,300 women) were counted as part of the sector 'wholesale and retail trade, restaurants and hotels', representing only 8 per cent of the total employees in this sector. In Egypt, according to the 1989 Labour Force Sample Survey, only 5 per cent of the total female labour force (237,400 out of 4.6 million) was involved in this sector, representing 17.7 per cent of the total employees (1.3 million) counted in this sector.[16] According to Charles, however, women are underrepresented in this sector in countries as different from each other as Sweden, the former GDR, Mexico and

Malta. Throughout the world, the largest concentrations of women workers are in public and private services ('community, social and personal services'); in this regard, Arab countries follow a global pattern.

Summary and Conclusions

In this chapter I have sought to bring the study of women's employment in the Arab world more in line with existing approaches in development studies, such as gender and development, Middle East studies of the political economy, and world-system analysis. In formulating an explanatory framework I have underscored gender, class, the state, development strategy, and the world-system as macrosociological determinants of women's employment. Using political economy typologies, I have argued that development strategies and state policies explain the differences in women's employment patterns. This is not to deny the salience of cultural understandings in the determination of female roles in Arab countries or in any other region, but to suggest that political and economic factors, and class and gender divisions, provide a more satisfactory explanation.

Female labour-force participation is still low in relation to that of other regions of the world, and, of course, low in relation to male labour-force participation. As part of an explanation, I have discussed the position of the Arab region within the world-system. Unlike the East Asian NICs, many Arab economies have been largely dependent upon oil exports. The oil economies chose a strategy which relied on oil, gas and finance; this minimizes the use of labour and offers insignificant employment opportunities for women. With regard to ISI, although it opened up some employment opportunities for women – for example, in state-run factories or in industrial plants in the private sector receiving state support – the capital-intensive strategy favoured male employment. In contrast, the utilization of an export-led development strategy, accompanied by an influx of multinational corporations into a country, tends to be associated with extensive use of female labour, leading to increases in female labour-force participation and in particular to increases in the female share of manufacturing, though often through subcontracting and home-based arrangements. Hence the higher levels of female employment in Morocco and Tunisia.

There can be no doubt that expanding education and employment opportunities have created a generation of Arab women who have become accustomed to working in the formal sector and indeed expect it. It should not be surprising that middle-class educated and employed women should be the ones agitating for more progressive social changes – for women as women and for women as workers. Nevertheless, in most Arab countries women remain an under-utilized human resource because of limited industrialization, because of the gender ideology stressing women's family roles, and because of ambivalence on the part of patriarchal state managers toward the full participation of women in economic development and in decision-making. As a result, labour-force attachment on the part of Arab women has not yet been established, and women have a long way to go before they attain the labour-force participation rates and access to salaried employment of other semi-peripheral regions, not to mention the advanced industrialized world.

Throughout the semi-periphery, manufacturing for export, increased trade, and foreign investment have tended to encourage female employment. In Tunisia and Morocco export-oriented garment industries contributed to the growth of the female labour force during the 1980s. But much of this employment is home-based or in small unregistered workshops where wages are low and social security nonexistent. It is likely that as Arab countries continue to pursue privatization and economic liberalization, women's employment will increase. However, the growth of small-scale manufacturing or home-based work, as distinct from employment in large and modern firms or in the public sector, or low-wage jobs in the expanding service sector, may not be in women's best interests.

Future research should examine how the proper utilization of female labour contributes to the wealth and well-being of societies, and how marginalization, neglect and under-utilization of women adversely affect economic development. More studies are needed on, among other issues: the interplay of supply and demand factors that affect women's employment and earnings; the impact of privatization, liberalization, and the expansion of the services sector on occupational trends for women, such as the growth of tourism-related and business-related jobs; male–female wage differentials and productivity differentials; employment policy, labour legislation, and social policies; education and employment linkages, including the match (or mismatch) of women's educational tracking and labour–market requirements; the effects of women's employment on household decision-making; the links between education, employment, and fertility. Documenting women's employment patterns is, or should be, an important part of development analysis. At the level of policy-making, investment in women's education and employment should be more widely appreciated as an integral part of human capital formation and utilization of the national human—resources base.

Notes

1. For a review of the literature and the debates, see Tiano 1987, Lim 1990, Moghadam 1990.

2. This is beginning to change with the establishment of The Economic Research Forum in Cairo, supported by the World Bank, which has produced a number of interesting studies on macroeconomic and microeconomic issues pertaining to Arab countries, Iran, and Turkey, including several quantitative papers on micro-level determinants of female labour-force participation. The present book is also intended as a contribution to the literature.

3. It will be recalled that early attempts to explain the South Korean or East Asian economic phenomena in cultural terms – the Confucian work ethic – have been dismissed as theoretically deficient. See Lie 1992. Nevertheless, a recent comparative study of women and work argues that culture is a significant deter- minant of women's access to economic resources and explains the differences in Marxist, Muslim, non-Muslim African, and Latin American Catholic patterns of employment. See Clark et al. 1991.

4. For a comparative study of changing family law in Western countries (from patriarchal to egalitarian), see Glendon 1977, 1989.

5. For a discussion of this pattern for Arab and Turkish women in the labour force, see Lewin-Epstein and Semyonov 1992 and Oncü 1980.

6. For a positive view, see Karshenas 1990. For a less sanguine view, see Gelb and Associates 1988.

7. There is now a growing literature which links the growth of female em- ployment to export-led growth. For a critique of the deterioration of labour conditions in the context of this development, see Standing 1989. From a some- what different intellectual tradition, Krueger (1983, especially ch. 3) argues that both growth performance and employment generation are 'better under export promotion than under import substitution', an argument made also by Perkins (1992), in her comparative study of Asian economies and women's employment. What should be added is that this obtains under a capitalist organization of the economy; the full employment and earlier high growth rates of the socialist economies require other explanations.

8. Two important points, however, are worth noting: (a) semi-peripheral countries continue to produce and export more traditionally peripheral-like prod- ucts, even though they may be less dependent on them than before, and (b) even when manufactures are exported to the core, they remain of the sort that has always defined the semi-periphery's role in the world division of labour. That is, the new industries of the semi-periphery are the old, declining industries of the core, which is now focusing on the export of professional services (such as banking, accounting, management consulting, and so on, but also higher educa- tion, especially in the USA) and high-technology goods.

9. On Tunisia, see ILO 1993: Table 2A.

10. On the labour force in Syria, see ibid., Table 3B.

11. On Jordan, see ibid., Table 5A.

12. This came to light during interviews by the author with employees and managers at Hikma Pharmaceuticals in Amman, 12 November 1994.

13. Similarly, in non-Arab but oil-exporting Iran, according to the 1986 census, some 990,000 women were part of the labour force (9 per cent), as against over 10 million men. See Moghadam 1993: ch. 6.

14. In the United States, the public sector has been most conducive to female advancement. The so-called 'glass ceiling' blocking the advancement of women and minorities is more firmly in place in the private sector than in the public sector, where affirmative-action goals are enforced. Standing, among others, has pointed out that not only are women's wages and employment conditions better on average in the public sector than in private wage employment, but that wage differentials between men and women are smaller in the public sector (Standing 1989: 25). See also von Ginniken 1991.

15. See ILO 1993, p. 56, Table 2A.

16. Egypt's 1986 census counted about 63,000 women in whole and retail trade, restaurants and hotels, compared with about 860,000 men, and out of a total female workforce of 1.5 million women. Enumeration had clearly changed, or improved, by the 1989 Labour Force Sample Survey, although privatization, the expansion of the services sector, and economic need may be propelling more women into the labour force and into services-related and tourism-related occupations.

References

Addi, Lahouari. 1992. 'The Structural Crisis of the Algerian Economy'. Paper presented at the annual meeting of the Middle East Studies Association, Portland, Oregon, USA (28–31 October).

Berquist, Charles, ed. 1984. *Labor in the Capitalist World-Economy*. Beverly Hills, CA: Sage.

Birks, J.S., I.J. Seccombe and C.A. Sinclair. 1988. 'Labor Migration and Labor Organization in the Arab World'. In Michael Adams, ed., *The Middle East*. New York: Facts-on-File, pp. 718–41.

Blumberg, Rae Lesser. 1989. *Making the Case for the Gender Variable*. Washington, DC: AID Office for Women in Development.

Boserup, Ester. 1990. 'Economic Change and the Roles of Women'. In Irene Tinker, ed., *Persistent Inequalities: Women and World Development*. New York: Oxford University Press, pp. 14–25.

CERED. 1989. *Femmes et Condition Feminine au Maroc*. Rabat: Direction de la Statistique.

Charles, Maria. 1992. 'Cross-National Variation in Occupational Sex Segregation', *American Sociological Review*, vol. 57, no. 1 (August), pp. 483–502.

Clark, Roger, Thomas Ramsbey and Emily Stier Adler. 1991. 'Culture, Gender, and Labor Force Participation: A Cross-National Study'. *Gender & Society*, vol. 5, no. 1 (March), pp. 47–66.

Deyo, Frederic. 1987. *The Political Economy of the New Asian Industrialism*. Ithaca, NY: Cornell University Press.

El-Naggar, Said, ed. 1989. *Privatization and Structural Adjustment in the Arab Countries.* Washington DC: International Monetary Fund.

Elson, Diane and Ruth Pearson. 1980. 'The Subordination of Women and the Internationalisation of Factory Production'. In Kate Young et al., eds, *Of Marriage and the Market: Women's Subordination in International Perspective.* London: CSE Books, pp. 144–166.

ESCWA. 1994. 'Executive Summary: Participation of Women in Manufacturing Industries in Western Asia'. Amman: ESCWA (mimeo).

Evans, Peter. 1979. *Dependent Development: The Alliance of Multinational, State, and Local Capital in Brazil.* Princeton, NJ: Princeton University Press.

Fiala, Robert. 1992. 'The International System, Labor-Force Structure, and the Growth and Distribution of National Income 1950–1980'. *Sociological Perspectives*, vol. 35, no. 2.

Gelb, Alan, and Associates. 1988. *Oil Windfalls: Blessing or Curse?* New York: Oxford University Press for the World Bank.

Gereffi, Gary, and Donald Wyman, eds. 1990. *Manufacturing Miracles: Paths of Industrialization in Latin America and East Asia.* Princeton, NJ: Princeton University Press.

Glendon, Mary Ann. 1977. *State, Law and Family: Family Law in Transition in the United States and Western Europe.* Cambridge, MA: Harvard University Press.

———— 1989. *The Transformation of Family Law.* Chicago: University of Chicago Press.

Heyzer, Noeleen. 1986. *Working Women in Southeast Asia: Development, Subordination and Emancipation.* Milton Keynes: Open University Press.

Hijab, Nadia. 1988. *Womanpower: The Arab Debate on Women at Work.* Cambridge: Cambridge University Press.

ILO. 1990. *Retrospective Edition on Population Censuses 1945–1989.* Geneva: ILO.

———— 1993. *Yearbook of Labour Statistics 1993.* Geneva: ILO.

ILO/INSTRAW. 1985. *Women in Global Economic Activity: 1950–2000.* Geneva and Santo Domingo: ILO and INSTRAW.

Institut National du Travail. 1987. *Revue Algérienne du Travail: L'Emploi en Algérie: Réalités et Perspectives.* Algiers (December).

Jenkins, Rhys. 1991. 'The Political Economy of Industrialization: A Comparison of Latin American and East Asian Newly Industrializing Countries'. *Development and Change*, vol. 22, no. 2 (April), pp. 197–232.

Joekes, Susan. 1982. 'Female-Led Industrialization: Women's Jobs in Third World Export Manufacturing: The Case of the Clothing Industry in Morocco'. Research Report No. 15, University of Sussex: Institute of Development Studies, Falmer.

———— 1987. *Women in the World Economy: An INSTRAW Study.* New York: Oxford University Press.

Joekes, Susan, and Roxanna Moayedi. 1987. *Women and Export Manufacturing: A Review of the Issues and AID Policy.* Washington DC: International Center for Research on Women.

Karshenas, Massoud. 1990. *Oil, State, and Industrialization in Iran.* Cambridge: Cambridge University Press.

Krueger, Anne O. 1983. *Trade and Employment in Developing Countries, Vol. 3: Synthesis and Conclusions.* Chicago: University of Chicago Press.

Lewin-Epstein, Noah, and Moshe Semyonov. 1992. 'Modernization and Subordination: Arab Women in the Israeli Labor Force'. *European Sociological Review*, vol. 8, pp. 38–51.

Lie, John. 1992. 'The Political Economy of South Korean Development', *International Sociology*, vol. 7, no. 3 (September), pp. 285–300.

Lim, Linda. 1990. 'Women's Work in Export Factories: The Politics of a Cause.' In Irene Tinker, ed., *Persistent Inequalities: Women and World Development*. New York: Oxford University Press, pp. 101–22.

Mabro, Robert. 1988. 'Industrialization'. In Adams, ed., *The Middle East*. New York: Facts-on-File, pp. 687–96.

Mehra, Rekha, David Burns, Paul Carlson, Geeta Rao Gupta and Margaret Lycette. 1992. *Engendering Development in Asia and the Near East: A Sourcebook*. Washington DC: International Center for Research on Women.

Miliband, Ralph. 1989. *Divided Societies: Class Struggle in Contemporary Capitalism*. Oxford: Clarendon Press.

Moghadam, Valentine M. 1990. *Gender, Development and Policy: Toward Equity and Empowerment*. Helsinki: WIDER Research for Action Series (November).

———— 1993. *Modernizing Women: Gender and Social Change in the Middle East*. Boulder, CO: Lynne Rienner Publishers.

Mujahid, G.B.S. 1985. 'Female Labor Force Participation in Jordan'. In J. Abu Nasr et al., eds. *Women, Employment and Development in the Arab World*. Berlin: Mouton for the ILO, pp. 103–30.

Niblock, Tim. 1993. 'International and Domestic Factors in the Economic Liberalisation Process in Arab Countries'. In Tim Niblock and Emma Murphy, eds, *Economic and Political Liberalization in the Middle East*. London: British Academic Press, pp. 55–87.

Oncü, Ayse. 1980. 'Women in the Professions: Why So Many?' In Nermin Abadan-Unat, *Women in Turkish Society*. Leiden: Brill.

Papanek, Hanna. 1990. 'To Each Less Than She Needs, From Each More Than She Can Do: Allocations, Entitlements, and Value'. In Irene Tinker, ed., *Persistent Inequalities*. New York: Oxford University Press, pp. 162–83.

Pearson, Ruth. 1992. 'Gender Issues in Industrialization'. In Tom Hewitt, Hazel Johnson and David Wield, eds, *Industrialization and Development*. Oxford: Oxford University Press, pp. 222–47.

Perkins, Frances. 1992. 'Integration of Women's Concerns into Development Planning: Market Interventions'. In ESCAP, *Integration of Women's Concerns into Development Planning in Asia and the Pacific*. New York: United Nations, pp. 105–204.

Pyle, Jean. 1990. 'Export-Led Development and the Underdevelopment of Women: The Impact of Discriminatory Development Policy in the Republic of Ireland'. In Kathryn Ward, ed., *Women Workers and Global Restructuring*. Ithaca, NY: ILR Press, pp. 85–112.

Reskin, Barbara. 1988. 'Bringing the Men Back In: Sex Differentiation and the Devaluation of Women's Work'. *Gender & Society*, vol. 2, pp. 58–81.

———— 1991. 'Labor Markets as Queues: A Structural Approach to Changing Occupational Sex Composition'. In Joan Huber, ed., *Macro-Micro Linkages in Sociology*. Newbury Park, CA: Sage Publications, pp. 170–92.

Richards, Alan, and John Waterbury. 1990. *A Political Economy of the Middle East:*

State, Class and Economic Development. Boulder, CO: Westview Press.

Saadi, Nouredine. 1991. *La Femme et La Loi en Algérie.* Casablanca: Éditions Fennec for UNU/WIDER.

Seddon, David. 1993. 'Austerity Protests in Response to Liberalisation in the Middle East'. In Tim Niblock and Emma Murphy, eds, *Economic and Political Liberalization in the Middle East.* London: British Academic Press, pp. 88–113.

Sen, Gita, and Caren Grown. 1987. *Development, Crises and Alternative Visions: Third World Women's Perspectives.* New York: Monthly Review Press.

Shannon, Thomas Richard. 1989. *An Introduction to the World-System Perspective.* Boulder, CO: Westview Press.

Standing, Guy. 1989. 'Global Feminisation Through Flexible Labour'. *World Development,* vol. 17, no. 7, pp. 1077–95.

Tiano, Susan. 1987. 'Gender, Work, and World Capitalism: Third World Women's Role in Development. In Beth Hess and Myra Marx Ferree, eds, *Analyzing Gender.* Beverly Hills, CA: Sage, pp. 216–43.

UNFPA/Ministère du Plan. 1984. *La Femme et la Famille Tunisienne à Travers les Chiffres.* Tunis: United Nations Fund for Population Activities, and the Ministry of Planning.

UNFT (Union Nationale des Femmes Tunisiennes). 1987. *La Femme au Travail en Chiffres.* Tunis: UNFT.

von Ginniken, Wouter, ed. 1991. *Government and Its Employees.* Aldershot: Avebury.

Wallerstein, Immanuel. 1979. *The Capitalist World-System.* Cambridge: Cambridge University Press.

——— 1989. *The Modern World World-System,* Vol. III. New York: Academic Press.

Ward, Kathryn. 1984. *Women in the World-System.* New York: Praeger.

World Bank. 1993. *World Development Report 1993.* New York: Oxford University Press.

3

Women as Mobilizers of Human Resources in Arab Countries

Huda C. Zurayk and Fadia Saadeh

Introduction

The role of women in development has become an important issue for planners in developing countries because of the potential untapped human resource that women represent. Whereas the role of men as a human resource that must be developed and used efficiently in production is never questioned, the participation of women in the labour force is complicated by the fact that the woman is the childbearer and carries the major responsibility in the child-rearing process. In Arab society, these functions of women in the family are given a very high value.

Much has been written about the role of women in development, and on the need to increase the economic participation of women in developing countries. There is general agreement that women's labour-force participation is important from a macroeconomic perspective. Moreover, the labour-force participation of women is considered to be beneficial from a micro-perspective, as it contributes to the welfare of the family for the poor, who form the majority of the developing world's population. Work is also seen to develop a woman's personality as well as to increase her status in society (Schuster 1981/82: 529).

This chapter approaches the subject of women's role in development from a wider perspective than that of labour-force participation, to consider women's role as a mobilizer of the labour force. The role of mobilizer includes influencing positively both the quantity and the quality of the labour force. The avenue for increasing quantity is to encourage women's entry into the labour force. The avenue for increasing quality is to influence the efficiency of the process of organization of the labour force, and the degree of productivity.

In the following section, we shall review the level of economic activity of women in Arab countries and attempt to delineate the obstacles that stand in the way of its expansion. Later on in this chapter, we shall examine the role of women in Arab society in stimulating the economic activity of women and in enhancing the efficiency and productivity of the total labour force.

The Economic Activity of Women

We have shown in previous work (Zurayk 1985), and so have others (Abu Nasr et al. 1985; Moghadam, Chapter 2, this volume), that the economic activity of women in Arab countries is low. Latest estimates of rates of economic activity by sex in Arab countries show that these countries have different levels and patterns of socio-economic development, yet there is a consistency in terms of the level of economic activity of women. In all countries the participation rates of women are much lower than those of men, and in a majority of countries the participation rates of women are less than 15 per cent. In fact, within this low level of participation, rates vary from less than or close to 5 per cent in Democratic Yemen, Egypt, Saudi Arabia and United Arab Emirates to over 20 per cent in Lebanon, Sudan and Mauritania in 1992.

These low levels of female participation are due in part to a misleading conceptualization of economic activity, to which we shall return later, as well as to a problem in measuring women's work. The measurement problem arises from the nature of the economic activity of women and from the cultural values attached to the work of women in Arab society. The standard definition of economic activity is 'that activity which is directed to the production of goods or services which is measurable in economic terms and in which, generally speaking, people are gainfully employed' (UN 1974: 100). Many of the activities of women, particularly in agriculture, are of this nature but are not easily recognizable as such because they are not organized on a full-time basis, as pointed out by Anker and Anker in Chapter 8 of this volume. Rather, such activities tend to involve work that is family-based, part-time, irregular or seasonal, and in some cases not easily classifiable in standard occupation terms.

These confusing qualities, in addition to the negative cultural values attaching to women's work, lead to an undercount of the economic activity of women in censuses and labour-force surveys. The woman respondent who is not a full-time wage earner, or the male household member answering for her, may not report the work she does, considering it part of household duties, or may be ashamed to admit to her work. Similarly, the interviewer, male or female, may be too ready to accept a woman who does not work full time outside the home as a housewife, and to record her as such without probing to find out whether she does part-time or family or seasonal work and/or work that may not fit within the standard classification of occupations (Zurayk 1985).

Because of these measurement problems, the statistics on economic activity do not tell us about women's economic activity in its totality. Special efforts are therefore called for to attempt to capture statistically the different dimensions of women's work. The statistics, however, probably cover fairly accurately the full-time participation of women. As such, the observations made about the low level of women's economic activity do at least describe accurately their full-time contribution. They point to the need for mobilization efforts to stimulate a more systematic entry of women into the labour force. Such mobilization efforts should be based on a clear understanding of the obstacles that stand in the way of a fuller labour-force participation of women. We attempt to review these obstacles as they pertain to Arab society in particular, and to suggest ways in which they may be overcome.

The household activities of women

1. The marital and reproductive patterns of women

As a result of certain demographic and social characteristics in Arab countries, we find a large proportion of women in the role of childbearers and childrearers. First, because of past patterns of fertility and mortality, a substantial proportion of females (35–45 per cent) in all Arab countries are in the reproductive age range of 15 to 44. This condition is likely to continue, even if fertility were to decline, because of the momentum of growth in the Arab region resulting from past patterns of reproduction (Sirageldin 1986: 10–11).

Second, marriage is early and universal – at least in those Arab countries for which information is available. In most Arab countries, close to 50 per cent or more of the age group 15 to 24 are married. Moreover, the proportion married in the age group 25 to 34 reaches 85 per cent or over for all countries except Lebanon. Very few women remain single beyond the age of 35.

Third, the level of fertility in Arab countries remains very high. The total fertility rate seems to be highest among Arab countries and in sub-Saharan Africa. It is interesting to note that the fertility levels are high irrespective of levels of socio-economic development. We can thus summarize with three observations: a substantial proportion of females in Arab countries are in the reproductive age group of 15 to 44; the great majority of these women are married; and they are reproducing at high rates of fertility. These observations indicate that women are occupied in the household and in family responsibilities resulting from their marital and reproductive patterns for a large proportion of their adult life, as Shakhatreh (Chapter 7 this volume) shows for Jordan.

2. *The economic value of household activities*

The fact that women spend a large proportion of their adult life in household activity contrasts with the reality that the economic value of this activity is not recognized in the statistical accounting systems. This lack of recognition is responsible for the profile presented by statistical systems of women as low contributors of economic value to society. In fact, household activity fulfils all the criteria used to define work. It involves an expenditure of energy and a contribution, direct or indirect, to the production of goods and services which, if it were not for the activity of women, would have had to be bought on the market by the family (Stevens and Boyd 1980: 187). What is produced by women in their household activity has economic value and as such should be accounted for as part of active labour (Benería 1981: 11).

Hence, before we speak of encouraging the entry of women into the labour force, we must adequately measure their economic contribution in household activity, mainly for the difference it makes to women's lives. One difference is that it counteracts the misleading profile presented of women due to the underevaluation of the economic contribution of their work. Recognition of the long hours of labour that women spend in household activity would serve to improve their image of themselves, raise their status in society, and possibly provide them with some of the benefits associated with working status, such as insurance and retirement benefits. Measuring women's economic contribution in the household is also important for delineating the periods of 'underemployment' in their marital and reproductive life – that is, those periods when it is possible for women to be free from home production sufficiently to be drawn into the labour market. Finally, recognizing the amount of effort a woman spends in household duties may underline the need for a greater contribution in those household activities in which men and adult children can equally play a role. It may also underline the need to reorganize the entry of women into the labour market, allowing for part-time employment and for leave. With such modifications in the organization of household and market activity, the woman would no longer have to face the equally difficult choices of either restricting her life to home production or of being overburdened with a double load of home and market production (Benería 1981: 21–2).

In the face of such discussion of the need to expand the concept of work, the problem of measurement of the value of household activity is often raised. The standard definition of work has tied economic value to income-earning activity. One alternative is to define work to include hours spent in use-value production of goods and services, and to exclude hours spent in recreation and leisure (Benería 1981: 23). To operationalize a measure on this basis, it is important to experiment on samples from culturally varied locations. Time-use studies present a method of documentation that can record in detail how the hours of a typical day are spent. Their advantages and disadvantages have been discussed elsewhere (Zurayk 1985: 43–5), and on balance they present a useful instrument for experimentation in this direction (Benería 1981: 19; Zurayk 1985: 43; Anker and Anker, Chapter 8 this volume).

3. *Accommodating women in their double role*

In addition to its economic value, there is tremendous social and family-life value in the household activity of women in Arab society. However, because of the importance of drawing women into the labour force, there is a need to develop the reorganization strategies and the support mechanisms that can accommodate women in their double role.

Sorenson (1983: 313) has categorized the pattern of employment of married women into four types. The first is the *conventional pattern* in which a woman who is working before marriage ceases to work either at marriage or at the birth of her first live child and never returns to work. The second is the *interrupted pattern* in which a woman stops working at marriage or at the birth of her first live child and returns to work some time after the birth of her last child. The third is the *double-track pattern*, which can be 'pure' in that the woman continues to work throughout her reproductive span, or 'not pure' in that the woman stops working at marriage or at the start of reproduction but returns to work before the birth of her last child. The final type is the *unstable pattern*, which refers to a woman who moves in and out of the labour market at different periods.

In Arab societies, the conventional pattern, in which a woman ceases to work at marriage or at the start of reproduction, is the most prevalent. In fact, examination of the labour-force participation rates in terms of age and sex groupings reveals that adult females tend not to work even before they enter marriage. For married women, the 'pure' double-track pattern produces a heavy burden and is not compatible with Arab values that encourage the presence of women in the home during child-bearing and childrearing. Women of high education and professional women may choose to follow this pattern, and in that they deserve the support of society and of their families. However, a preferable pattern for married women in general may be the 'not pure' double-track or the interrupted pattern. It is not sufficient, however, simply to register the preference for these patterns. There is a need to develop support mechanisms that will make it possible for – and, indeed, encourage – married women to follow these preferred patterns.

The discussion above suggests the need for support mechanisms which can be summarized under three headings:

(a) Mechanisms that assist women to enter the labour force during or following the reproductive period: these include provision of nursery services and day-care centres, the application of societal pressure on employers to employ women on an equal-opportunity basis, and the introduction of refresher courses in various specialized subjects for women to regain lost, and acquire new, knowledge and skills.

(b) Reorganization of time-basis employment: this includes introducing part-time or shared employment of women, as well as acceptance of maternity and other leave for women.

(c) Reorganization of the process of housekeeping: this includes increasing the contribution of husbands and adult children toward housekeeping activities, as well as encouraging extended family living, which is a traditional pattern in the Arab heritage and can provide support for the mother in child-rearing activities.

The level of skills of women

Data on labour-force participation of women in the Arab world show the same or slightly higher rates of labour-force participation for females in the age group 15 to 24, who are mostly single, as for succeeding age groups. This result reveals that entry of women into the labour force is restricted not only by marital and reproductive responsibilities but by other factors as well. In this section we shall investigate the level of preparedness of women to enter the labour force.

In determining the level of preparedness of women, we shall utilize information on their educational levels. Azzam et al. (1985: 27–31) have shown that labour-force participation of women in Arab countries is positively related to levels of literacy. We can also illustrate this relation with data from a survey consisting of a sample of 2,752 households in Beirut city in 1983–84 (Zurayk and Armenian 1985). That sample shows that in most age groups the participation rate of women rises with education, for the single, married and separated/divorced/widowed groups. The participation of women of low education is very weak except for single women.

Data on illiteracy rates for males and females 15 years of age and older in Arab countries in 1985 shows very high rates of illiteracy for females, with only Bahrain, Jordan, Kuwait and Lebanon showing less than 50 per cent illiteracy. Nevertheless, the rate of illiteracy is still close to one third of adult females in these four countries. At the other extreme, it reaches over 85 per cent for Mauritania, Somalia, Sudan and Yemen Arab Republic. Illiteracy among females is also shown to be higher than among males for all Arab countries.

Information on levels of education, including the level of attainment for the literate population, is available only for the proportion that is 25 years of age or older. Data shows that, with the exception of Kuwait and Qatar, 15 per cent or less of females in this age category have received secondary education. The situation of males is again better than that of females.

In projecting the skill levels of future generations, we look to data on school enrolment of females and males. We find school enrolment in primary level for females to be over 50 per cent for most countries, and to have reached over 75 per cent for almost half of the countries, in 1992. Yet for the Yemen Arab Republic the rate is very low, in stark contrast to what has been achieved for males in that country (see Lackner, Chapter 5 in this volume, for a full discussion of Yemen). Mauritania, Somalia, Sudan and Morocco also suffer from low rates of enrolment of females in primary education. As for secondary level, the proportion of females enrolled was less than 50 per cent in most countries in 1992. It thus seems that, with regard to future generations of adult women, high rates of illiteracy will persist in a few countries.

On the other hand, adult women in most countries will have improved their educational level, while the proportion attaining the secondary educational level will remain modest. One must be careful, however, to examine the quality of education that females are receiving. It is probable that the education they receive is not of a kind that develops women's view of themselves and mobilizes them to enter the labour force. It is even more probable that the education does not prepare them for the needs of the labour market in Arab countries. Sirageldin (1986) emphasizes the latter as a very serious problem for future generations.

In terms of the current generation of adult women, it is apparent that education – a major enabling factor to entering the labour force – is at very low levels. This forms an obstacle to the entry of women into the labour force, and is partly responsible for the low levels of participation that we observe. Both literacy programmes for women and the provision of work opportunities to match current skill levels are called for. We shall return to the latter point in the following section.

Society's view of women's work

Another factor which influences the entry of women into the labour force is the generally negative view that Arab society has of women's work. This results in part from the value system that encourages the segregation of the sexes, and that considers the married women's duty towards her family to be the priority. Nevertheless, in many Arab countries restrictions against women's entry into certain professions are now relaxing. However, much still needs to be done in terms of changing the value system relating to women's place in society (Azzam et al. 1985: 6).

Values can be influenced through the following institutions: the family, school, religion, political parties and the mass communication system (Zurayk 1983: 107). Schooling and mass communication have particularly wide application, and can be used to instil new values in terms of women's role in society. Unfortunately, studies have shown that these systems continue to project the traditional view of the accepted sphere of women's activities (Kallab 1983; Abdel Kader 1982). In textbooks and mass communication programmes, we generally see the woman as mother and housewife, and sometimes she appears in the traditionally accepted jobs of teacher and nurse.

The availability of jobs for women

When assessing information on women in the economically active group in all Arab countries by size, and by the percentages currently or once married, illiterate and in employment, we note in particular the large size of this age group and the fact that the vast majority are currently outside the labour force. These observations have often raised the fear that jobs are not available for absorbing this large potential addition to the labour force. However, the key factors here are, one, the high proportion of women who are or have been married; and, two, the large percentage who are illiterate. It follows that the women will not be ready or able to enter the labour force all at once. As support mechanisms are instituted, married women will be encouraged gradually to enter the workforce. Many of them will be handicapped, however, by their low level of education. Thus policies to expand the entry of women into the labour force must provide both the support mechanisms and the opportunities for productive employment consistent with the present levels of skill. This is the short-term solution. In the longer term, the market demand for labour should be carefully assessed and developed, and both men and women must be adequately prepared to meet that demand.

The Woman as a Mobilizer of Human Resources

The potential for the woman to act as a mobilizer will now be examined in relation to her activities both within and outside the family. Her role as a mobilizer is viewed in terms of her influence on the entry of women into the labour force, and on the efficiency of organization and the productivity of that force. While the obstacles to the entry of women into the labour force have been discussed in the previous section, the problems of labour-force organization and productivity in Arab countries have not been considered because they fall outside our sphere of specialization. Nevertheless, we are concerned with one very important problem in this regard: the lax attitude to work and productivity which characterizes the workforce in Arab countries, particularly in the public sector.

The woman as a mobilizer in the family

The family is the primary institution in society in which children are socialized, and in which values are nurtured and developed. The woman is the main person in the family responsible for childrearing and as such she is potentially able to exert considerable influence over her children's attitude towards work and productivity in general, and towards the work of women in particular.

One of the most effective avenues of influence is the woman's own behaviour in terms of work and productivity inside and outside the home. It has been shown that women whose mothers have worked are themselves more likely to join the labour force, and that their occupations are likely to resemble their mothers (Stevens and Boyd 1980). The impact of the example a working mother sets is not, however, restricted to her family, but propagates itself through the family's network of contacts. Its mobilization effect depends on the positive profile projected of a working woman's life. As such the example of the Western working woman does not provide a positive model because her situation has, in concert with other social and economic factors, served to undermine family living. The lesson learnt is not, therefore, to oppose women working, but to emphasize the importance of implementing support mechanisms that can help promote both a healthy and happy family life and the participation of women in the labour force.

In Arab countries, women's low rate of participation in the labour force indicates that they do not at present generally play a sufficiently strong mobilizing role through example. Their main effort at mobilization in the family is, therefore, through childrearing activities. However, even in these activities the effect is not likely to be great, for three main reasons. First, the data have shown that women in Arab countries are largely illiterate and of low education, so that the potential for introducing a change in values through childrearing is limited. Second, women in Arab countries have a low level of awareness of the various life options that could exist for them, and of their right to choose among these options. Third, even though it is in the woman's own interest to encourage the transformation of societal values, the conflict that such action may create in the family might discourage her from directing her efforts to this issue.

In addition to the options of setting an example and of childrearing, a third way that women can play a mobilizing role in the family is through their full participation in the process of deciding how many children to have. The fewer children she has, the easier it is for a woman to enter the labour market following the birth of her last child. However, the same three reasons of low level of education, inadequate awareness and fear of conflict may again prevent the woman from fully exercising her potential in this regard.

The woman as a mobilizer outside the family

1. *The working woman*

We will examine in this section the mobilizing potential of women through their economic activity outside the household. The ability of women to exert influence in the workplace comes both from the type of occupation they have and from the seniority of their positions. Examining the employment of females in the various occupational categories, we note that women form a substantial proportion of professionals in almost all Arab countries, and that – except for Egypt and Syria – they are severely underrepresented in administrative and management occupations. The proportion of women in clerical occupations in Egypt, Jordan, Lebanon and Tunisia, and in service occupations in Kuwait, Lebanon, Morocco and Tunisia, was over 20 per cent in 1992. Their role in agriculture is subject to undercount and is likely to be substantial in all countries with a large agricultural sector.

The association between level of education and rates of economic activity can explain why females are relatively numerous in the professional occupations. Here women are likely to come into contact with many people, and would have earned their status and power of influence through example and reputation. On the other hand, and as Moghadam discusses in Chapter 2 of this volume, we find relatively few women in occupations that are directly involved with organization and productivity of labour, or in administrative and managerial positions. It is these occupations that women must seek to enter in greater numbers because of the opportunity they provide for influencing the organization of the labour force, particularly as it relates to the contribution of women.

The contribution of women to service occupations has been noted to be mostly in the occupations of teacher and nurse (Azzam et al. 1985: 6). The occupation of teacher is very valuable, for it provides women with a second avenue of influence, other than their role in the family, over the attitudes of children toward work, and especially women's work. The women serving as teachers are, moreover, educated women who are expected to be more aware than many mothers of the obstacles to productive work, and to the work of women in Arab society. Thus, through their role as teachers, women have the opportunity to influence children from all backgrounds. The outcome is not as positive as may be desired, however, because of the low quality of education the teachers themselves have received in some cases, and because of the relative safety of propagating society's values rather than motivating for change.

Other service occupations with the potential to influence values are in the sphere of mass communication, such as journalism or script-writing for television and radio programmes. Although no detailed information is available on the availability of jobs in such occupations, it is probably accurate to say that women play a relatively small role in those sectors of the mass communications system relating to programming and the determination of content, where influence is the greatest. Women must attempt to occupy such positions because of their strategic importance in mobilizing human resources.

We come, finally, to the role of women in clerical occupations. Here women tend to be employed mostly in the secretarial sector. This serves to reinforce the secondary position of women vis-à-vis men, who are inevitably found in the boss's position.

We consider next the position of women as mobilizers in terms of age seniority on the job. Comparison of the distribution of economically active males and females by age indicates that in almost all countries a larger proportion of working males, as compared to working females, are in the age group 35 and over. The fact that the male labour force is larger in this age range means that the number of women achieving age seniority is small relative to men. Thus the working woman's potential for wielding influence through age seniority on the job seems rather limited.

2. *The woman in volunteer work*

In most Arab countries, educated women have entered the field of volunteer work in non-governmental organizations, and have attained high positions in these organizations. Their work is not recognized as economic activity because it does not fit the standard definition of an income-earning contribution. Nevertheless, through their volunteer work many women have become public figures and are therefore in a position to influence attitudes towards work and the work of women.

3. *The woman as policy-maker*

Unfortunately, in the Arab countries few women have attained policy-making positions in the government sector. Such positions are very important for the opportunity they offer to enact policies that can serve to mobilize efforts in a number of directions. Many women call for the introduction of a Ministry of Women's Affairs in Arab countries, staffed largely by women. A better strategy would be for women to attain policy-making positions in those ministries most crucial to the needs of women – namely, education, health, social affairs and labour. Through such positions women can initiate policies that will strongly support moves toward a change in values and in the organization of work.

Conclusions

Women in Arab countries are to be found in a number of key positions, from which they are able to wield influence on the quantity and quality of the labour force. At home they are mothers; in the workplace they are professionals, health workers and teachers; in public life they are leaders in volunteer non-governmental organizations; but they have almost no presence as policy-makers in government. In order to take advantage of these key positions to mobilize human resources, women have to be mobilized themselves. In summary form, the following actions are required:

- Improvement in the literacy and general educational level of women, as well as in the quality of the educational system and its suitability vis-à-vis the demands of the labour market.

- Introduction of mass communication programmes that aim to change attitudes to work and to women's work in particular.

- Development of support mechanisms to enable a married woman to enter the labour force at a chosen time in her marital and reproductive life.

- Creation of income-earning opportunities for women consistent with the low levels of skills currently existing.

References

Abdel Khader, S. 1982. 'The Image of Women in Drama and Women's Programmes in Egyptian Television'. Ph.D. dissertation, Faculty of Mass Communication, Cairo University.

Abu Nasr, J., N. Khoury and H. Azzam, eds. 1985. *Women, Employment and Development in the Arab World*. Berlin: Mouton Publishers.

Azzam, H., J. Abu Nasr and I. Lorfing. 1985. 'An Overview of Arab Women in Population, Employment and Economic Development', in J. Abu Nasr, N. Khoury and H. Azzam, eds, *Women, Employment and Development in the Arab World*. Berlin: Mouton Publishers.

Benería, L. 1981. 'Conceptualizing the Labour Force: The Underestimation of Women's Economic Activity'. *Journal of Development Studies* 17, pp. 10–28.

Kallab, H. 1983. *She Cooks and He Reads.* Institute of Women's Studies in the Arab World, Beirut University College (in Arabic).

Schuster, I. 1981/82. 'Recent Research on Women in Development'. *The Journal of Development Studies* 18, pp. 512–35.

Sirageldin, I. 1986. 'Women and Demographic Change in the Arab Gulf: Relationships to Social and Economic Realities'. Paper presented at the Arab Gulf States Seminar for Women on Population and Family, Abu Dhabi, 3–5 March.

Sorensen, A. 1983. 'Women's Employment Patterns after Marriage'. *Journal of Marriage and the Family* 45, pp. 113–21.

Stevens, G., and M. Boyd. 1980. 'The Importance of Mother: Labour Force Participation and Integrational Mobility of Women'. *Social Forces* 59, pp. 187–99.

United Nations (UN). 1974. *Towards a System of Social and Demographic Statistics.* Studies in Methods, Series F, No. 18. New York: United Nations, Department of International Economics and Social Affairs.

Zurayk, H. 1983. 'Economic Activity of the Arab Woman'. *Al-Mustaqbal Al-Arabi*, vol. 48, no. 2, pp. 94–107 (in Arabic).

——— 1985. 'Women's Economic Participation'. In F. Shorter and H. Zurayk, eds, *Population Factors in Development Planning in the Middle East.* New York: The Population Council.

Zurayk, H. and H. Armenian, eds. 1985. *Beirut 1984: A Population and Health Profile.* Beirut: American University of Beirut.

4

Women and Development in the Maghreb Countries

Salma Galal

Introduction

As in other regions, issues related to women and development have been intensely discussed, researched and promoted in the Arab region. The UN Decade for Women (1975–85) was launched to promote equality and development, but women and men in developing countries continue to suffer from poverty, ignorance and disease. There is a growing awareness that the contribution of women in development (WID) is a matter of serious policy and action. The development process results in inequitable benefits and distribution of resources among men and women. Women are placed in a disadvantaged position by gender discrimination, economic marginalization, and the burden of their multiple roles. The Fourth World Conference on Women (Beijing, September 1995) addresses old and new problems facing women, and assesses the advances made since the Nairobi Conference in 1985.

The *1989 World Survey on the Role of Women in Development* (UN 1989) summarized the factors contributing to the deterioration of women's status in developing countries as follows:

- the economic crisis, including the national debt, affected work conditions, hence low-paid labourers were preferred;
- the inability of some economic sectors to integrate women appropriately;
- the decrease in women's incomes, especially in agricultural areas;
- the gap between men's and women's incomes, and the phenomenon of 'feminization of poverty';
- the long-lasting effects of illiteracy, malnutrition and illness.

The Arab countries have undergone rapid social change due to oil-financed development, and change has also occurred in the status of women. Oil prices, however, have fluctuated and the Maghreb countries in particular have been adversely affected by rising prices and by labour migration. As these countries have limited resources, the World Bank and the International Monetary Fund (IMF) became their primary sources of finance, particularly during the process of structural adjustment. This and other forms of dependency on the industrial nations has been a feature of the Maghreb countries since independence. Their limited resources made them economically dependent on the remittances of labourers who migrated to France, Germany and elsewhere. The worsening economic situation, the rural-to-urban migration, and the male out-migration are factors creating the need for women to earn cash income, especially in Morocco and Tunisia.

The Maghreb countries are not only experiencing economic difficulties (and, in the case of Algeria in 1994, a political crisis as well); they are also undergoing a modification in societal structure. Women in rural and urban areas in the Maghreb countries are faced with problems related to poverty, lack of skills and means of generating income, as well as social and cultural constraints. The choices available to them are not an individual matter in these countries but are rather a family and community affair. Positive improvements in the status of women have occurred in the areas of life expectancy, literacy, education and employment. Nevertheless, high rates of fertility, maternal and child mortality, illiteracy, poverty, and limited participation in public life continue (see Table 4.1 for comparative basic indicators).

This chapter concerns the present situation of the population, and especially of women, in the Maghreb countries, with a focus on health, fertility, employment, education, and legal conditions in Algeria, Morocco and Tunisia. Further, it seeks to explicate women's role in development and identify future policy options for their enhanced integration in the process.

A socio-economic profile

The constitutional monarchy of Morocco and the Republic of Tunisia were formed following independence from France in 1956, while the Republic of Algeria was established in 1962 after a long and bloody revolt. In all three Maghreb countries women participated in the national movements leading to independence. In the decades since independence,

Table 4.1   Basic indicators: Algeria, Morocco, Tunisia

	Algeria	Morocco	Tunisia
Total land area (1000 km²)	2381.7	446	163.6
Agricultural % of total	16.6	65.5	47.1
Population in millions	25.59	25.7	8.22
Density per km²	9	50	44
Urban population (% share)	52	48	54
Labour force participation rate (%)	24	33	30
GNP per capita ($)			
1983	2520	710	1290
1990	2330	970	1450
Population below poverty line (%)			
urban	20	28	20
rural	–	32	15
Human development index 1992	0.553	0.549	0.690

Sources: World Bank 1988; UNDP 1994.

the processes of urbanization, industrialization, inflation and migration have affected women in both their productive and reproductive roles. Traditionally, women's maternal role was highly respected and valued. The number of children born, especially boys, empowered women and enhanced their social status. Yet in the Maghreb, as indeed throughout the world, there is a discrepancy between the social value of motherhood and housework and its economic value. Furthermore, there are two schools of thought concerning women's employment: one supports the equality of woman and her right to work, and the other insists on her staying at home and thus remaining faithful to the 'Arab-Islamic heritage'. The economic need is stronger, however, especially among women from the poorer sections of society. But many women lack both an adequate income and the knowledge to manage their productive activities and increasingly diverse roles.

Population and Economic Policy of the Maghreb Countries

Algeria is the largest of the Maghreb countries, although only 16.6 per cent of its area is agricultural and inhabited, mainly along the Mediterranean coast. The average annual deforestation is about 2.3 per cent. It has a population of 25.6 million, with some 52 per cent in urban areas.

In 1991, the natural population growth reached 2.7 per cent. The Five-Year Plan of 1985–90 assigned great importance to the magnitude of social needs to be satisfied. The main demographic characteristics of Algeria are the high natural population growth (2.7 per cent), the youthfulness of the population (47 per cent under 15 years of age), the rapid rural-to-urban migration, and the need for employment-generation (ILO 1984a).

Once a capital-surplus country, Algeria has in more recent years been experiencing serious economic difficulties. The GDP was $42.2 billion in 1990, distributed as follows: 41 per cent services, 46 per cent industry, and 13 per cent agriculture. The official average annual rate of inflation was 6.6 per cent for the period 1980–90. External public debt was about 30.5 per cent of GNP. Increasing slowly, Algeria's per-capita GNP in 1990 was $2,330 (UNDP, *Human Development Report 1993*).

The population of Morocco, a mixture of Berbers and Arabs, totals 25.3 million, with some 48 per cent in urban areas. Agricultural activity is predominant, and 65 per cent of the land is under agricultural use. Access to safe water, however, is available for only 57 per cent of the population; rural people in particular are at a disadvantage. In 1990 the GDP of Morocco totalled $25.2 billion, of which 51 per cent was derived from services, 33 per cent from industry, and 16 per cent from agriculture. The annual inflation rate decreased from 7.2 per cent in 1980 to 5.7 per cent in 1991. The external public debt is 115.6 per cent of GNP. The per-capita GNP increased from $710 in 1983 to $970 in 1990 (UNDP, *Human Development Report 1993*). Economic reform programmes were initiated in 1983 with the following main objectives:

- to improve access to water supplies for rural and urban populations;
- to increase production and exports in agriculture, forestry, pastoral and fisheries sectors;
- to strengthen national development management capabilities;
- to improve investment efficiency in the public and private sector;
- to develop income and employment-generating activities for rural and urban communities.

Tunisia has a population of 8.2 million, with an average growth rate of 2 per cent, of which 54 per cent live in urban areas. Agricultural land accounts for about 47.1 per cent of the country. Industry is mainly on the coast, where the density of the population is highest. The GDP was $11.1 billion in 1990, distributed as follows: 16 per cent agriculture, 32 per cent industry, and 52 per cent services. Per-capita GNP increased to $1,450 in the late 1980s. In spite of the improvement in the economic growth rate, urban employment and rural underemployment are still serious problems. It is estimated that the unemployment rate is 12 per cent. The Seventh National Plan (1987–91) was intended to go a long way toward improving labour requirements. The demand for jobs is very high: the economy does not generate enough jobs, and women's demand for employment is increasing due to rising inflation rates and declining real family income (ILO 1984a). The other major concern is to bring the balance of payments under control and maintain equilibrium among the regions of the country.

With a population growth rate of 2.8 for Algeria, 2.4 for Morocco and 2.1 for Tunisia, high fertility rates, and nearly half the population under the age of 15 – Morocco 45 per cent, Algeria 47 per cent, Tunisia 40 per cent – the base of the population pyramid is broad. Age dependency is high – Morocco 85.4 per cent, Algeria 97.3 per cent, Tunisia 76.8 per cent (UNDP 1990) – and this increases the burden on the active labour force. Such high population growth can only worsen unemployment and the distribution of available resources.

Women, Health and Welfare

There is a reciprocal relationship between health and development. In 1978 the conference of Alma Ata declared primary health care part of development and set as the goal for the year 2000 'the attainment ... of a level of health that will permit [the peoples of the world] to lead socially productive lives', contributing to a better quality of life. In recent decades health indicators such as life expectancy, infant mortality rate (IMR) and maternal mortality rate (MMR) have been used as indicators of development. Whereas life expectancy in the Maghreb countries was between 40 and 51 years in 1965, it rose to 63 for Morocco, 66 for Algeria and 68 for Tunisia in 1990–95, indicating improvement in the quality of life. Vaccination coverage has expanded, and most of the population has access to health services, especially in Algeria and Tunisia; however, Morocco's maternal and infant mortality rates remain relatively high (see comparative data in Table 4.2).

In Morocco, although the family-planning programme was adopted in 1965, the total fertility rate is 4.5/1000 (see Table 4.2). Contraceptive users are 36 per cent; the majority of young women (51 per cent) believe that postpartum breastfeeding protects them from conceiving

Table 4.2 Population indicators: Algeria, Morocco, Tunisia

	Algeria	Morocco	Tunisia
Population age structure (%)			
0–14 years	47	45	40
15–65 years	49	52	56
65 and above	3	3	4
Life expectancy [a]	66	63	68
Population growth rate (%)	2.8	2.4	2.1
Crude birth rate (/1000)[a]	35	33	27
Maternal mortality rate (/1000)	2.1	2.7	2.0
Infant mortality rate (/1000)[b]	65	72	45
Vaccination coverage[a]	90	84	92
Female mean age at first marriage	21.0	22.3	24.3
Total fertility rate (/1000)[a]	5.0	4.5	3.6
Contraceptive users (%)	36	36	50
Availability of health services (% population)[c]	90	62	90
Availability of safe water (% population)[d]	99	73	65
Availability of sewage system (% population)[d]	59	65	45

Notes: [a] = 1990–95
    [b] = 1988
    [c] = 1987–89
    [d] = 1988–90

Source: UNDP, *Human Development Report 1990, 1991, 1992, 1993.*

(*Studies in Family Planning* 1990: 119). Cultural expectations require the newly married to demonstrate their fertility by having their first child very soon, ideally a boy. The vaccination coverage is 84 per cent and the IMR 72/1000, but mothers who lose their children will try to compensate by giving birth to more children. Although 62 per cent of the population have access to health services, many women of the lower socio-economic strata believe that modern medical facilities belong to the better off (Mernissi 1975). Traditionally, in rural areas the woman is the preserver of the family's health and sometimes even the healer.

Midwifery is a respected and honoured profession, but it carries a humble material reward.

In Algeria, the relative youth of the population has imposed a heavy burden on the country's socio-economic development. Still the total fertility is 5/1000 and the contraceptive use 36 per cent. As with the other Arab countries, fertility rates are high in the 20–24 age group, but even higher in the 25–29 age group (Omran 1990). Although the IMR has decreased from 150/1000 in 1970 to 65/1000 in 1990, it is still high. Having experienced the death of some of their children, women compensate by giving birth to more children. The national plan of 1985–90 established the necessity of stabilizing the birth rate, especially by spacing births and by raising women's educational level and enhancing their opportunities for employment.

In contrast to Algeria, the Republic of Tunisia adopted a demographic policy to slow down its population growth in order to improve development almost immediately following independence in 1956. The birth rate was reduced from 46/1000 in 1970 to 27.1/1000 in 1990. Contraceptive use was 50 per cent in 1991. However, low-income families value children as additional wage earners (Richter-Dridi 1981). In 1987 Tunisia was honoured by the United Nations for its achievements in population policy (Arab Council for Childhood Development 1989).

Education

The World Conference on Education for All, held in March 1990 in Thailand, set as a goal, in the 'World Declaration on Education for All', the eradication of illiteracy by the year 2000 (UNESCO 1990). This very ambitious goal is not likely to be achieved: despite intensive efforts to combat illiteracy, the results have been very slow in developing countries. Moreover, the absolute numbers are increasing, owing to population growth which is 2.8 per cent in Algeria, 2.4 per cent in Morocco, and 2.1 per cent in Tunisia. Projections based on analytical studies conducted by UNESCO indicated that the countries in which illiteracy decreases by less than 10 per cent for a period of ten years exhibit an overall increase in the number of illiterates (Galal and Nassar 1985). All Maghreb countries had lower rates than this, as indicated in Table 4.3 (2.28 in Algeria, 0.95 in Morocco, 2.25 in Tunisia). In 1990, female illiteracy in Algeria, Morocco and Tunisia amounted to 64 per cent, 54 per cent and 43 per cent, respectively (see Table 4.3). Although

Table 4.3   Illiteracy trends: Algeria, Morocco, Tunisia

	Algeria		Morocco		Tunisia	
	1970	*1990*	*1970*	*1990*	*1970*	*1990*
Adult illiteracy (%)	75	48.6	78	50.5	70	34.7
Female illiteracy (%)	89	64	90	54	83	43
Male illiteracy (%)	61	39	66	30	56	26
Yearly mean decrease rate (1970–85)	2.28		0.95		2.25	
Expected yearly rate of decrease to reach the goal for 2000	6.82		5.92		7.13	

Source: UNDP, *Human Development Report 1990.*

Algeria and Tunisia allocate one third of their budgets to education (Chemli and El-Solhi 1990), it is obvious that the expected lower rates will not be achieved by the year 2000. Like health and education, social services are bottomless barrels, capable of absorbing the whole budget and entire effort with no immediate outcome.

As a number of chapters in this book argue, education is an important indicator of women's role in development. Besides providing a woman with better opportunities for employment, education facilitates her effective participation in the general issues of her society and country. It gives a woman the power and the confidence to make decisions in her various domains, on the personal, family and community levels. The exposure to education and work that a woman experiences also influences her role as the manager of family resources.

In Algeria, fully one third of the budget has been allocated to education, an indicator of Algeria's mass education policy. The male:female ratio of enrolment is 105:85. Female share is 43.6 per cent in primary, 41.3 per cent in preparatory, and 44.8 per cent in secondary education. Although the pupil:teacher ratio is between 22 and 28, drop-out rates for girls and boys go up to 9.8 and 9.2, respectively (UN/ESCWA 1989). Similar female educational problems prevail in Morocco.

In Morocco, schooling has been obligatory for all children aged 7–13 since 1963. Previously, Quran classes were attended by children aged 4–7 in every community (Holl 1979). In the years 1984–87 the ratio of school enrolment for boys:girls was 96:62. Over 2 million children were in primary education in 1987–88 and about 1 million in preparatory education. The female share is 38.6 per cent in primary and 40.8 per

Table 4.4 Students enrolled, female percentage and male:female ratio, at different educational levels (1987–88): Algeria, Morocco, Tunisia

Country	Primary	Preparatory	Secondary	University	Vocational and teacher
Algeria					
Total (1000s)	3481	1400	357	132	669
Female (%)	43.6	41.3	44.8	–	30
Male:female enrolment ratio	105:85		62:45		
Drop-outs (%)	8				
Morocco					
Total (1000s)	2177	972	291	169	279
Female (%)	38.6	40.8	38.9	34.2	33
Male:female enrolment ratio	96:62		39:27		
Drop-outs	–				
Tunisia					
Total (1000s)	1339		438	408	258
Female (%)	44.7		43.1	36.7	31.2[a]
Male:female enrolment ratio	127:108		45:33		
Drop-outs (%)	13				

Note: [b] = 1981
Sources: UN-ESCWA 1990; UNDP, *Human Development Report 1989*; World Bank 1988.

cent in preparatory education. This female percentage did not differ much from that in 1980–81. About 42 per cent of primary-school pupils continue their education (UN/ESCWA 1989).

In Tunisia, the first girls' school was founded in 1900. In 1944, Arabic was introduced to classes to encourage parents to send their daughters to school. Since 1958, education for children aged 6–14 has been compulsory and free. The enrolment male:female ratio was 127:108 in the years 1984–87. The female share is 44.7 per cent in primary, 43.1 per cent in secondary, and 36.7 per cent in tertiary education (see Table 4.4). Unfortunately, drop-out rates are higher for girls than for boys. To deal with its older, illiterate population, Tunisia started a mass literacy campaign in 1966. In the one hundred centres of the *Union Nationale des*

Table 4.5 Economically active population by industry and percentage female: Algeria, Morocco, Tunisia

	Algeria (1987)			Morocco (1982)			Tunisia (1984)		
	No.	Female	% F	No.	Female	% F	No.	Female	% F
Agriculture, hunting, forestry, fishing	714,947	9,753	1	2,351,629	362,426	15	475,370	95,750	20
Mining and quarrying	64,685	3,142	5	63,360	2,250	4	38,030	1,920	5
Manufacturing	471,471	40,632	9	930,615	336,877	36	317,740	176,560	56
Electricity, gas, water	40,196	1,579	4	22,462	1,300	6	86,700	5,050	6
Construction	677,211	12,372	2	437,464	3,371	1	264,870	3,250	1
Wholesale, retail trade, hotels, restaurants	376,590	14,399	4	498,130	23,738	5	153,860	10,350	7
Transportation, storage	207,314	9,029	4	140,981	4,128	3	n.a.	n.a.	
Finance and insurance	125,426	17,751	14	n.a.	n.a.		47,440	20,670	44
Community, social and personal services	945,560	234,803	25	1,006,912	280,974	28	307,330	56,710	18
Others and not adequately defined (NAD)	149,241	83,718	56	n.a.	n.a.		95,080	17,940	19
Unemployed/not previously employed	862,117	57,642	7	547,704	166,216	30	52,930	13,850	26
Unemployed/previously employed	279,161	7,618	3	n.a.	n.a.		192,310	31,580	16
Total EAP	5,341,102	492,443	9	5,999,260	1,181,280	20	2,031,660	433,630	21

Source: ILO 1990 (Table prepared by V.M. Moghadam).

Femmes Tunisiennes (UNFT), literacy classes were held for women, in addition to instruction in cooking, sewing and raising children (Richter-Dridi 1981).

Women and Employment

Women have always worked, mainly in and around the household economy. It was with the institutionalization of work that its definition changed. In rural areas, female participation in different tasks is a necessity – a *sine qua non*. However, the official statistics on women in agriculture, housework or handicraft are insufficient and undercount much of rural women's productive activity, as discussed in this volume by Moghadam (Chapter 2), by Lackner (Chapter 5), and by Anker and Anker (Chapter 8).

Economists maintain that the Maghreb countries suffer from basic structural economic problems, namely the predominance of traditional agricultural patterns along with weak modernization and insufficient development of industry. It is further noted that budgetary resource limitations, employment difficulties exacerbated by the return of those working previously in European countries, and lack of integration of production processes limit employment generation (ILO 1984a). Data from ESCWA and the ILO indicate that, although the agricultural sector retains an important place in the economies of the Maghreb (though less so in Algeria), industrialization has been proceeding, and more of the labour force are moving into industry and services. However, as Moghadam points out in Chapter 2, labour-force participation remains low for women, and their employment status is not necessarily that of salaried employees in the modern sector. In Morocco, 39 per cent of the labour force is in agriculture, while in Algeria the figure is 14 per cent and in Tunisia 23 per cent (see Table 4.5). The labour-force participation rate is 33 per cent in Morocco, 24 per cent in Algeria, and 30 per cent in Tunisia (see Table 4.1). Very little is known about infor-mal-sector activity by the urban poor in slums and squatter settlements, or about people engaged in socially frowned-on informal activities like domestic service, petty trade, peddling and hawking; the extent to which women are involved in these activities is also unclear at this time. It is known, however, that many women work as dressmakers or seamstresses, which allows them to stay at home and not go against tradition.

Hijab believes that demand, opportunity and skills are the main factors influencing women's participation in remunerated employment

Table 4.6 Economically active population by occupation and percentage female: Algeria, Morocco, Tunisia

	Algeria (1987)			Morocco (1982)			Tunisia (1984)		
	No.	Female	% F	No.	Female	% F	No.	Female	% F
Professional, technical and related workers	598,748	165,108	28	324,941	78,172	24	55,770	9,810	18
Administrative and managerial workers	57,303	3,363	6	n.a.	n.a.		25,880	1,880	7
Clerical and related workers	418,438	74,786	18	252,259	64,497	26	213,240	57,040	27
Sales workers	282,927	4,839	2	455,022	17,717	4	42,550	800	2
Workers in services	346,063	65,101	19	427,531	162,528	38	174,910	28,120	16
Agriculture, animal husbandry, fishery	682,095	8,501	1	2,380,106	384,140	16	469,530	95,440	20
Production related workers: transport, operator	1,446,091	36,571	3	1,707,184	393,085	23	692,380	122,050	18
Workers not classified by occupation	368,159	68,914	19	452,217	81,141	18	117,750	71,280	61
All unemployed	1,141,278	65,260	6	n.a.	n.a.		244,610	45,430	19
Total EAP	5,341,102	492,443	9	5,999,260	1,181,280	20	2,036,620	431,850	21

Sources: ILO, *Yearbook of Labour Statistics 1991*, Table 2B; and *Retrospective Edition on Population Censuses 1945–1989*, Table 2C (Table prepared by V. M. Moghadam).

(Hijab 1988). In Chapter 7 of this volume, Shakhatreh analyses household-level determinants while Moghadam (Chapter 2) considers structural factors. Whatever the main causes, the percentage share of the female labour force has doubled since 1965 to about 26 per cent for Morocco, 7 per cent for Algeria, and 21 per cent for Tunisia in 1987. As can be seen in Tables 4.5 and 4.6, there are some similarities and some differences in the distribution of the economically active population, and the female labour force in particular, across the three countries.

Algeria's industrialization policy, aiming at the development of basic infrastructures, created more than 1 million jobs between 1967 and 1978 (ILO 1984a). The number of migrant workers to France and other European countries increased, reaching approximately 1 million (Khoury and Farag 1987). Due to inflationary pressures on real family income and urbanization, women's demand for jobs has been increasing at over 10 per cent annually (ILO 1984a), although by 1990 women made up only 8 per cent of the economically active population. Similar to other Maghreb countries, 72 per cent of working women are under 40 years of age. Some 30 per cent of them work as professionals and another 30 per cent in services. After marriage young women prefer to quit their jobs and stay at home.

In Morocco, the highest female shares in the economically active population are in manufacturing, agriculture, and public and private services. However, underreporting, especially of rural women's work, is a problem of census definition as well as of cultural values. Housework and agricultural work done by women in rural areas overlap and are difficult to separate. In urban areas, however, activities within the home and outside form distinct spheres; this often involves a challenge to established social norms. In the case of employment as an agricultural labourer – a position of low social standing – things are different: only a very needy rural woman would take such work, as it might affect her children's social mobility. Children, it should be noted, constitute 4 per cent of the labour force.

In industry women mainly work in textiles (where two-thirds of the workforce are women) and the food industry (Joekes 1982). Women who work in traditionally female jobs, like sewing and embroidery, are socially accepted, and those who work as teachers and midwives are even respected. In 1979 the proportion of women working in higher governmental offices was 13 per cent (Howard-Merriam 1984), and it grew in the 1980s. Male applicants have an advantage over female applicants, as men are considered to be the family breadwinners. Maternity leave is frowned upon, particularly in the private sector.

Tunisia has to face restrictions on the immigration of its labour force introduced by European countries, as well as urban migration due to rural underemployment. As a result, unemployment is high for both men and women. As in many Arab countries, female workers are concentrated in textiles, often with low levels of education and consequently on low wages. Midwifery and teaching are socially accepted professions, while nursing is less acceptable. Eighty-five per cent of all working women are under 40 years of age.

The Framework of Laws and Legislation

The constitutions of the Maghreb countries guarantee equal rights for all citizens. The civil laws are mainly derived from French law. With the independence of these countries, women gained their voting right. Family laws and personal status legislation are drawn from the Sharia (Islamic law), which gives men and women different rights. It should be added that in Tunisia and Algeria women judges serve in courts of justice, which is a rarity in Arab countries. Attempts to reform family laws are still an issue in many Arab countries, but none of them breach the Sharia (Hijab 1988). According to the Quran, women have the full right to hold and manage property in their own name, to inherit and to bequeath wealth. Quranic rights to property do not always translate into real property rights for women in many Muslim societies, however.

Labour laws provide equal rights and opportunities for men and women. Legislation regarding maternal protection, such as maternity and child-care leave, are adequate for the minority of women in the formal sector. They are more successfully applied in the public sector than in the private sector, where regulation is lacking (ILO 1984b). Women often do not know their legal rights, partly because they do not participate in the law-making process, and partly because they are kept uninformed about it. Particularly in rural areas, customs and traditions tend to be more powerful than laws, and the family is the main institution and decision-maker regarding women's lives.

The Moroccan Personal Status Code of 1957–58 stresses the wife's right to divorce her husband on her own initiative provided this is stipulated in the marriage contract. Nevertheless, a woman taking advantage of this right could be ostracized by her family (Holl 1979). In such cases, mothers keep custody of boys until puberty and girls until marriage. Polygamy is restricted and could be grounds for divorce; a second wife has to be informed of the previous marriage (Hijab 1988).

Working women qualify for maternity protection after having paid fifty-four days of social-security contributions over a ten-month period preceding the interruption of work. The maternity leave entitlement is twelve weeks, during which 50 per cent of the wages are paid for ten weeks. During this period dismissal is prohibited. The working women's legislation started in 1947 with the employment regulation (LS 1947– Mor. 1), and was followed in 1972 by the social-security measures (amended in 1973) (ILO 1984b).

The Algerian Family Code of 1984 gives the wife the right to divorce in the case of infirmity, imprisonment, abandonment, absence of physical union for over four months, and prejudice. If the husband initiates divorce, the wife is entitled to compensation; she is also entitled to housing if she is raising children. Polygamy is restricted and the wife's permission is required. Custody is given to mothers until boys reach 10 years of age (and may be extended to 16 years) and until girls are married (*Journal Officiel* 1984). Prior to the passing of this law, concerned women demonstrated several times between 1981 and 1984 for its implementation. The single-party parliament was divided into two schools of thought, one insisting that Algeria must remain faithful to 'Arab-Islamic heritage' and the other stressing women's equality with men, the proof of which was demonstrated during the struggle for independence (Hijab 1988). The National Charter of Algeria that was promulgated in February 1986 affirms the role of women in the family and in society, and recognizes that their contribution to social and productive activities is necessary for the development of the country.

The ordinance of 1975 on conditions of work (private sector) and that of 1971 on social insurance in agriculture, as well as the individual labour-relations act of 1982, and the social insurance act of 1983, guarantee working women maternity protection where they have contributed ten months' social-security contributions or were employed for the three months preceding leave. As in Morocco, maternity leave is twelve weeks, at 50 per cent of wages, during the course of which dismissal is prohibited (ILO 1984b).

The Tunisian Personal Status Code of 1956, amended in 1964, 1966 and 1981, is the most progressive in the Arab world. Divorce can only be granted in court. A divorced wife is housed until she remarries. Polygamy is prohibited. Bigamous men and women are liable to imprisonment. Custody is determined by the best interests of the child. The Personal Code provides for equality in all fields; nevertheless, women still receive a smaller share of inheritance, and the man is deemed the head of the family (Hijab 1988). There have been female judges in Tunisia since 1966.

The Labour Code of 1966 gives women maternity protection and allows part-time work. The family receives advantageous tax treatment if the wife works – only half of her wages will be taxed (Mernissi 1978). Maternity leave is thirty days if the mother has contributed to social insurance for at least two of the four preceding quarters. Two-thirds of the average daily wage is paid. Again, dismissal is prohibited during maternity leave (ILO 1984b).

Social and Political Participation of Women

In the Maghreb, political participation is in general very low and sometimes sporadic, partly due to the multiple roles of women and lack of time, and partly due to social norms or husbands' refusal. In addition to official women's federations, there are voluntary organizations, mainly of a social and cultural nature, with activities related to special issues such as handicapped children, literacy classes for girls and women, handicrafts, and family planning. Women of the elite sectors of society tend to initiate such associations. Sometimes, as a result of their different socio-economic backgrounds, these women are not successful in achieving their goals. In Morocco, for example, the Union des Femmes Morocaines was initiated by the king and female officials and employees, while the Female Worker Cooperative is not well known among women (Howard-Merriam 1984). In recent years, however, the number of women's non-governmental organizations (NGOs) in the Maghreb, as elsewhere in the Arab world, has been expanding rapidly.

In Morocco, women have been entitled to vote (directly and through a proxy) since the independence of Morocco, but their participation in the political parties has been limited. In 1982 the first women were elected to a parliamentary executive committee (Howard-Merriam 1984). In Tunisia women have voted since 1956, but the numbers of female representatives in parliament has remained low. Nevertheless, the women's organization Union Nationale des Femmes Tunisiennes had thousands of members as early as 1960 and over the years has successfully concentrated its efforts on the family-planning programme and the literacy campaign. Tunisia had 6,000 NGOs in 1988 – one of the largest contingents of NGOs in an Arab country; some of them are religious in nature, others serve their own members, and some are community-oriented (El-Monsif 1989).

Women's Participation in Development

Having reviewed the Maghreb region in terms of its socio-economic and demographic profile, and the position of women with respect to health, welfare, the legal system, education, employment, and political participation, we now shift the focus to married women and their options in the development process in the Maghreb. The high rate of marriage in the Maghreb and the importance of the family in the Arab world compels us to consider the various roles that women who are wives and mothers can assume in the development process and in the employment structure. In our view, married women have at least three different options as regards their participation in development. They can be housewife and mother, housewife and mother with home-based work, or housewife and mother with outside employment.

Housewife and mother

The role of housewife assists the regeneration of the (mostly male) labour force, while mothers can contribute to development by raising children prepared appropriately for the developmental process. This is one of the ways that women can act as 'mobilizers of human resources', as discussed by Zurayk and Saadeh in Chapter 3 of this volume. Though pre-school years are the most formative in a child's life, mothers are often unaware of their responsibilities. Therefore training of women and guidance from institutions and community workers could assist them in raising healthy children with a positive self-image, who would learn to set realistic goals and recognize and deal with problems as they encounter them. The Arab Maghreb Union may be the organization most appropriate for integrating 'child development' initiatives within the programme aiming to eradicate illiteracy by the year 2000 (UNESCO 1990). It is obvious that this input will have a long-term impact, but the developmental process requires a capable human resource base. While fulfilling their roles as housewives and mothers, women may be distanced from national and social issues; but they can become part of the mainstream process as soon as they start employment. When their major task is fulfilled, that is, mothers can be integrated into the labour force at a later stage. However, the state has to support their induction into the labour market at that stage by obliging employers to assign a certain percentage of jobs to them.

Housewife and mother with home-based work

Women who are in need of an income – such as in the case of female-headed households, low-income families or those in rural areas – but who face major societal constraints tend to prefer home-based work. It might be their first step towards outside employment. Changes in individual and societal attitudes take place only gradually. These women will probably remain unaware of their legal working rights and of the cooperative movement. They could be supported by home-visiting advisers, or they could start their own cooperative.

Morocco has long had a legal framework for home-based activities within its legislation on home working: Decree No. 1428 of March 1940 (ILO 1989). Algeria has practical experience in this respect in rural areas (Bou-Saleh 1990), integrating home-based work with industry.

Housewife and mother with outside employment

As shown in Table 4.6, Tunisia is the leader in female-labour force participation, with 21.3 per cent, followed by Morocco with 19.7 per cent, while Algeria with 6 per cent lags far behind. As long as the infrastructure fails to support working mothers by providing nurseries and kindergartens, the female share will not increase.

Women's labour-force participation in the Maghreb countries, as in the whole Arab world, remains a major problem for evaluation and planning. Census data collection leads to an undercount of women's work as women's activities often fall outside the sphere of production *per se*, and thus outside census definitions of 'economic activity'. A large proportion of women, especially in rural areas, are not full-time wage earners; rather, their work is irregular, seasonal, part-time and not in accordance with the accepted occupational standards. In addition, male respondents to census questionnaires tend not to concede female work due to cultural inhibitions (El-Bakri 1990; Anker and Anker, Chapter 7 in this volume).

In the future there will be fewer job opportunities within the state sphere, suggesting that men too will have to reorient themselves toward home-based work or small-scale enterprises.

Working women in urban areas

The integration of women into industrial development was one of the items under the UNIDO 1990–95 plan. Women are intended to be equal beneficiaries, especially in small-scale industries in urban areas. As long as small-scale industries are not integrated within the industrial plan, it could not be sustained for long.

The changing pattern of the family from an extended unit to a nuclear one necessitates working women in urban areas finding nursery care for their children during working hours. (In Morocco there are only 342 and in Tunisia 361 such nurseries [UN-ESCWA 1989].) These nurseries could also serve as information centres for those raising children. Similar centres can be established in rural areas; interested community leaders could be trained for this purpose, so that poverty and ignorance are not passed on to children.

What is clear is that policies should recognize women's vital role in the family and in society, and should allow women to combine these roles in a manner that is conducive to both family life and child welfare, on the one hand, and to social development, on the other. The Conference on Socio-Economic Challenges for the 1990s: Arab Women's Contribution to Development (Cairo, 20–23 May 1990) considered various strategies for the integration of women into the economy. The conference opted for what was called 'the third option' – that is, it rejected the option of full-time domesticity with no formal economic activity, and that of full-time work with no or little family time, in favour of policies to humanize the pattern of work for both men and women, including flexible working hours for women (UNDP 1990: Final Report).

Working women in rural areas

With the exception of the urban poor, rural women have historically been the most disadvantaged group of women in socio-economic terms. Their incorporation into the process of development is a necessity if the gap between urban and rural is not to widen further. It is necessary to assess the needs of rural women in order to design appropriate skill-training programmes, whether in food processing or marketing of products. In addition to small-scale enterprises, agro-industry is also appropriate in rural areas (UNIDO 1989). In southern Algeria, a state-owned company with subsidiaries throughout the country supplied women with raw materials to make products, and collected the finished products for sale in the company stores. Women were paid for their work at fixed piece rates. In addition, this company trained girls for such production work (Bou-Saleh 1990).

It is important to understand that people below the poverty line are very difficult to integrate into the development process. Once their survival needs are met, however, they are more likely to participate as well as to benefit.

Future Considerations

About half of the population in Maghreb countries live in rural areas where different patterns of development might be considered. Although development is understood in strictly economic terms, social, psychological, cultural, and other dimensions should be considered as well. However, whereas economic achievements are measurable and quantifiable, social-psychological changes take more time; assessing them is a qualitative and more difficult task.

While the legal frameworks in the Maghreb countries have undergone a number of changes, reaching a progressive stage especially in Tunisia, the implementation of laws has to be supervised and monitored, as there is a discrepancy between theory and practice. The world over, in periods of economic depression women are the first to be made redundant; this is usually accompanied by statements that their 'true place' is in the home. In the Maghreb countries legislation should ensure that even in the private sector a share of employment must be reserved for women, given that they are a vulnerable group comprising, *inter alia*, female-headed households. Another form of discrimination against women lies in the difficulty they have in obtaining loans. Consequently certain employment options for women will remain impossible without more favourable loan terms.

The broad population base in the Maghreb countries suggests harder times ahead for the younger generation in the labour market. Home-based work for both sexes has to be reconsidered, legalized and regulated. Morocco has already taken steps in this direction (ILO 1989).

Communities need national support if they are to develop their human resource base and their infrastructure. Education has to relate to community needs and community development as an integral part of its curriculum. As we have seen, child labour represents about 4 per cent of the total labour force in Morocco and is expected to rise. In Algeria, although only 0.4 per cent of the labour force are children, the primary-education drop-out rate is almost 10 per cent, thus indicating that children are needed to support family income. Working children have to attain a basic level of education, such as writing and calculation, in addition to vocational sciences. The integration of education into apprenticeships will improve the quality of their vocational training.

Women's participation in development has to be approached differently in rural and urban areas. In both sectors women should have a number of options available to them from which to choose. Women can contribute to development as housewives and mothers through their role in the socialization process by working at home or by entering the paid labour force. According to their circumstances and stage of life, women should be able to decide which option is the most suitable for them. Of course they should be able to make *informed* choices; and preparation for choices and responsibilities requires education and training. As with the consultations held by NGOs in the three countries, whether in family planning, literacy or vocational training, women have to be consulted regarding their educational and working options. In each village and urban area there should be community leaders trained in counselling or other services that provide the necessary information.

References

Arab Council for Childhood Development. 1989. *The State of the Child in the Arab World*. Cairo.

Bou-Saleh, Fatiha. 1990. 'Women and Rural Life: The Case of Algeria'. Paper prepared for the UNDP Conference on Socio-Economic Challenges for the 1990s, Arab Women's Contribution to Development, Cairo, 20–23 May.

Chemli, M. and El-R. El-Solhi. 1990. Personal interviews at the 16th Regional Conference of Arab National Commissions for UNESCO, 22 November.

El-Bakri, Z. 1990. 'A Profile of Arab Rural Women'. Paper prepared for the UNDP Conference on Socio-Economic Challenges for the 1990s.

El-Monsif, W. 1989. 'History of Voluntary Work'. Paper presented at the Arab Conference for NGOs Participation and Development, Cairo, October/November (in Arabic).

Galal, A. and S. Nassar. 1985. *Strategy of Education after Illiteracy Eradication and Continuous Education in ARE*. Hamburg: Institute of Education/UNESCO (in Arabic).

Hijab, N. 1988. *Womanpower – the Arab Debate on Women at Work*. Cambridge: Cambridge University Press.

Holl, R. 1979. *Die Stellung der Frau im zeitgenossischen Islam: Dargestellt am Beispiel Marokkos*. Frankfurt am Maine, Bern and Cirencester.

Howard-Merriam, K. 1984. 'Women's Political Participation in Morocco's Development: How Much and For Whom?' *The Maghreb Review*, vol. 9, nos 1–

2, p. 12.

International Labour Organization (ILO). 1984a. 'Employment and Manpower Problems and Policy Issues in Arab Countries: Proposals for the Future'. Papers and proceedings of an ILO regional symposium held in Geneva, January 1983.

———— 1984b. *Women at Work, Protection of Working Mothers: An ILO Global Survey (1964–1984)*, No. 2.

———— 1989. *Conditions of Work Digest*, vol. 8, no. 2.

———— 1990. *ILO Yearbook of Labour Statistics, Retrospective Edition on Population Censuses 1945–89*. Geneva: ILO.

———— 1991. *Yearbook of Labour Statistics 1991*. Geneva: ILO.

Khoury, N. and A. Farrag, eds. 1987. *Population and Human Resources Development and Planning in the Arab World: Concepts and Methodologies*. Geneva: ILO/Cairo University/Institute for Statistical Studies and Research (in Arabic).

Joekes, S.P. 1982. 'Female-led Industrialisation. Women's Jobs in Third World Export Manufacturing: The Case of the Moroccan Clothing Industry'. Sussex: IDS Research Reports.

Journal Officiel d'Algerie. 1984. 12 June.

Mernissi, F. 1975. 'Obstacles to Family Planning Practice in Urban Morocco'. *Studies in Family Planning*, vol. 6, p. 418.

———— 1978. *Country Reports on Women in North Africa: Libya, Morocco, Tunisia*. Addis Ababa: ATRCW-UNECA/CSDHA.

Omran, A. 1990. *Population of the Arab World - Past and Present*. New York: United Nations Fund for Population Activities (UNFPA).

Richter-Dridi, I. 1981. *Frauenbefreiung in einem Islamischen Land: Ein Widerspruch? Das Beispiel Tunisien*. Frankfurt am Maine.

Studies in Family Planning. 1990. vol. 21, no. 2, March/April.

UNESCO. 1990. *World Declaration on Education for All*. UNESCO: Paris.

United Nations (UN). 1986. *Compendium of Statistics and Indicators on the Situation of Women*. New York: United Nations.

———— 1989. *1989 World Survey on the Role of Women in Development*. New York: United Nations.

United Nations Development Programme (UNDP). 1990. *Conference on Socio-Economic Challenges for the 1990s: Arab Women's Contribution to Development*, Cairo, 20–23 May.

———— *Human Development Report, 1990, 1991, 1992, 1993, 1994*. New York: Oxford University Press.

United Nations Economic and Social Commission for Western Asia (UN-ESCWA). 1989. *United Arab Statistics Abstract 1980–1988*. Amman: ESCWA.

World Bank. 1988. *Social Indicators of Development*. Baltimore, MD: Johns Hopkins University Press.

5

Women and Development in the Republic of Yemen

Helen Lackner

Introduction

This chapter examines government policies towards women in the People's Democratic Republic of Yemen and the Yemen Arab Republic, and attempts to identify trends which may determine such policy in the Republic of Yemen after completion of the transition period in 1993. After a short summary of the political, economic and social environment in which policies were defined, there is a description of women's living conditions, including their role in production. This is followed by an analysis of a number of social indicators: political involvement, women's legal status, participation in the labour force, access to education and healthcare. As will be seen, and has been argued previously (Molyneux 1982; Lackner 1985a), women fared better in PDRY than in YAR and this was a direct consequence of state policy.

The Republic of Yemen was born in May 1990 through the uni-fication of the former People's Democratic Republic of Yemen (PDRY) and the Yemen Arab Republic (YAR). At the time of unification, Yemeni women had very high hopes. Women in the YAR hoped that PDRY legislation on the family and women's status would prevail, thus giving them a stronger case and considerable protection against polygyny, as well as a higher status in social life and encouragement to obtain education and work. Women in the PDRY hoped that the higher living standards which they believed existed in the YAR would spread to their part of the country and they would benefit from improved material living conditions.

Along with many other hopes of ordinary Yemenis, men and women, these have been disappointed in the first three years of the Republic of Yemen. The 1992 Personal Status Law is far closer to the YAR's Family Law, giving women no protection against polygyny and vesting all authority with the husband within the nuclear family and the father in the extended family. As a result the situation of women in the former YAR has not improved, while women in the former PDRY live in constant fear of their husbands marrying second wives – which serves as an effective threat in domestic disputes even though it is very rarely implemented.

Background: The Two Yemens

In the twentieth century, prior to the 1962 revolution, what became the YAR had been kept isolated from the outside world and its social, economic, technological and political changes. The revolution was followed by an eight-year civil war during which no 'development' policies could be implemented, except in the military sector. Between 1970 and 1990 an economy which can be described as almost medieval gave way to another with the characteristics of the late twentieth century, based on services, administration and a weak productive sector. Politically, a centralized state asserted its control over almost the entire population and territory. Social relations were deeply affected by images of the outside world as seen on television and related by migrants.

Some socio-economic developments were of particular relevance to women: in particular, migration, technological innovations and communications. Migration has been primarily a male phenomenon, affecting at its peak (from the late 1970s to the early 1980s) up to a third of the adult male population. Given that over 90 per cent of the country's population was rural, the impact of migration was also mainly felt in the rural areas. Migrants were usually farmers who went to work as unskilled labourers or small businessmen in Saudi Arabia, Kuwait, Abu Dhabi and, to a lesser extent, other oil-exporting states. They often stayed away for up to two years at a time, during which period the women in the household were effectively (though not nominally) in charge of house and farm management.

The PDRY became a single political entity at independence in 1967. The hinterland had been a collection of statelets ruled by tribal and other traditional leaders, under British protection and often selected and enthroned by the British. They were grouped in the Eastern and Western Aden Protectorates. Aden itself was ruled as a crown colony and populated largely by immigrants (from highland Yemen, India and Somalia, with, of course, British military and administrators). After four years of organized armed struggle led by a movement with rural origins, the British left in 1967 and a single state was created, the People's Democratic Republic of Yemen.

Ruled throughout its existence by the same organization, the Yemeni Socialist Party (the successor to the National Liberation Front), the PDRY was the only socialist Arab state. While its policies were clearly distinct from those found elsewhere, various aspects of international socialist ideology and practice were reflected in the development of the PDRY, and the regime's policies shifted from an initial 'ultra-leftism' associated with left politics of the 1960s to a more conventional form of socialism comparable to that found in Eastern Europe in the 1980s. Women's emancipation remained an objective throughout the period, but it was promoted differently in each political phase of the regime. In Aden women's situation had already been far more liberal than else-where during the colonial period, and women were given more oppor-tunities after independence. Emancipation of women in rural areas was an early cause of hostility to the regime as more conservative rural men saw efforts at bringing women out of the home as an attack on their rights as heads of households.[1]

The regime faced enormous difficulties. Although economically its ambition was to redistribute wealth, Yemeni reality dictated a redistri-bution of poverty: Aden's port and base had been the main source of revenue, and they vanished at the time of independence. Politically, the regime was torn between the specific realities of Yemeni social relations and the abstract language brought by fraternal socialist thinkers. With respect to its international situation, the regime had to face active hostility from its neighbours and received very little foreign investment for its economic and social development programmes. Socially the regime established a modern infrastructure throughout the country, giving the population schools (with Yemeni staff), medical centres and communi-cations; unfortunately the lack of internally generated revenue meant that most of this had to be financed with foreign assistance (see, for example, Kristiansson, Nasher and Bagenholm 1984).

The existence of the two Yemens notwithstanding, unity became an official slogan in both Sana'a and Aden. Throughout the 1970s and 1980s there were forces calling for unification and they were supported by the realities of social, economic and even political life, which were far more similar than was claimed by the regimes. For example, both economies had emerging state and private sectors, the aim of which was to create a 'modern' economy; and both were striving to establish central state control over societies divided by tribe and status, through the creation of 'national' physical and social infrastructures. These strategies were implemented against the background of a single nation and culture, strengthened by migration within Yemen which ensured that almost every Yemeni had relatives in the other part of the country.

Factors that maintained the separation of the two states were nonetheless strong. These included rivalry between the regimes and the self-interest of the political classes which would suffer from unity. There was also the matter of the apparently irreconcilable political choices of the two regimes, one aligned with the socialist world and the other with the USA and the right-wing regimes in the Arabian Peninsula. Of particular significance was the opposition of the Saudi Arabian regime to what it saw as the threat of a large, populated, united Yemen on its borders.

From the mid-1980s onwards, both parts of Yemen experienced political uncertainty and increasing popular dissatisfaction with the power structures. In the PDRY, Yemenis had lost faith in the abstract slogans of the Yemeni Socialist Party (YSP). The regime's major achievements – its health, education and communications investment – were taken for granted by a population whose expectations were based on Kuwaiti living standards. Other policies had either led to disappointment through bad implementation (such as the land reform), or had always been unpopular (such as restrictions on migration). Finance became an issue when repayment of earlier multilateral loans fell due. The Soviet Union and its allies faced problems of their own and were increasingly unwilling and unable to support the PDRY, materially or politically. In this context the regime was shattered in 1986 by the worst ever power struggle within the YSP's leadership. Fighting led to the death of over 5,000 people, including the surviving leadership of the armed struggle. Its result was the division of the remains of the YSP into a weakened faction in power in Aden and another in exile in Sana'a. The politically discredited and militarily weakened PDRY regime faced increasing balance-of-payments difficulties, lack of resources and international isolation as a result of the collapse of the Eastern bloc.

The situation in the YAR was hardly better. The remittances boom was over; the rising cost of living was not matched by increased incomes from farming, the civil service or the private sector. Benefits expected from oil production remained elusive. Corruption was rampant, thus alienating the population. The gap between the few really rich and the mass of the people was both increasing and becoming more visible through conspicuous consumption such as the construction of luxury villas, while the number of beggars multiplied. The state's finances suffered from increased debt despite the export of oil which started in 1986. The regime's credibility dropped as stated policies were openly flouted and popular grievances, however justified, were ignored. Politically the regime's forcible integration of opposition forces into a supposedly democratic structure left the population largely indifferent, as real power was seen to be elsewhere. Tension with the regime in Aden and uneasy relations with the exiled section of the YSP were further problems, while border clashes with Saudi Arabia were a constant feature of life after the discovery of oil in the border region.

In the context of the internal crises of the two regimes, momentum towards unification increased. Sustained over the years by unification committees which had achieved a number of fundamental agreements, including a united constitution, this momentum speeded up in the late 1980s with the discovery of oil in a PDRY area bordering YAR and close to Saudi Arabia. The two states reached agreement and set up a company for joint exploration. The introduction of freedom of movement for Yemenis within the country in 1988 was a highly popular political gesture which gave unification real meaning for the population. Agreement on unification was rushed through and a United Yemen announced, ahead of schedule, in May 1990. A transitional period ended with free national elections for a multi-party parliament in April 1993. Because the Saudi regime had been weakened by the drop in oil revenues and by the increasing internal challenges from both 'liberal modernizing' forces and those who challenged official Wahhabism on fundamentalist religious grounds, it was unable successfully to oppose Yemeni unification.

The transitional period was a very difficult one, made even more so by international events. The Gulf crisis gave Saudi Arabia an opportunity to expel most of its Yemeni population: over 800,000 were evicted and many deprived of their possessions. This conflict brought to the fore differences between the two leaderships. Whereas Ali Abdullah Saleh of the north had for a long time been close to the Iraqi ruler, the YSP leadership had an equally long history of hostility to Iraqi Ba'athism. Political differences between the YSP and the General People's Congress[2] became increasingly bitter, focusing on policy and on the distribution of power and political positions in the post-transition period. Political tension in the country was sustained by a series of actual and attempted assassinations of political figures, most of the targets being YSP members.

The economic crisis worsened. Although oil exports rose rapidly, the quantities involved and world prices meant this had less impact on the economy than hoped. At the same time, the currency collapsed (assisted by the surreptitious intervention of currency dealers). Inflation soared, incomes and production stagnated, and foreign aid was seriously reduced. The reintegration of the returned migrants was an added burden.

Despite a free press and the creation of numerous political parties, dissatisfaction rose as the population throughout Yemen found their expectations disappointed. Instead of the hoped-for expansion of the reasonably competent administration from the PDRY to the whole country, corruption spread everywhere. High prices ensured that the consumer products previously widely available in the YAR were out of most people's reach. Given all these factors, social tensions rose to unprecedented levels, and took forms which had not been seen anywhere in Yemen under the earlier regimes. In September 1991 the president and vice president were greeted by hostile demonstrators in Aden, demanding lower prices and maintenance of social benefits. Spontaneous riots occurred in October 1991 in Sana'a, sparked off by popular revulsion against the military's flouting of the law. More seriously, in December 1992 riots against high prices and corruption took place in Ta'iz, Hodeida, Sana'a and Dhamar.

The Status of Women in the Two Yemens

Women's lives in Yemen depend primarily on three factors: their ascribed position in society, whether they live in rural or urban areas, and their wealth. In the past, their legal status depended on whether they lived in the PDRY or in the YAR.

Yemen has a complex social structure based on ascribed status, which affects women more than men in daily life. The highest group is that of the *sada*[3] families, whose women are strictly secluded, even in the villages. In some situations this deprives a poor family of female labour, and thus worsens its living standards. Yet, throughout Yemen *sada*, except the most modernized, keep their women veiled and at home, only going out under exceptional circumstances. The bulk of the population is composed of tribal people (*qabila*, pl. *qaba'il*) whose men in the past divided their time between farming and fighting. *Qabila* village women are not veiled and participate actively in production, particularly agriculture and the building of their own houses. Below the true tribes are the tradesmen, whose status has improved markedly in recent decades. The lowest social stratum is composed of a variety of service workers, collectively known as *muzzayin, akhdam* and *hujur*, of various origins, some of them reputed to be descendants of slaves, active in occupations such as personal grooming, artistic activities and cleaning.

Throughout the period under consideration, Yemeni women have been and are subject to the male-dominated customs of Yemen and to the restrictions imposed by Muslim law. They are subject to the authority of their fathers and, later, their brothers, husbands and eventually sons, who have the right to make decisions concerning their lives and activities. Women are expected to end social contact with unrelated men at the onset of puberty or even earlier, and thereafter their social life is restricted to mixing with women. This segregation is not as strictly enforced in the rural areas, where women continue to work alongside men in the fields throughout their lives. Everywhere women remain virgins until marriage, and strict sexual fidelity is demanded in all sectors of society. Women's activities are restricted to the household, where they have power and authority based on their age and seniority. Outside the home women have no say. All major political, social, economic and religious decisions are taken by men singly or in groups, and women are largely excluded from this decision-making.

In the YAR, women's political participation was negligible. Although women had the right to vote and to be members of political bodies, only a very few women from the highest social groups took an active part in political life. No women held positions in the government and only very few in the institutions of the General People's Congress (GPC). In the PDRY, women had the right to vote once they reached the age of 18 and to stand for election in the Local and Supreme People's Council alongside men and equally with them once they were 24 or over. Their level of participation in elections was high: in the 1983 Local People's Council elections, 80 per cent of the electorate participated, including a majority of women. Their representation in political institutions, however, was not impressive. In the Supreme People's Council that was elected in 1978 there were 6 women out of 111 members; in that elected in 1986, there were 10. There were no women ministers; nor were there any women on the Political Bureau of the Yemeni Socialist Party. In the Central Committee, the number of women remained very low. Women's representation in the Local People's

Councils was higher, particularly in the Aden area, but still quite low. In 1983 there were 34 women elected out of 305 councillors throughout the country.

In terms of principle and policy there were substantial differences between the two regimes' policies on women. These were particularly evident in the laws on marriage and family affairs, which are the aspects of legislation – civil or religious – that most affect women. The constitution of the PDRY stated that all 'citizens are equal in their rights and duties irrespective of their sex, origin, religion, language, standard of education or social status'.[4] This statement declaring the constitutional equality of the sexes gave women support in their demands for greater equality as well as providing the services necessary to ensure it. The major piece of legislation in support of women was the 1974 Family Law. This liberal law, comparable in the Arab world only to the Tunisian Family Law, was a unique achievement in favour of women.

Contrary to tradition, wherein marriage is an alliance between two families or the strengthening of family relations, the law stated that 'marriage is a contract between a man and a woman, equal in rights and responsibilities, made on the basis of mutual understanding and respect with the aim of creating a cohesive family which is the cornerstone of society.'[5] The minimum age for marriage was set at 18 for men and 16 for women. Unlike in traditional Muslim marriages where male guardians act on behalf of the bride, this law insisted that the bride herself must sign the marriage register. Moreover, unlike in many Muslim countries, where men may have more than one wife, the PDRY Family Law allowed such only under exceptional circumstances. Article 11 stated that,

> Marriage to a second wife is not permitted except with permission in writing from the relevant summary court. Such permission shall not be granted except where one of the following circumstances is proven to the satisfaction of the court:
> 1. If the wife is sterile, subject to confirmation by a medical report, provided that the husband had no knowledge of the condition prior to marriage.
> 2. If according to medical evidence the wife is suffering from a chronic or contagious incurable disease.

The Family Law's household management proposals were particularly progressive, stating that 'both husband and wife shall participate in bearing the expenses of marriage and establishing the conjugal home according to their means.' Further, 'both husband and wife shall share in bearing the costs of their married life and where one party is unable to do so the other party shall be responsible for maintenance and the costs of married life.' Similarly, 'both father and mother share responsibility for the maintenance of children according to their means.'

Another major aspect of marriage which this law attempted to regulate was the brideprice, which was not to exceed YD 100 (about $300). The law transformed divorce procedures, putting an abrupt end to centuries of practice: 'Unilateral divorce is prohibited'. To be legal a divorce had to go through a court, and the court would not approve a divorce unless the People's Defence Committee and the General Union of Yemeni Women supported it. Either partner could petition for divorce on equal grounds, but a woman had one additional ground, namely if her husband married a second wife.

This law made a considerable difference to marital relations in the PDRY. Although it was by no means fully enforced, it created possibilities for women to control their own lives. The effort at enforcement was to prevent polygyny. Rules on bridewealth were widely ignored and the amounts paid corresponded, rather, to possible income from migration. However, the law allowed determined women to exercise their rights: for example, although under-age marriage persisted, particularly in the countryside, it became possible for a young woman to reject a marriage partner she did not want. Should her parents be insistent and unwilling to accept her refusal, she could appeal to the local GUYW and the People's Defence Committee, who might support her and help her persuade her parents of the error of their ways.

In contrast to the PDRY, women's legal status in the YAR was determined by the Sharia and its interpretation by local Muslim authorities, be they Zeidi or Shafi'i, which was the basis of written laws. Many practices experienced as 'laws' were in reality traditions; but, if infringed, they were upheld by the relevant authorities. Most of them restricted rather than increased women's rights. In the YAR marriage was a contract between two families represented by the bridegroom and the male agent (usually the father) of the bride. While the bride's consent should, theoretically, be given, the law did not insist on it being actively expressed. Similarly, the bride should have reached menarche, but again this was not always enforced. Regulations for the conduct of married life clearly indicated women's subordination. Men were entitled to obedience from their wives, who had to live in the matrimonial home, obey their husbands and do the housework; they could not leave the home without the husband's permission, and could not refuse intercourse. A husband's duties were to provide the home and maintenance both in terms of food and other necessities including clothing, and to treat all his wives equally if he had more than one (see Myntti 1979, 1985; Makhlouf 1979).

Bridewealth was one of the two sources of women's independent income. It was not usually paid in full at the time of marriage; rather, a substantial part was retained to be paid on divorce or desertion by the husband (if proved in the wrong). The part paid was handed over to the bride. This was her own personal wealth and not to be treated as part of the household income. Often the only substantial amount of money she handled in her life, it was usually used to buy gold, which can be kept easily and seen, thus giving the woman increased status. The amounts involved in bridewealth increased dramatically in the early 1970s due to the high cash incomes that migrant workers earned in the oil-producing states. In the early 1970s, prior to the emigration boom, bridewealth was around YR 5,000 ($1,250); by the late 1970s it was close to YR 100,000 ($25,000) and rose even higher in the early 1980s. Since then the reduction in remittances and the changed fortunes of the oil-exporting states have resulted in continued fluctuation of bridewealth rates.

Divorce was a constant threat to women's security in the YAR. In the late 1970s the divorce rate was quite high: 70 per cent of all first marriages ended in divorce. While there were certain circumstances in which women were legally entitled to initiate divorce (such as a husband's insanity, his physical disability, desertion without maintenance for over two years, conviction for a criminal offence), the procedures were complex and of little assistance in most cases of marital dispute. Although Islam allows women to require that the marriage contract give them the right to initiate divorce, this was rarely done. In practice divorces were initiated by men and were in fact unilateral repudiations, without any recourse to proof of misbehaviour: all a man had to do was state in front of two witnesses that he was divorcing his wife; if this statement was repeated three times the divorce was final and irrevocable.

In the YAR, as elsewhere in the Arab world, men are responsible for the maintenance of children from a marriage even after divorce, and in theory can take up care and custody when a boy reaches 7 years of age and a girl 10. In practice children are usually left with their mothers until adulthood, though problems arise in cases when the woman remarries and her new husband is not keen on having children from an earlier marriage in the household. After divorce a man is responsible for the maintenance of his former wife during the 'waiting period' –

that is, a period of about three months during which the woman may not remarry. This period is meant to ensure that the woman is not pregnant with the husband's child. If the woman is divorced during pregnancy, the husband must maintain her until the birth of the child.

When women are divorced, they usually return to the parental home or that of a brother. If no relative will take them in, they have to live alone and maintain themselves, which usually means taking up low-paid jobs in the villages or small towns, either as agricultural labourers, bread makers, washer women, cleaners, and so on, according to their ascribed status and their ability and training.

Apart from bridewealth, inheritance is the other main means for women to obtain wealth of their own. They are theoretically entitled to inherit half the share received by a male with identical relationship to the deceased. In practice women often waive their rights and allow their brothers to take over what property they are entitled to, either formally or by letting them manage it, and only take whatever their brothers give them on their own initiative, usually in the form of cash 'gifts' on religious festivities. This reluctance to claim what is theirs by right is based on the possibility of their having to return to their family homes and be dependent on their brothers for maintenance. When the legacy takes the form of a share in the family house, women do retain it as they may find themselves going to live in the room which belongs to them at some future date; but agricultural land and other income-generating property are almost always left under the 'management' of male relatives. On the whole, women are extremely conscious of their dependence on males and of their need to maintain status.

The 1992 Personal Status Law

Issued as a Presidential Council Decree, the 1992 Personal Status Law of the Republic of Yemen contains clauses specifically affecting women in the areas of marriage, divorce and custody of children. In all these matters, this law is clearly closely based on the Muslim Sharia and is therefore very similar to the situation prevailing in the YAR. It does, however, state that marriage is a partnership between the couple involved,[6] and that 'any contract established on the basis of compulsion on the husband or wife is invalid'.[7] It permits a man to marry up to four wives (Article 12) and accepts male authority within the family. Concerning divorce, it gives both partners equal right to petition (Article 47), and states that a judge has to take responsibility for cases initiated by women. It does not, however, put an end to repudiation of a wife, though all divorces have to be brought before the court for registration. In cases of separation, custody reverts to the father at the age of 7 for boys and 10 for girls.

This law confirms many of the fears expressed by women throughout Yemen since unification. Most women had been looking forward to an end to polygyny, which distorts relations between couples. They had hoped to be encouraged to participate more actively in public life, professionally and politically. However, this law makes it clear that the trend of Yemeni politics in the 1990s is not moving in that direction.

Women's Activities in the Rural Sector

Women play a major role in agriculture throughout Yemen. Their role in cultivation varies according to a number of factors: social status, land tenure, region and crop. Almost everywhere, women are responsible for the care of cattle and other livestock. Conditions of animal husbandry and the number of household animals kept are significantly different in the highlands and the coastal areas. Except for range-land grazing and camel husbandry, which are the responsibility of children and men respectively, animal husbandry is almost entirely the province of females. In the highlands camels are sometimes fed by women in the same way as cows, and this can be an additional burden on their time.[8]

In the coastal plains, a household can keep more cattle and they are grazed outdoors; cattle-owning households may have up to half a dozen head, as husbandry is far less demanding of time and effort. In the highlands, cows kept according to traditional Yemeni husbandry practice require the full-time labour of one person per cow.[9] Cattle are the most prized livestock, particularly in the highlands, where their milk is the major source of calcium and milk products for the population. *Samn baladi* (home-made ghee) is a high-status food, as is its by-product, *laban* or *haqin* (buttermilk, smoked and prepared with chillies). These uses of milk both take priority over giving children unprocessed milk to drink. Families usually keep one cow, very rarely two. Cows are not grazed but hand-fed sorghum stalks wrapped in alfalfa. This force-feeding of the cows takes place for a total of between three and four hours daily and is usually done by elderly women: it is a fairly relaxing activity which the women enjoy as it provides opportunities to sit and talk with neighbours while working. In addition to hand-feeding, cows have to be watered and washed and their sheds occasionally cleaned.

Donkeys are kept as beasts of burden throughout the country. Camels are mainly found in the lowlands. Chickens are popular everywhere, despite the increase in chicken farms in recent years, while rabbits are quite rare. The care of chickens takes little time as they are given left overs from human meals and left to scavenge; at night they are kept in cages or in the house to keep them out of reach of marauding foxes and other predators. Goats and sheep are mostly herded by children in the village, who take them out into the fields for grazing and are paid to do this according to the number of head they look after; however, their pens have to be kept clean and this is women's work. In addition, in towns and where no grazing is available they are fed alfalfa, which is either cultivated (it is cut and collected by the women of the household daily from the fields, and this can take between half and one hour) or bought in the market.

The vast majority of cultivation tasks are performed by women in most parts of the country, but there are differences in detail which require further study in order to identify clearly female activities according to crop, task, agro-ecological zone, and social status. The exceptions are certain areas such as Wadi Rima in Tihama, and women of the *sada* group who would lose status by working the land. Cash crops are generally not considered to be women's work: qat[10] in particular is usually cultivated by men, and women's only role in its cultivation may be weeding; again this is not seen as weeding the qat but rather as collecting animal fodder. The well-known (but still unexplained) exception to this rule is the area of Jabal Sabr, above Ta'iz, where women own and cultivate *qat* for their own benefit and even sell it themselves in the souk. Other cash crops such as coffee and grapes remain male preserves, although in the last decade women's work in cultivating other fruits and vegetables has increased, though they do not participate in marketing.

Having dealt with the exceptions, let us now examine mainstream agriculture. Most fields are cultivated with cereals, sorghum, millet, wheat and barley, mostly rain-fed but sometimes irrigated. The vegetables most commonly cultivated are leeks, tomatoes, potatoes, and alfalfa for animals. In these crops women do most of the work, with the exception of ploughing and threshing which are mainly male activities but sometimes involve women. The application of chemical fertilizers and pest-control agents is now defined as a male task, although traditionally women spread manure on the fields; nevertheless there are areas, particularly in the southern governorates, where women do apply fertilizer. On the whole, however, this appears to be an example of a task being transformed from a female to a male province when it passes from traditional methods to modern technology.

Women's tasks include sowing, planting, transplanting, thinning, weeding, most harvesting, winnowing, pulling out roots, manure application and, in some areas, irrigating. These tasks require different amounts of women's time according to the season and the amount of land cultivated, the amount of alfalfa to be cut daily, and so on. At peak harvesting times, women spend up to eight hours a day in the fields; harvesting can also take place at different times according to the crops, particularly on irrigated land. For example, in Hadramaut women on average contribute 39 per cent of the labour in wheat farming (Ahmed and Tarmoon 1984). In harvesting and winnowing women do 80 per cent of the work. Alfalfa is almost entirely a women's crop. Date production is mainly a male activity, but women do 48 per cent of the trimming, 52 per cent of the picking and 80 per cent of the sorting. Women are to be seen throughout the day working in the fields in Wadi Hadramaut throughout the year.

The participation of women in village productive life is taken for granted. In addition to their agricultural tasks, women are exclusively responsible for looking after the house. Girls are trained from an early age to participate in all the activities which will be their lot for life. A woman's responsibilities can mean an average working day of up to sixteen hours for a woman who has many small children, fields to cultivate and livestock to keep, without any assistance from a male relative. It is therefore not surprising that under 10 per cent of rural women are literate. Aside from not having the time to attend school, even if the men in the family allowed it, schooling seems largely irrelevant to rural women whose workloads and responsibilities are very heavy and not those of a literate culture.

All rural women are responsible for housework, ranging from water and fuel collection to cooking, cleaning and child care. These tasks can take varying amounts of time depending on circumstances. Cooking usually takes up about two hours of the day, and house cleaning about half an hour. How much time is devoted to child care depends, obviously, on the number and age of the children. The time taken to collect water can vary from nothing if the house has running water to one or two hours daily when water has to be collected from a remote well or spring and either carried on the woman's head or by donkey, often up steep hills.

The acquisition of fuel takes two main forms: the collection of firewood, done once or twice weekly and sometimes taking half a day or more, and the manufacture of dung cakes, which can take about five hours weekly in all, and includes careful collection of animal droppings near the house. With the introduction of bottled gas and paraffin cookers, as well as the almost total disappearance of trees, this is a task which is rapidly disappearing except for the very poorest women for whom it becomes increasingly arduous and time-consuming. In 1991, in Khawlan, an extremely deforested area of the Central Highlands near Sana'a, I came across women gathering cacti and other succulents for fuel over 10 km away from their homes because they could not afford gas.

Thanks to the remittances which reached most households in the 1970s and 1980s, many villages now have electricity for at least a few hours every evening, and in urban areas the vast majority of houses use electric power. By the end of the 1980s, at the national level 20 per cent of all dwellings were connected to the public grid, and 25 per cent to private networks, while 50 per cent of housing units were lit with paraffin.[11] Electrification has transformed life for women: it has brought television and video, thus introducing into the most remote mountains real and imaginary ways of life totally foreign to the daily realities lived by women and children, and encouraging unrealistic ambitions. It brought refrigerators and the possibility of conserving food, as well as various food-processing appliances (mainly the mixer), which reduced labour time in the kitchen. As such, migrants' remittances and state initiatives alike have improved some women's living conditions through provision of village water supplies, either from standpipes or with piping to each house from boreholes. As a result, most urban women and increasing numbers of rural women have reasonable access to water, though not necessarily to safe water, as the piping is often unhygienic and prone to leaks. In addition, drainage facilities are rare, thus increasing the risk of water-borne diseases.

A worker's remittance also tended to be used to build an independent house (encouraging the break-up of the extended family in favour of the nuclear one), and to buy a vehicle, used both for family purposes (visits to hospitals and relatives) and for business by the returned migrant or one of his male relatives (taxis, transport of goods, and so on). Road construction has enabled people to purchase fuels to replace wood and dung cakes. Most families in rural areas and almost all urban families now use a combination of fuels, including bottled gas, paraffin cookers and some firewood/dung cakes (used almost exclusively for the manufacture of a certain type of bread).

Improved communications, such as roads and telephones, have broadened people's access to the new facilities existing in the country: hospitals, schools, large urban shopping centres. Shopping has become part of life – not only for clothing, kitchen equipment and other similar necessities but also for food. The increase in acreage devoted to growing *qat* at the expense of food crops, the heavy labour demands and low yields of refined sorghum cultivation and the unreliability of rain, the absence of young men to carry out heavy farm labour, and the low subsidized prices of imported grains are factors that have combined with the increased availability of cash remittances to ensure that much traditional cultivation was neglected. Instead traditional diets were changed and most foods bought: sorghum gave way to imported refined wheat; dried powdered milk became a basic item; fresh vegetables and meat are consumed in larger quantities. Moreover, soft drinks and other items lacking nutritional value have become big sellers and use up much available cash that could be spent on nutritious food.

Women in Urban Areas

Yemen has been undergoing very rapid urbanization. While only 10 per cent of the population was urban up to the late 1970s, in 1990 the urbanization rate was 30 per cent. This is due to considerable rural-to-urban migration in recent years, one of the many by-products of the emigration boom. Returning migrants have often built houses in the towns, and increasingly in the 1980s in the capital itself, where they hope to find work. In addition to functioning as the main residence of the migrants themselves and their nuclear families, these houses also serve as bases for rural relatives visiting while seeking official documents (which often takes a matter of weeks rather than hours). The arrival of a large number of immigrants from different parts of the country has deeply affected the stability and social cohesion of the main towns, and played a major role in the social transformation of contemporary Yemen (Lackner 1985b; YAR 1985).

Urban life, whether in a major city or smaller town, has many obvious advantages for women, at least in the beginning. Moving to town provides an immediate improvement in status (real or imagined), manifested by veiling – usually the adoption of the most concealing of the Yemeni forms of outdoor covering, the *shirshaf*. Other immediate benefits are a dramatic reduction in workload as certain tasks cease to be practised in towns: cultivation of the fields, trips in search of fuel or water. Only a few head of small livestock can be kept in urban houses. Thus women's workload is reduced to housework, which is itself made easier by electricity, purchased fuels, and running water in the house. For most rural women, this represents the ultimate in leisurely living, and seems like a dream holiday. For women who have got used to it, memories of the harshness of rural living conditions ensure continued appreciation of urban life and help to overcome the boredom it produces.

Urban life has its own constraints and customs: life is centred around housework, child care and socializing. While the mornings are devoted to housework and cooking, afternoons focus on meetings with other women.[12] Socialization is circumscribed by a woman's position in the social structure and her wealth. Unlike rural women, who – with the exception of *sada* – all work, in towns only the lowest social group of poor women walk unveiled and work outside the home. *Qabila* women are mainly involved in housework, child care and looking after their chickens and sheep. They are increasingly interested in fashion, the unfolding dramas of the television soap operas, and events in the neighbourhood. As many of them do need an income, they try to earn money through activities compatible with the status to which they aspire, activities which can be carried out at home or focus on afternoon women's gatherings – sewing, knitting, selling cloth, sometimes cooking.

Urban life for most women is tending to develop features comparable to that of women in industrialized countries in the 1950s: it is focused on the home, children and television. The break-up of the extended family (through separate housing, physical and social distance) is creating a level of isolation for urban women which is only partially relieved by the afternoon gatherings and frequent visits from rural and other relatives. Relationships with husbands have not become significantly closer, as men's lives still follow quite separate social patterns.

Women in the labour force

A major problem in the study of women's role in the labour force is the lack of sex-disaggregated data – a problem shared with many other countries (see, for example, Benería 1981; and Dixon 1982). The definition of participation in the labour force, in the Republic of Yemen and elsewhere, focuses on wage labour and on relationships that are part of the modern sector in the economy. In practice most women work in the rural areas, and their labour is subsumed under the category 'family' labour and thus excluded from the labour statistics such as they are. What is more, the only data on the labour force published in the *Statistical Yearbook* since unification concern foreign labour.

In the YAR, the total labour force was estimated to be 1.85 million people in the early 1980s, with only 5.6 per cent female participation. In the PDRY it was government policy to encourage women to join the labour force. Women's participation in the official labour force rose from 17 per cent (54,350) in 1973 to 20 per cent (91,000) in 1984 (World Bank 1984). As can be seen, the percentage increase was small, but it represented almost a doubling in absolute numbers. The main success of this policy was in Aden, as elsewhere few women entered the labour force. Difficulties were largely due to cultural factors and the fact that socially women's employment was viewed with some scepticism. While women's traditional activities in the rural areas in agriculture and in construction were accepted as the norm (but excluded from the official data), in the urban environment and in decision-making circles some activities were considered more suitable for women than others.

This remains true in the new situation of united Yemen and results in a status-ranking of jobs in which education and clerical work are considered acceptable occupations for women, while factory work or construction are regarded as of low status. Work in the health sectors suffers from traditional prejudices: whereas to be a doctor is to have a high-status occupation even for women, nursing and other paramedic activities are of very low status. This is a serious problem as there is a great shortage of female health staff and most women prefer to be treated by other women, and may even not attend medical facilities unless women staff are available. In 1990, at the time of unification, women formed 13 per cent of the total official labour force.

Women contribute enormously to the economy, although most of their labour is not included in official statistics. A survey of women's work in rural areas of a number of northern governorates indicates that women do between 70 and 75 per cent of all agricultural work (YAR 1985). Of females aged 10 and above, 72.4 per cent are economically active, and over 97 per cent of these are engaged in agricultural activities ranging from the care of livestock to cultivation of most crops, as described above. Despite these important activities, and the fact that in some cases where men have migrated the only male participation is that of 'supervising' relatives who take decisions on behalf of the absent husbands, very few women are recognized as farmers in their own right. In the PDRY, although a few women were trained in the use of modern agricultural machinery, generally the mechanization of agriculture, as elsewhere in the Third World, has meant a transfer from women's to men's work. The introduction of new techniques has also been mainly aimed at men by men through the limited agricultural extension service. This service is very new in Yemen and has not up to now treated women as serious agricultural producers, despite their important role, particularly on small family farms.

Women working in the towns are divided into two main categories: (1) women who work in low-skill labouring and servicing activities, and (2) women in the professions. The first category comprises mainly the poorest women, often divorcees or widows who are inadequately supported by their male relatives, or women whose husbands are unable to maintain them and their children, either directly or through sending sufficient remittances. In many cases, these working women come from the lowest social strata and from immigrant groups. A few particularly poor women are employed by the municipalities in street cleaning and related activities. Female factory workers in Sana'a, Ta'iz and Hodeida are mostly from low-status and immigrant communities. By contrast, factory workers in the former PDRY also include poor women from higher-status groups, as factory work was considered more acceptable than work in agriculture. Work in the modern sector can thus help women to rise above ascribed status in order to earn a living.

Home-based work for women is of two kinds: that done in a woman's own home and that performed in someone else's, including grooming for festivities and the more recent innovation of domestic service. This can range from cleaning and laundering to cooking and child care, as well as more traditional activities such as decorating women's bodies with *henna* and *naqsh*, preparing brides for their weddings, and so on. Employment of full-time servants is becoming more common among the richer Yemenis, but this work is rarely done by Yemeni women. It is more commonly done by Somalis or even, increasingly, by domestics especially imported from Southeast Asia. Women working in their own homes bake bread, which they sell in the streets, along with cloth, sewing and other handicrafts; they also cook for parties and so on.

At an intermediate level there are increasing numbers of female teachers, office staff, and health-sector workers. These women are still very few in number, though proportionately more are found in Aden, Ta'iz and Hodeida than in Sana'a, which, despite being the capital, still suffers from its more restrictive Zeidi tradition. In the 1980s, with the increase in the number of young women graduating from university in the PDRY, a substantial proportion of them migrated to the YAR where they were appointed to civil service posts and to other official positions at the junior and middle management level, as there were far fewer women of YAR origin with the necessary qualifications. This occurred either when young women followed their husbands to the YAR or because there they were assured of urban jobs, whereas in the PDRY there was a government effort to increase the number of qualified civil service staff in the rural areas, and there were fewer positions available in the capital.

Highly educated women constitute the other category of working women. On the whole they come from the higher-status groups, and most have been educated abroad, though nowadays many younger ones have had at least part of their education at home. They are involved in professional activities and their family status allows them to operate at senior levels alongside men with only limited cultural constraints. They are found in all sectors and some of them have reached very senior positions, but their numbers are very small.

Education

Girls' schooling in the PDRY has undergone extraordinary expansion. In the last year of colonial rule there were 13,397 students, most of whom attended primary schools in Aden. In the PDRY's last year as a separate state, 112,406 girls attended Unified School,[13] compared to 227,586 boys, representing 33 per cent of total attendance at that level; at the secondary level 32 per cent of the 33,279 students were girls (Republic of Yemen 1991). In the YAR, by contrast, only 27 per cent of attendance at primary and intermediate level was female and only 13 per cent at secondary level. In absolute terms this means that, while there were almost four times as many girls attending the lower levels of schooling, by secondary level there were only 300 more female secondary students in the YAR, which had a population five times that of the PDRY.

Data for the Republic of Yemen show that there is still much to do to ensure adequate educational coverage of the population, girls in particular. Data for school attendance in relation to the total age group show that attendance is still low, particularly for girls: in 1991–92 only 32 per cent of girls in the primary-school age group were enrolled (by comparison with 85 per cent of boys), the ratio decreasing dramatically as the educational ladder is climbed, with 14 per cent of girls aged 13–

15 attending intermediate school (compared with 55 per cent of boys), and 5 per cent of girls aged 16–18 in secondary schools (compared with 26 per cent of boys) (see Republic of Yemen 1991: xiii). This level of attendance suggests that the problem of adult illiteracy is reproducing itself within the younger generation, particularly girls. Given the relationship between education and fertility, this is a matter for serious concern.

Adult education was given considerable attention in the PDRY, and a number of mass-literacy campaigns took place; in addition there were continuous programmes in Aden and other towns to give adults the opportunity of obtaining regular school qualifications. Although they did not achieve the aim of educating the whole population, they did have considerable impact. In the YAR there were literacy classes in the towns and some in villages. Neither has proved very effective, and rural female illiteracy is still estimated at over 90 per cent.

With respect to teaching, by the time of unification the PDRY had achieved 100 per cent Yemeni teachers throughout the school system, whereas in YAR only 37 per cent of teachers were Yemeni at the lower levels, and only 27 per cent in secondary schools. This significant foreign influence on Yemeni children has a number of negative features: often these teachers have a low opinion of Yemeni culture and try to force their own culture on the students. Many foreign teachers also encourage fundamentalist interpretations of Islam and thus contribute to the country's political problems.

The universities of Sana'a and Aden, which have been established for a number of years, reveal interesting differences in their gender composition. In 1989-90 Sana'a University had 4,480 women students, representing only 14 per cent of its total enrolment, while Aden University had 1,576 representing 41 per cent of all its students.

While proportionate investment in education was clearly far higher in the PDRY than in the YAR, education is a recognized priority in unified Yemen, where the stress is on creating a common syllabus and trying to improve educational standards.

Health and population policy

Human health is affected as much by public-health measures as by the medical services available. In the PDRY, while considerable efforts went into the provision of clean water, including a number of rural water-supply projects, the associated issue of drainage was long ignored. Similarly in the YAR, small local private and cooperative water projects multiplied in the late 1970s and 1980s, again with no attention to the fundamental question of drainage of used water. Despite these efforts nationally in the late 1980s only 20 per cent of dwellings were served by a public-sector water project, 10 per cent by a private-sector one, while 40 per cent used a well outside the dwelling, 17.5 a stream, and 7 per cent a reservoir (see Republic of Yemen 1991). Given that these data include the urban areas, it is clear that a supply of clean and accessible water is still a dream for most rural Yemeni women.

Both governments recognized the importance of providing primary health care, but they were unable to train and field sufficient numbers of male and female primary health-care workers, particularly in the rural areas. In addition, despite their rhetoric, both governments were influenced by the medical lobbies and therefore promoted the construction of large, visible, high-status hospitals. The cost of construction and running these has long been known to be wildly disproportionate to the benefits they produce in terms of public health.

In 1990, the southern governorates had 314 primary health care units (41 per cent), and 32 of the 74 hospitals in the country (43 per cent), which represents a substantially higher level of service given that they had a population five times smaller than that of the YAR. Since 1982, doctors have been graduating from Aden University, including substantial numbers of women, thus giving Yemeni women far better opportunities of seeing female doctors and ensuring a wider presence of doctors in the rural areas. In addition, the medical system in the PDRY provided a free service to the population and the practice of private medicine was illegal, thus ensuring that patients got treatment through the state service rather than having to pay in the afternoon for the services doctors were 'too busy' to provide in the mornings in the public sector.

In the Republic of Yemen private medicine competes with the state sector, and the system allows pharmacy owners to sell as many drugs as they can, regardless of their clinical necessity. With regard to improving standards of public health, a more dirigiste perspective, one that supports the development of rural primary health-care services and the provision of water and drainage, might have a great impact on many of the country's social problems.

The Yemeni population is increasing at a rate of 3.1 per cent per annum, and the total fertility rate has risen steadily since 1975 when it was 7.9, to 8.6 in 1979, and to 8.3 in 1986. While fertility in the PDRY was lower, largely thanks to the educational efforts of the government, the national fertility rate was estimated at 7.5 in 1990 (UNDP 1992: 171). These figures are very high and reflect continuing high infant mortality (114 per thousand), low levels of female education, limited education among the population at large, and inaccessibility of contraceptives.[14]

In 1990 a National Population Strategy was adopted with the following objectives to be achieved by the year 2010: lowering the death rate by 50 per cent; lowering the fertility rate to below 5; reducing population growth to 2 per cent; improving quality of life through higher school enrolment ratios; improving primary health care, emphasizing preventive care; improving living conditions through increased per-capita income and work opportunities; and improving population distribution.

Conclusion: Prospects for the Future

The general political, economic and social difficulties of the first years in the life of the Republic of Yemen have deeply affected women, who have been at the sharp end of these events. At a time of crisis the all-male political leadership has not increased its commitment to women's emancipation, but on the contrary has restricted official concern about women to matters of population policy and education.

The main political threat to the regime, in Yemen as elsewhere in the Arab world in the 1990s, comes from Muslim fundamentalism. As has been seen elsewhere, and is exemplified particularly in Saudi Arabia, the most visible indication of success for fundamentalist ideology is found in the restriction of women's rights. In an already male-dominated society where, as a result of social transformation, men feel weakened and experience a loss of control over external events, they tend to strengthen their grip over their women to demonstrate publicly their power and authority. This usually takes the form of controlling women's freedom of movement, ranging from seclusion in the home to legislation requiring a male guardian's permission for a woman to travel alone. Within the same ideological sphere, veiling is a form of seclusion forced upon women outside the home. Of great practical use, the keeping of women at home takes them out of the labour market; this can be seen as an advantage for some unskilled and unqualified men who would find it difficult to compete with women openly in the labour market.

In view of women's political weakness, policies more favourable to women are unlikely to emerge in the Republic of Yemen while the main opposition to the regime comes from fundamentalism. During such a period, the authorities are likely to give in to fundamentalist pressure on matters relating to women, while resisting it in other spheres, as women have few means of putting effective political pressure on the government.

However, given the importance of women's status for national development, government concern for social issues will help to improve women's living standards. The known link between quality of life, education and fertility has been officially recognized in the National Population Strategy. Therefore the actions which may be taken to achieve its objectives will be of great assistance to women. To achieve all the Population Strategy's objectives, women must be given better access to preventive and curative health care, to education beyond primary level, to contraception, and to good income-generating opportunities. There is no doubt that if all this were achieved, in addition to their existing civil rights, Yemeni women would be far more satisfied with their lot than they are today. Concentration on social objectives can therefore be a good strategy to assist the process of development for women in the Republic of Yemen, and this fits in with stated government aims.

Notes

This chapter is based on two separate studies on women in the YAR and PDRY which were prepared for the ILO in 1986. The author wishes to thank the following people for assistance with data collection, reading and commenting on earlier drafts of this paper: Paul Barker, Khaled Hariri, Hermione Harris, Fatima Huraibi and Fathia Manqush.

1. For details on the PDRY and women's positions, see Molyneux 1982; Basharaheel, Bafaqih and Thabet 1983; Lackner 1985a, 1985b. For information on the PDRY's economic situation, see World Bank 1984.

2. The General People's Congress was created in 1982 as part of Ali Abdullah Saleh's effort at top-down democratization of the regime. It was composed of elected and nominated members, mainly traditional leaders, tribal and religious, and of the leaderships of the unrecognized opposition movements.

3. *Sada* (sing. *sayyed*): a group of people found throughout the Muslim world, who claim direct descent from the Prophet Mohammed. They are traditionally the religious educated classes, and often form the political elite.

4. Constitution, Article 35.

5. All the following quotations are from Family Law.

6. Republican Decree, Law No. 2 of 1992 Concerning Personal Status, Article 6.

7. Ibid., Article 10.

8. For further information on the agricultural sector, agricultural policies,

and the gender division of labour in the rural sector, see Hendrix-Holstein and Huraibi 1978; Carapico and Tutwiler 1981; FAO 1981: Adra 1983; Ahmed and Tarmoon 1984.

   9. For a study of women's use of time in Yemeni rural life, see Lackner 1983.

   10. *Qat* is a mildly narcotic bush, the fresh leaves of which are chewed in Yemen and the countries on the other side of the Red Sea. It is not physically addictive, but is a social activity with most men chewing for many hours on end in groups and talking. For a detailed study of the social role of *qat*, see Weir 1985.

   11. Data derived from Republic of Yemen 1992a.

   12. Daily life in a small town in the Central Highlands is well described in Dorsky 1986. This book describes the main phases of women's lives and the dynamics of their social relations in the late 1970s, the period when the migration boom and remittances were at their peak. The stratification Dorsky witnesses is still very much influenced by tradition, though its undermining by wealth, and the rise of merchant families, are already visible in her work.

   13. Unified School was introduced in the late 1970s to combine primary and intermediate schools and give education a more vocational orientation.

   14. For more information on health, fertility and population issues, see UNFPA 1984; International Statistical Institute 1984; UNFPA and UNDIESA 1985; YAR 1986.

References

Adra, N. 1983. *The Impact of Male Migration on Women's Roles in Agriculture in the YAR*. Unpublished.

Ahmed, J.M., and A.M. Tarmoon. 1984. *An Evaluation Study of the Impact on Women of the Wadi Hadramaut Agricultural Development Project*. Aden, mimeo.

Basharaheel, M.A., A.A. Bafaqih and S. S. Thabet. 1983. *Woman and Development in Democratic Yemen* (in Arabic). Aden, mimeo.

Benería, L. 1981. 'Conceptualizing the Labour Force: The Underestimation of Women's Economic Activities'. In N. Nelson, ed., *African Women in the Development Process*. London: Frank Cass, pp. 10–28.

Carapico, S., and R. Tutwiler. 1981. *Yemeni Agriculture and Economic Change*. Milwaukee: American Institute for Yemeni Studies.

Dixon, R.B. 1982. 'Women in Agriculture: Counting the Labor Force in Developing Countries'. *Population and Development Review*, vol. 8, no. 3 (September), pp. 539–66.

Dorsky, S. 1986. *Women of 'Amran, A Middle Eastern Ethnographic Study*. Salt Lake City, UT: University of Utah Press.

Food and Agriculture Organization (FAO). 1981. *Review of Rural Development Strategy and Policies in YAR*. Rome: FAO.

Hendrix-Holstein, L., and F. Huraibi. 1978. *The Position of Rural Women in Radá'*. Unpublished.

International Statistical Institute. 1984. *Yemen Arab Republic Fertility Survey, 1979*, 2 vols.

Kristiansson, B., A. Nasher and G. Bagenholm. 1984. *Nutrition, Growth and Health among Preschool Children in PDR Yemen, 1982–1983*. Stockholm: Rädda Barnen.

Lackner, H. 1983. *Domestic Practices in the Rada' District, YAR.* Arnhem.
——— 1985a. *PDR Yemen, Outpost of Socialist Development in Arabia.* London: Ithaca Press.
——— 1985b. 'Labour Immigration and Its Socio-Economic Impact on the Sending Areas, the Literature Reviewed with Reference to the Experience of the PDRY'. Unpublished M.Sc. dissertation, University of London.
Makhouf, C. 1979. 'The Legal Status of Women among the Awlad'. *'Ali' Anthropological Quarterly*, vol. 40, no. 3.
Molyneux, M. 1982. *State Policies and the Position of Women Workers in the People's Democratic Republic of Yemen.* Geneva: ILO.
Myntti, C. 1979. *Women and Development in YAR.* Eschborn: GTZ.
——— 1985. 'Women, Work, Population and Development in the YAR'. In J. Abu-Nasr, N. Khoury and H. Azzam, eds, *Women, Employment and Development in the Arab World.* The Hague: Mouton.
PDRY (People's Democratic Republic of Yemen). 1974. *The Family Law.*
——— 1978. *Constitution.*
——— 1984. *Statistical Yearbook 1983.* Central Statistical Organization.
RIRDP. 1983. *Domestic Practices in the Rada' District.* Arnhem.
——— 1983. *Household Water Use in al Beida Province.* Arnhem.
Republic of Yemen. 1991. *Statistical Yearbook 1990.* Ministry of Planning and Development, Central Statistical Organization, Sana'a.
——— 1992a. *Statistical Yearbook 1991.* Ministry of Planning and Development, Central Statistical Organization, Sana'a.
——— 1992b. Republican Decree, Law No. 20 of 1992 Concerning Personal Status.
UNDP. 1992. *Human Development Report.* New York.
UNFPA. 1984. *Report on the Evaluation of UNFPA-sponsored Country Programme in Democratic Yemen 1979–1984 and the Role of Women in It.* New York.
UNFPA and UN Department of International Economic and Social Affairs (UNDIESA). 1985. *Population Policy Compendium PDRY.*
Weir, S. 1985. *Qat in Yemen.* London: British Museum Publications.
World Bank. 1984. *PDRY Special Economic Report Mid-term Review of the Second Five Year Plan 1981-1985.* Washington DC.
YAR (Yemen Arab Republic), Central Planning Organization. 1985. *A Study on the Participation of Yemeni Women in Economic Activity* (in Arabic). Sana'a.
——— Central Statistical Office. 1986. *Preliminary Results of the 1986 Census* (in Arabic). Sana'a.

6

Female Higher Education and Participation in the Labour Force in Lebanon

Samih Boustani and Nada Mufarrej

Introduction

As in other Arab countries, the gap between the occupational status of Lebanese men and women is still very wide. Progress has been enjoyed by Lebanese women in professional fields, however. This improvement has been due to the changes in the level of women's education (see, for example, Azzam, Abu-Nasr and Lorfing 1985). Although women's associations and international agencies identified the problem long ago and called for improvement in women's educational level, it took the shock of war to achieve this end. The military events that took place in Lebanon in 1975 marked a turning point in attitudes towards female education and employment (Abu-Nasr 1979). These events highlighted the importance of developing human resources, helping in part to negate traditional and bigoted notions about female education and employment. Female education, which up to the mid-1970s had been the prerogative of women from educated and/or well-to-do families, became by the mid-1980s a necessity for women from every walk of life. Nevertheless, it remains obvious that the educational trend is still biased towards men rather than women, due mostly to parental preferential treatment.

On the other hand, the civil war absorbed much of Lebanon's financial resources and led to an increasing deterioration in the purchasing power of the Lebanese pound. Accordingly, female integration in the labour force became a necessity rather than a choice. The Lebanese woman thus became, due to force of circumstance, a fully fledged partner in the family economy (see, *inter alia*, Lorfing and Abu-Nasr 1980a, 1980b; M. Chamie 1985).

The pre- and post-1975 voluntary migration from some rural to particular urban areas, coupled with the forced displacement of a considerable number of Lebanese from one region to another, resulted in the expansion of Greater Beirut to around one-third of Lebanese territory; an uneven concentration of the population; and the creation of new, *de facto*, urban agglomerations in regions that had been, until recently, considered rural (see J. Chamie 1981; Fa'our 1981). This internal migratory movement reduced the agricultural area in favour of the construction of housing. The unexpected change generated a financial instability in the lives of both the original residents of the suburban areas and the ex-rural occupants. Traditionally, both sectors produced foodstuff through the cultivation of crops and the maintenance of their livestock. Now, due to the urban expansion into rural areas, agriculture and farming have vanished, giving way to the new living conditions.[1]

The emigration of Lebanese men to some Arab countries created a void in the labour market, which the Lebanese women tried to fill. However, changes in the female participation in the labour force are, generally, governed by the rates of social and economic change. Consequently, an understanding of these changes calls for a survey of formal employment in Lebanon, of the demographic trends prevailing in the 1979–90 period under study, and of the economic activity of these females.

Data

Lebanon's database ranks among the world's poorest, be it in terms of main economic indicators, socio-economic data, or, most specifically, demographic variables. In fact, since 1932 no comprehensive demographic census has taken place. Thus, Lebanon relies for its statistical data on several sources of follow-up surveys. These surveys, however, have not been part of a consistent comprehensive scheme, but rather a response to emerging needs at specific points in time over the years.

In 1970, a survey named 'Population Active au Liban' was undertaken by the Direction Centrale de la Statistique of the then existing Ministry of Planning. This survey recorded demographic and socio-economic information from a sample of 30,000 households. This exercise was followed in 1971 by a 'National Fertility and Family Planning' survey that was based on 10 per cent of the Lebanese female population aged between 15 and 44 years, as well as an 'Internal Migration' survey that studied the trend of movement from rural areas to the capital Beirut. In 1979, Evelyn Richards of Beirut University College implemented a survey on the 'Employment Status of Women in Lebanon'. This survey covered 240 establishments in the area of Greater Beirut; employers were asked to indicate their preference for potential employees by sex, marital status, age and the level of education, as well as the salary and benefits they were willing to offer. A preparatory study for the implementation of a drinking-water system for Beirut covered 13,000 hectares. It was carried out in 1983 by BECEOM, ACE and SEURECA (see Republique Libanaise 1984a, 1984b). A Housing and Population Survey was undertaken in 1984 by the Région Métropolitaine de Beyrouth (RMB), under the auspices of the Council for Development and Reconstruction (CDR), but remained unpublished. It covered an area of 23,000 hectares of Greater Beirut and collected demographic, housing and economic information; as such, it represents the vital element in the execution of a physical plan for the region. Some of this information is published in what is generally known as the *Livre Blanc*, whose distribution has been limited. In 1986, CDR, with the financial backing of the European Economic Community, carried out an industrial census that covered the 11,000 industrial establishments that have more than five workers on their payrolls. This ad hoc census was followed in 1987 by an updating survey that included artisanal industries.

These various surveys did not for the most part focus on economic and demographic issues; instead they tackled certain qualitative aspects of the subject matter surveyed. Most of the data in this chapter's tables are based on these aspects.

Formal Employment

Lebanon's reputation as an East–West crossroads is due to its different – at times interacting, at times conflicting – cultures. On the one hand, being a Middle Eastern country and one of the previous territories of the once great Ottoman Empire, it certainly and inevitably upholds Middle Eastern culture and customs. On the other hand, being an ex-French colony and a fertile land for Western missionaries to build on, it has been affected by Western culture and customs. Consequently, Lebanese women have been influenced by this mixed cultural and behavioural milieu. Whereas school programmes and especially university curricula are based on Western models which presuppose equality between men and women, women nevertheless have to interact within

Table 6.1 Summary schedule of the most important rules concerning women in the social security law in Lebanon

Title	Chapter	Article no.	Sub-article	Decree no. and date	Main contents
I	I	13	2b 2c	13955 of 26 September 1963	Creation of a sickness/maternity fund that covers among others: (1) Maternity (pregnancy, delivery and post-delivery). (2) Temporary inability to work resulting from maternity, and entailing suspension of the insured's earnings.
I	I	14	2a 2b 2c	as above	Members of the insured family eligible for cover: (1) Parents over 60 years of age or suffering from a mental or physical disability that prevents them from earning a living. (2) Husband in the same condition as 1. (3) Children up to 16 years of age. In the case of disability or engagement in studies, age limit can be extended to 25 years (provided that she is widowed or divorced but has custody of children).
I	I	15	1b 1c 3	as above	Maternity services shall comprise: (1) Medical examination and care before delivery; necessary services during delivery; and care after delivery. (2) Maternity benefits in cases of temporary incapacity arising from delivery. (3) Pathological pregnancy is treated as a sickness.
I	II	17	2b1 2b2 2bc	As modified by Decree No. 2653 13 January 1972	Medical services in cases of maternity: (1) Care and tests before, during and after delivery. (2) Necessary medications. (3) Hospital stay, medical care and surgical operations.
I	II	18	4	as above	Determination of the number and nature of pre- and post-natal examinations by the Social Security Fund.

Title	Chapter	Article no.	Sub-article	Decree no. and date	Main contents
I	IV	26	1	13955 of 26 September 1963	(1) An insured woman is entitled to maternity benefit over a ten-week period, on the condition that she abstains from work and collects no earnings throughout the period (2) Maternity benefit is equal to two-thirds of the average day's earnings.
II	VI	46	2a	as above	Family allowances are due to: (1) Each infirm dependent child, with no age limit. (2) Each single non-salaried daughter up to the age of 25. (3) Each legitimate wife living at home, when she has no remunerated occupation. (4) Under-age children (up to five children).
II	VI	47	a	as above	Each child is entitled to a single family allowance. In cases of both parents meeting the conditions to claim rights, family allowance goes to the father unless the mother has custody.
VI		50	1d 1e	as above	A woman is entitled to end-of-service indemnity if: (1) She leaves her job in the course of the 12 months following her marriage. (2) If she reaches the age of 55 yrs (60 yrs for men).
		I		595 of 4 February 1971	The rate of the insured's contribution is set at 30% of the tariff established by the Social Security Fund.
		I		5203 of 23 March 1973	Lebanese undergraduates are covered in the case of sickness or maternity.
		I		7431 of 16 March 1974	Abrogation of the insured's share in the cost of medical acts in the case of maternity; however, not in the cost of hospital care, operating theatre and other expenses.

Source: ARGUS of Lebanese Documents' *Social Security Law*, Bureau of Lebanese and Arab Documentation, 1983.

a male-dominated society. These contradictions are not systematically governed by rules and regulations in the National Charter, even though it considers both sexes equal in terms of rights and obligations, which implies the non-existence of legal discrimination.[2]

The most important Lebanese law in the context of this study is the Social Security Law issued on 26 September 1963. Although it establishes the Lebanese woman as an essential part of the Lebanese labour force, giving her equal and sometimes apparently preferential rights, it gives men discriminatory rights in other circumstances. Table 6.1 summarizes the main elements of the Social Security Law's rules and regulations that are of greatest importance to women – mainly those relating to maternity. These rules concern about 18 per cent of the total female population – those who are economically active and of reproductive age.

The Social Security Law gives an expectant mother the right to medical cover before, during and after delivery. This medical service includes care and tests, necessary medications, hospital stay and surgical operations. The law even compensates a woman for any temporary disability resulting from maternity. A Lebanese woman is entitled to ten weeks partially or fully paid maternity leave; this renders maternity a natural part of a woman's working life, safeguarding her job and giving her ample time to nurse her infant. This law has also given the Lebanese woman preferential treatment inasmuch as it abolished her contribution to the cost of medical treatment in the case of maternity (Decree No. 7431, dated 16 March 1974), equal to 30 per cent of the tariff recognized by the Social Security Fund (Decree No. 595, dated 4 February 1971) but retained her obligatory contribution to the cost of hospital care, operations and other expenses.

This preferential treatment extends to retirement. Any woman who reaches the age of 55 years (as compared to 60 years for men) or who leaves work in the twelve months following her marriage, has the right to her end-of-service indemnity. Of course, what is here termed preferential treatment might also reflect the legislator's unconscious belief in the woman's primary role as housewife. It should be noted that insured persons (excluding the above-mentioned cases) who want to quit their jobs before a specified twenty-year working life must prove that they are leaving the labour force for good before they are entitled to a certain percentage of their indemnity.

In the case of medical-services cover, a woman's husband is only eligible if he is either over 60 years of age or is mentally or physically handicapped and thus unable to earn a living. Her children are only eligible if she is widowed or divorced but retains custody. This latter is not the case if her husband is not a beneficiary of the above-mentioned cover, although a man's non-salaried wife and children under 16 years of age are always entitled. In the same way, a woman is not entitled to a family allowance for an unemployed husband even if he is over 60 years of age or has a mental or physical handicap, whereas a man is entitled to a family allowance for his unsalaried wife and single daughter who is less than 25 years of age (see Al-Amin 1979).

In 1973, Lebanese undergraduates became entitled, under Decree No. 5203, to medical-care cover in cases of sickness and maternity. This extension of the law may have played an important part in encouraging females to join the ranks of the labour force.

Demographic Trends

This section aims to examine demographic data relating to economically active Lebanese women, specifically those with a university education. In this chapter, we will use the term 'highly educated' to denote those with educational attainment beyond secondary school. Before reviewing the essential factors that govern Lebanese women's occupational preferences, it may be useful to delineate the employment categories that attract the majority of university-educated women.

Professional Personnel
- Scientific and liberal professions
- Engineers and architects
- Medical doctors and dentists
- Educational personnel
     elementary
     complementary
     secondary
- Other liberal professions

Administrative Personnel
- Directors, higher administrators, officers
- Administrative personnel
- Secretaries, typists, etc.
- Accountants, cashiers
- Other administrative personnel

Commercial Personnel

- Commercial personnel, saleswomen
- Wholesale and retail traders/commercial managers
- Commercial technical assistance
- Shopkeepers, employers, etc.

Table 6.2 indicates a sharp population growth between 1970 and 1975, which was counterbalanced by negative growth between 1975 and 1980. The Lebanese population grew between 1980 and 1985, but a very limited increase in the rate of growth was registered between 1985 and 1990. The growth rates of the Lebanese population are 5.3 to 2.4 per cent, 1.7 per cent and 0.2 per cent, respectively. Variations, positive or negative, are explained by the fluctuations in the vital rates – namely, fertility, migration and life expectancy. The total fertility rate, which was between 3.9 per cent in 1970 and 4 per cent in 1990, bore a direct relation to the prevailing military situation, decreasing with an escalation of fighting and increasing in periods of so-called calm. The rate of migration is very hard to estimate due to the exodus that takes place with every bout of violence and the return of the natives at its end. Life expectancy for females, which incidentally has always been greater than that for males, increased from 58 years in 1970 to 70 years in 1990. In the period under study, the crude death rate registered its highest level over the 1980–85 period of 8.2 per thousand.

Despite the military conflict, a development plan for the educational sector was partially executed in the period 1975–90, and many public schools in several regions in Lebanon were reopened and re-equipped. The massive destruction, mainly in the cities, the waves of interregional displacement, and the consequent creation of new *de facto* urban agglomerations and application of the same educational plan to these regions as an emergency measure, were the factors that forced a number of private schools to move their premises to these improvised urban sites. Thus, secondary schools spread regionally. Coupled with a decrease in the population under 15, this had a positive effect on the level of female, especially secondary-school, education. The student/teacher ratio decreased, and elementary and primary education were no longer seen as sufficient for women. The spread of secondary education made the idea of university education much less far-fetched than in previous years. The division of the once central private and public university campuses into regional institutions, the reconstitution and re-equipping of the Lebanese University – the only public university – and the creation

Table 6.2 Distribution of Lebanese economically active and highly educated population by sex, 1970–90 (thousands)

Distribution		1970	1975	1980	1985	1990
Population	Male	1,080	1,404	1,234	1,336	1,355
	Female	1,046	1,366	1,218	1,332	1,337
	Total	2,126	2,770	2,452	2,668	2,692
Economically active	Male	445	608	550	635	657
	Female	93	138	116	146	148
	Total	538	746	666	781	805
Economically active	Male	49	57	103	123	139
with higher educational	Female	18	24	42	66	75
attainment	Total	67	81	145	189	214

Sources: Etude du reseau de distribution d'eau potable de la ville de Beyrouth et ses banlieus, 1985–90; Republique Libanese, Ministère de l'Industrie et du Petrole et Conseil du Developpement et de la Reconstruction, *Mise a jour du Recensement Industriel*, 1989; ECWA, Statistical Abstract of the ECWA Region (various years); UN, *World Statistics in Brief*, 1988; Republique Libanese, Conseil du Developpement et de la Reconstruction, *Schema Directeur de la Région Métropolitaine de Beyrouth*, 1986; Republique Libanese, Ministère de l'Industrie et du Petrole et Conseil du Developpement et de la Reconstruction, *Recensement Industriel*, 1986; ECWA *Demographic and Related Socio–Economic Data Sheets*, 1982; UNESCO, Trends and Projections of Enrolment by Level of Education and by Age, 1975; Republique Libanese, Ministère du Plan, Direction Centrale de la Statistique, *Population Active au Liban, 1970*, 1972.

of new, mainly applied courses, rendered higher education more accessible, especially to those females who previously faced opposition to their attempts at leaving family homes to live on far-away campuses, or who were victims of parental preferential treatment due to scarce financial resources. Some women were motivated to improve their level of education because jobs open to those with a secondary education (for example, elementary teaching and unclassified secretarial work) are very low-paid. Worsening economic conditions made a university degree the prerequisite for better-paid jobs, and employment on the part of single women a grave necessity. In some cases, girls from wealthy families regarded university education as a way of passing time, meeting future husbands or improving their chances of meeting one. For the most part, Lebanese women with university education hold an arts degree, and only in a few cases, a degree in the sciences.

Highly educated married women who had previously been economically active as single women, or who had married directly after attaining a degree and who had become economically unproductive either voluntarily or due to their husbands' opposition to their employment, returned to the labour force out of economic necessity.

The proportion of highly educated economically active women out of the total female population increased from nearly 1.7 per cent in 1970 and 1975 to 6.5 per cent in 1990, while educated economically active women came to constitute 35 per cent of the total of the highly educated economically active population as compared to nearly 27 per cent in 1970. These percentages reflect the positive changes in the level of female education in both absolute and relative terms. The change in the education of Lebanese women had a direct and noticeable effect on female economic activity. In fact, the female economic activity rate (that is, the proportion of economically active women out of the total female population) increased from 8.9 per cent in 1970 to 11.1 per cent in 1990. The disproportionality between the rate of growth of the female population of 1.2 per cent per year over the period under study and that of the economically active female population of 2.3 per cent per year shows the importance of the evolution that has taken place in the social and economic conditions of women in Lebanon. A better indication of the correlation between higher education and economic activity is the increase in the percentage of highly educated women in the economically active female population: from 17.4 per cent in 1975 to 50.7 per cent in 1990. The average increase of 4.2 per cent per year of highly educated females entering employment implies that most newly graduated females are absorbed in the labour market (see, for example, Maalouf and Abu Rjeily 1987).

Economic Activity of Highly Educated Females

This section reviews the different types of economic activities undertaken by highly educated Lebanese women. As in most countries, the definition of economically active includes salaried and unpaid family workers but not housewives, whose contribution, as it is well known, is not included in the gross domestic product.

The increase in the number of highly educated females has left its imprint on the employment market. In fact, while highly educated women constituted around 3.3 per cent of the economically active population in 1970 and 1975, this proportion increased to 9.3 per cent in 1990. This female educational boom became observable in 1980. Highly educated females increased in number from less than 1 per cent of the total Lebanese population in 1970 and 1975 to 1.7 per cent in 1980, 2.5 per cent in 1985 and 2.8 per cent in 1990, while in absolute terms, the number of highly educated females tripled between 1975 and 1990. The rise in the number of highly educated women can be regarded in part as the outcome of the serious work that culminated in conferences on the integration of women in the labour market, and in part as the consequence of the spread of higher education facilities all over Lebanon, as discussed in the previous section. It is interesting to note that the sex ratio of highly educated males to females dropped from 4.6 in 1970 to 1.3 in 1990. These figures show the improvement in the educational level of females and their improved integration into the labour market. This integration has mainly resulted from the changing – that is, increased – requirements of the service sector. It should be pointed out that no development plans were drafted, nor previous studies undertaken, to direct the increased flow of secondary-educated females towards university courses, or from there towards employment choices. Between 1970 and 1990, female employment options became very diversified.

The impact of the employment of highly educated women will be far-reaching. It will help create low-level jobs relating to housework and thus have a multiplier effect in terms of total female employment. Second, it will affect the fertility rate of these highly educated career-oriented women, who will automatically tend to bear fewer children, due to the disruption caused to their careers by pregnancy, birth and maternity leave, as well as the increased financial obligations that arise with a larger family. In this context, the survey conducted by Evelyn Richards has shown that employers were reluctant to hire married women due to the restrictions family obligations would impose on a woman's dedication to her job. This study, it should be said, reflects the attitude prevailing ten years ago; this is now beginning to change gradually, along with women's attitudes to childbearing.

The agricultural sector has been excluded from this study due to the negligible number of highly educated females (and males for that matter) economically active.

Participation of Highly Educated Women in the Labour Force

The participation of highly educated women in the labour force increased between 1970 and 1990; nearly doubling in both absolute and relative terms between 1970 and 1980, and tripling between 1975 and 1990.

Table 6.3 Distribution of highly educated economically active women by economic sector in Lebanon (thousands)

	1970	1975	1980	1985	1990
1 Agriculture, hunting, foresting and fishing	0.4	–	1	0.5	1
2 Mining and quarrying	–	–	–	–	–
3 Manufacturing	3	4	5	5	6
4 Electricity and water	–	–	–	–	–
5 Construction	–	–	–	–	–
6 Wholesale and retail trade, restaurants and hotels	1	2	3	16	18
7 Transport, storage and communication	–	–	–	1	1
8 Financing, insurance, real estate and business services	2	4	3	3.5	3.5
9 Community, social and personal services	12	14	30	40	44
Non-defined	–	–	–	–	–
Total	18	24	42	66	75

Source: Author's calculations on the basis of the sources in Table 6.2.

While around 3.3 per cent of the economically active population in 1970 and 1975 were highly educated females, this percentage increased to 6.3 per cent in 1980, to 8.5 per cent in 1985, and to 9.3 per cent in 1990. Women's occupational spectrum widened, especially after 1975, and a number of changes took place.

As can be seen in Table 6.3, the increase in the level of highly educated women's economic activity was noticeable mainly in two sectors: community, social and personal services; and trade, restaurants and hotels. In the former, the number of highly educated women increased nearly threefold between 1975 and 1990, against a minimal increase between 1970 and 1975. This expansion is explained by the national needs that arose in the aftermath of each bout of violence, especially those that occurred in 1975, 1978, 1982 and 1989: highly educated Lebanese women enrolled in the fields of medicine, nursing, midwifery, teaching, social work and every type of civil assistance. The age range of women active in this sector is between 20 and 40 years. This reflects the direct effect of war on highly educated women's participation in this and other sectors. Furthermore, the number of highly educated women registered as active in sector 9 (community, social and personal services) as opposed to highly educated men, increased from 28 per cent in 1970 to 34 per cent in 1975, to reach 72 per cent in 1990. The total number of women active in this sector grew at an average annual rate of 5.5 per cent, while the number of highly educated females grew at an average annual rate of 15.5 per cent in the same period. This trend reflects the deep concern of highly educated women about their changing social environment and their choice of a profession suited to their physical nature. Although the marital status of highly educated females active in this sector is difficult to determine, a limited survey of women in the 20–40 age bracket has shown that more than 80 per cent of them are dedicated to their jobs and aware of the obstacle marriage can represent to their advance.

The second sector that registered an increase in the participation of highly educated women is the trade (wholesale and retail), restaurants and hotels sector. The increase has been in both absolute and relative terms. The number of highly educated females active in this sector doubled between 1970 and 1975 and increased ninefold between 1975 and 1990. While this sector accounted for 5.6 per cent of highly educated economically active women in 1970 and 8.3 per cent in 1975, this proportion increased to 24 per cent in 1990. The most important change, however, in both absolute and relative terms, occurred between 1980 and 1985. This change can be explained by the negative effect of the sporadic military flare-ups and the ensuing destruction, which led to the closure of several financial institutions. Accordingly, women with higher education shifted their field of activity from sector 8 to sector 6, given that no special educational preparation was needed for the shift.

As regards sector 8, or financial, insurance, real estate and business services, the trend of change was variable. In the early 1970s, Lebanese women started to turn towards types of university courses that until then had not been very popular with women: namely, economics, finance, accounting, business administration. Hence, the female labour supply in these fields doubled by 1975. However, due to the reasons stated in the previous paragraph, the number of highly educated economically active females in this sector decreased in both absolute and relative terms by 1980. In 1990, a slight increase was registered in absolute but not in relative terms. The sex ratio of highly educated men to women in this

Table 6.4   Women University Age-Specific Activity Rate, Lebanon

WUASAR[1]	1970	1975	1980	1985	1990
20–24	5.1	5.2	10.9	14.7	14.0
25–29	4.5	4.6	11.2	14.3	12.9
30–34	4.8	5.6	11.6	14.0	14.5
35–39	4.3	4.9	8.0	11.2	14.7
40–44	4.1	4.5	6.9	8.1	10.5
45–49	2.6	3.1	5.8	6.6	8.8
50–54	2.4	1.7	4.9	6.8	8.5
55–59	2.3	1.6	2.2	4.5	8.0
60–64	1.8	0.3	1.2	2.0	2.9
65+	0.8	0.2	0.4	0.4	1.5
Total	32.7	31.7	63.1	82.6	96.3
WUCAR[2]	3.1	2.3	5.2	6.2	7.3

[1] WUASAR (Women University Age–Specific Activity Rate): Number of university-level females working in each age group/Total number of women in each age group × 100.
[2] WUCAR (Women University Crude Activity Rate): Sum of WUASAR/Total female × 100.

Source: Estimated by the author based on the sources in Table 6.2.

sector decreased from 5 in 1970 to 3.4 in 1990. The marital status of women active in this sector is different from those in sector 9. A quick survey showed that 85 per cent of active women were either married or engaged to be married, the rest being single and aged between 20 and 25 years of age.

The participation of highly educated females in the manufacturing sector has seen a gradual rise, less dramatic than that in sector 9. Although the annual growth rate of the participation of highly educated females in this sector is 3.5 per cent between 1970 and 1990, the male/female sex ratio remains too high, in spite of having dropped from 10 in 1970 to 7.5 in 1990.

To sum up: in 1990, 50 per cent of highly educated economically active females worked in community, social and personal services, compared to 1 per cent in the Agricultural sector. This indicates that certain sectors have a sex-biased concentration of the highly educated economically active population. This concentration could be incidental, but in most cases it is voluntary, arising from ingrained beliefs or from the physical nature of women as compared to that of men.

Table 6.4 sheds light on the most important age groups of highly educated economically active females. It is clear from this table that the pattern of these women's participation in economic activity is set by the age bracket 20–44 years. The effect of the war on this distribution is most obvious in the year 1990 for the age group 35–39 years, where highly educated economically active women constitute 14.7 per cent of the total females in this group. At the aforementioned age bracket, the women's university age-specific activity rate is already declining, except for the year 1990, when it was the highest. It is interesting to note that this age group was the 20–24 age group in 1975 – that is, those freshly graduated from universities. The participation of the females of this age bracket in the economic activity increased the crude activity rate from 3.1 per cent in 1970 to 7.3 per cent in 1990. In short, it is clear from the distribution of highly educated females by age that the concentration is in the primary sector of the economy.

Employment of University-Educated Females

The number of highly educated employed women has increased per se in the period under study. The most dramatic change took place in 1980. The number of highly educated employed females increased by a factor of 3.5 between 1975 and 1980 and by a factor of 5 between 1975 and 1990. While the number of highly educated economically active females grew from 19.4 per cent of total active females in 1970 to 50.7 per cent in 1990, the number of highly educated employed females grew from 6.5 per cent of total active females in 1970 to 24 per cent in 1990. These two sets of figures indicate a female drop-out from the labour market, one of the main reasons for which is marriage.

Table 6.5 shows that the professional, technical and related workers employment category – that is, medical doctors, dentists, engineers, architects and secondary teachers – has followed a normal trend between 1970 and 1990, if the figures are compared in five-year spans. However, we note that the number of highly educated females employed in this category doubled between 1970 and 1990. The bulk of the change has taken place since 1980. The smooth increase registered between 1970 and 1980 reflects the effect of the female's environment on her choice of specialization. Since 1980, the increase has reflected the social, demographic and economic changes discussed earlier, namely, displace-

Table 6.5 Distribution of employment among highly educated females in Lebanon (thousands)

	1970	1975	1980	1985	1990
Professional, technical and related workers	6	7	8	10	12
Administrative and managerial workers	–	–	17	20	22
Clerical and related workers	–	–	–	1	1
Others	–	–	–	–	0.5
Total	6	7	25	31	35.5

Source: Author's calculations on the basis of the sources in Table 6.2.

ment, the spread of university campuses right across Lebanon, and expansion of the range of courses available in the Lebanese University to include applied sciences. (It should be noted that some university courses necessary for qualification in this employment category are very costly and beyond the means of many, given the prevailing economic situation.) However, although enrolment in these courses in the Lebanese University has increased noticeably, most of the women have not yet graduated and hence are not included in our figures. The coming years will show a dramatic change in the employment figures under this category.

The most prominent subgroups in this category are medical doctors, dentists and teachers. However, most highly educated female employees here belong to the educational sector: that is, elementary and secondary teachers, university deans, professors and instructors, and other teaching personnel. In 1970, of the 6,000 women employed in the first category, 40 per cent belonged to the educational sector, compared with 70 per cent of the 12,000 employed in 1990. This increase, in both absolute and relative terms, has been the result of the educational boom that took place after the war, and which is, in its turn, the result of the spread of educational facilities. In 1985, an increase was registered in the number of female medical doctors and dentists as compared to previous years, while no dramatic change has taken place in the engineering, architectural or scientific professions.

Table 6.5 shows the snowball effect of the Lebanese war on administrative and managerial highly educated female workers. Whereas up to 1980 the number of females belonging to this category was negligible, the number employed in this category subsequently increased dramatically compared to previous years, to the point where they were double the total registered in the first category. The most important subgroup under this category and the one that is mainly responsible for the change is that of social workers. Their job description ranges from social relief work, care for displaced people, first aid to war victims, anti-drug work, and social and child-care counselling. The demand for employment in this subgroup increased greatly after the 1975 events, due to the social problems that erupted and the changes that took place. It should be noted that 85 per cent of the Lebanese people have been subjected to at least one forced displacement in the past fifteen years. For some it has been a temporary displacement, while for many others it has been a lasting physical, mental and economic severance.

A number of women employed mainly in non-professional jobs and belonging to the middle or lower socio-economic classes, and who have started their working lives at the bottom of the hierarchy, have enrolled in university programmes while working in order to improve their employment prospects. Once graduated, only 25 per cent of this category were able to climb up the social ladder; nevertheless, their salaries were increased.

Prewar female university course choices tended more towards majors related to teaching, such as languages and physical sciences. However, these choices were channelled in the postwar period toward the medical sciences and related specializations, such as nursing, physio- and psychotherapy, nutrition, laboratory work and hospital administration.

Overview of the Integration of Highly Educated Females in the Labour Force

Table 6.6 underlines the main elements that directly affect the absorption and participation of highly educated Lebanese females in the labour market. However, the building of an econometric model in this situation is futile: for even though these elements are important, the regressions will suffer from the very strong or multico-linear relationship between the independent variables, thus leading to erroneous and misleading implications. Hence, because of their social and economic implications,

Table 6.6 Analysis data for integration of highly educated females in the labour force in Lebanon

			HEF			
	EA *(000s)*	E *(000s)*	CAR *(000s)*	ME *(000s)*	MM *(000s)*	Sex ratio
1975	24	7	2.3	1	−1	101.5
1979	18	6	3.1	2	4	102.5
1980	42	25	5.2	2	−1	102.5
1985	66	31	6.2	3	−2	100.1
1990	75	35.5	7.3	3	−2	101.5

HEF	= Highly Educated Females
EA	= Economically Active
E	= Employment
CAR	= Crude Activity Rate
ME	= Married Employed
MM	= Migratory Movement
Sex ratio	= M/F × 100

Sources: Constructed on the basis of previous tables in this chapter.

we have chosen three out of the six variables to run different sets of simple regressions. The task consists of measuring the interrelation of each of these three variables with each other, as well as with the other variables. The first chosen variable, the Economically Active Highly Educated Females (HEFEA), usually indicates the possible pattern of integration in the labour market. The second, the Highly Educated Employed Married Females (HEFME) distinguishes between married and single females, the marriage institution being very important in the Middle East. The third and last is the Highly Educated Females' Migratory Movements (HEFMM), which measures the internal and external migratory movements of highly educated women. Table 6.7 shows the values of the correlation coefficients between variables.

It will be noticed that several pairs of variables are very highly correlated: HEFNA and HEFE; HEFEA and HEFCAR; HEFME and HEFCAR; HEFEA and HEFME; HFME and HEFE; HEFEA and HEFMM; HEFMM and HEFE. These seven interrelations could be grouped under three headings: labour market availability; manpower availability; and external forces.

Table 6.7   Coefficient of correlation between different variables

HEF/r × 100	EA	E	CAR	ME	MM	Sex ratio
EA	100	97.1	96.0	85.7	−73.8	−60.0
ME	85.7	84.4	91.1	100	−31.0	−46.1
MM	−73.8	−72.3	−59.3	−31.0	100	61.0

Sources: Constructed on the basis of previous tables in this chapter.

Labour market availability

The contribution of highly educated Lebanese women to economic activity is identical to that of men due to their equal rights and obligations. Curiously, however, the specialization of a highly educated woman is always much closer to her field of employment than is that of the man. This means that a woman rarely performs a job for which she is not educationally prepared. An acceptably high correlation, 85.7 per cent, was noted between highly educated economically active females and highly educated married employed females. This implies that marriage is not really a hindrance to a woman's integration into the labour market. It should be noted that in 1990, 30 per cent of highly educated recently graduated and employed females were married. The relation between highly educated economically active females and the migratory movement of highly educated females is negative and not very strong, as is indicated by the correlation coefficient whose value is −73.8 per cent. Table 6.6 indicates an increase in highly educated employed females from 29 per cent of economically active females in 1975 to 47.3 per cent in 1990.

We conclude that labour market availability at the level of highly educated females is related to educational training, vocational training, marital status and the permanent area of residence.

Manpower availability

Such availability depends on employment opportunities and job security. The first implies those existing opportunities in the labour market that are compatible with these women's higher education; while job security consists of benefits offered, such as medical assistance and schooling aid, as well as working hours and the guarantee of job continuity. In this regard, women have shown a preference for working in the public sector and in important private establishments. The correlation co-efficient between HEFEA and Highly Educated Employed Females (HEFE) is 97.1 per cent during the 1970–90 period, which implies the availability of these benefits to highly educated females. The correlation coefficient between HEFE and HEFME is 84.4 per cent, which is acceptable and implies that marriage does not exclude female employ-ment. The presence of a relatively weak negative relationship between HEFE and HEFMM is noticeable from the correlation coefficient, which is equal to −72.3 per cent.

Women working in the public sector see themselves as better off, if not financially then qualitatively, than those in the private sector due to the fact that their jobs are protected from internal migration and forced displacement, and that they are able to take longer leaves without pay.

External Forces

As shown in Table 6.7, the correlation coefficients between HEFMM and HEFCAR, and between HEFMM and HEFME, are very weak and equal to −59.3 per cent and −31 per cent respectively. This means that the relation between the female migratory movement and their crude activity rate, and the relation between the former and married employed women, are very weak and have to be rejected.

Conclusions

Highly educated Lebanese women are in general subject to a dual way of life. On the one hand, they are at the heart of a household and a male-dominated society; on the other hand, they have a place at the centre of economic activity. Because of this, the Lebanese woman finds herself most of the time forced to sacrifice her job and professional aspirations for the sake of her family, due to the very demanding performance required of her, especially by the private sector.

Various chapters in this volume discuss traditional gender patterns as obstacles to women's advancement. In Lebanon, it took the shock of the Lebanese war to rid Lebanese society of several of its traditional patterns and to bring about social, demographic and economic changes that had a positive effect on female education and employment. In summary form, these changes include:

1. Increased acceptance by parents of their daughters' mobility, even before marriage.

2. Greater freedom for Lebanese teenage girls to widen their scope of education.

3. Better educational opportunities due to the spread and diversification of higher educational institutions, public as well as private, across the various regions of Lebanon.

4. Widening of the female employment spectrum as a result of the introduction of new educational disciplines, in response to changing labour-market demand.

5. Tougher economic conditions and very low per-capita income, leading to the forced entry of several Lebanese women into the labour market and their fighting for economic survival beside their partner.

6. Rendering of migration and foreign jobs lucrative to single, and sometimes to married, highly educated women due to a deteriorating Lebanese currency vis-à-vis foreign currencies.

For all the improvements in women's educational level and their increased and more confident presence in the labour market, they still have a long way to go to reach the level of Lebanese men – which, incidentally, could in itself be improved. Several centuries' head start could not be wiped away in fifteen years of war and strife. Although the number of highly educated females more than quadrupled between 1970 and 1990, while the number of males increased by a factor of less than three, highly educated females still constituted only 9.3 per cent of the total active population in 1990, as compared to 17.3 per cent of highly educated males. Efforts should be redoubled to do away with the bigotry that still exists among both parents and employers, and educational facilities should be greatly improved.

Table 6.8   Population by age group and sex, Lebanon 1970–90 (thousands)

Age	1970 F	1970 T	1975 F	1975 T	1980 F	1980 T	1985 F	1985 T	1990 F	1990 T
0–4	147	301	201	410	185	376	182	369	174	354
5–14	295	606	370	754	317	646	311	632	325	651
15–24	184	376	269	548	214	437	255	519	263	537
25–49	232	565	359	719	327	654	391	776	373	755
50–64	83	170	113	226	108	214	123	244	132	265
65+	53	105	54	113	67	125	70	128	70	130
Total	1,044	2,123	1,366	2,770	1,218	2,452	1,332	2,668	1,337	2,692

Sources: As in Table 6.2

Table 6.9   Student enrolment by level of education and sex, Lebanon 1970–90 (thousands)

Level	1970 F	1970 T	1975 F	1975 T	1980 F	1980 T	1985 F	1985 T	1990 F	1990 T
Primary	168	370	180	379	186	389	197	392	188	382
Intermediate	53	124	72	171	79	166	117	225	130	250
Secondary	27	69	29	170	45	102	68	137	84	170
General	11	36	9	120	32	73	50	101	62	125
Vocational	16	33	20	50	13	28	18	36	22	45
Higher	13	39	12	44	31	85	43	108	44	114
Total	261	602	293	764	341	742	419	862	446	916

Sources: As in Table 6.2

Table 6.10 Non-schooled population of 15 years and over, by level of education and sex, Lebanon 1970–90 (thousands)

Level	1970 F	1970 T	1975 F	1975 T	1980 F	1980 T	1985 F	1985 T	1990 F	1990 T
Primary	98	213	165	336	256	536	334	745	400	817
Intermediate	59	130	65	150	76	228	146	315	176	356
Secondary	25	70	43	149	60	193	98	235	117	238
Higher	5	28	12	37	17	66	32	90	53	122
Total	187	441	285	672	409	1,023	610	1,385	746	1,533

Sources: As in Table 6.2.

Table 6.11 Economically active population by age group and sex, Lebanon (thousands)

Age	1970 F	1970 T	1975 F	1975 T	1980 F	1980 T	1985 F	1985 T	1990 F	1990 T
10–14	8	16	11	20	10	20	3	13	3	13
15–24	32	120	54	199	41	159	48	168	49	174
25–49	43	303	58	400	52	364	81	455	81	468
50–64	7	74	11	97	10	95	11	107	12	111
65 +	2	23	3	28	3	28	3	38	3	39
Total	92	536	137	744	116	666	146	781	148	805

Sources: As in Table 6.2.

Table 6.12 Economically active population by type of activity and sex, Lebanon (thousands)

Type of activity	1970 F	1970 T	1975 F	1975 T	1980 F	1980 T	1985 F	1985 T	1990 F	1990 T
1 Agriculture, hunting, forestry and fishing	21	101	28	126	26	126	35	168	35	169
2 Mining and quarrying	0	–	–	1	–	1	–	1	–	1
3 Manufacturing	18	95	27	135	23	118	7	65	9	75
4 Electricity, water	–	6	2	8	–	7	–	6	–	5
5 Construction	–	35	–	50	–	43	–	49	–	51
6 Wholesale, retail trade, restaurants and hotels	6	92	25	130	7	113	38	220	38	225
7 Transport, storage and communications	2	38	–	54	2	47	4	45	2	48
8 Financing, insurance, real estate and business services	3	19	5	26	4	23	4	31	4	31
9 Community, social and personnel services	43	150	41	213	54	185	60	193	60	196
10 Activities not adequately defined	1	1	1	1	–	3	–	3	–	4
Total	94	538	129	746	116	666	146	781	148	805

Sources: As in Table 6.2.

Table 6.13 Employment by type of profession, secondary and university level of education and sex, Lebanon (thousands)

Level of education / Sex and type	1970			1975			1980			1985			1990		
	S	U	T	S	U	T	S	U	T	S	U	T	S	U	T
1 Professional, technical, and related — F	5	6	20	5	7	20	4	8	18	7	10	24	7	12	-
— T	14	15	53	19	21	73	13	15	51	22	22	70	23	23	-
2 Administrative, managerial — F	-	-	-	-	-	1	17	17	34	21	20	43	22	22	-
— T	2	3	11	3	4	16	20	20	40	28	23	51	27	27	-
3 Clerical and related — F	2	-	10	4	-	17	3	-	12	4	1	17	4	1	-
— T	11	3	45	15	3	65	10	2	44	15	3	64	15	5	-
4 Sales — F	-	-	3	-	-	4	-	-	4	-	-	5	-	-	-
— T	5	3	66	7	3	96	7	3	95	7	3	100	10	3	10
5 Services — F	-	-	21	-	-	30	-	-	19	-	-	16	-	-	-
— T	1	0.2	63	1	0.3	84	1	0.3	86	1	0.3	91	1	0.3	-
6 Agriculture, animal husbandry, forestry, fishing and hunting — F	-	-	21	-	-	28	-	-	20	-	-	27	-	-	-
— T	0.2	-	100	0.2	0.8	126	0.2	0.8	118	0.3	1	158	0.4	1	16
7,8,9 Production related, transport, equipment, operators, labourers — F	-	-	18	-	-	27	-	-	24	-	-	33	-	-	-
— T	1	0.2	184	1	0.3	262	1	0.3	208	1	0.3	222	1.4	-	22
X Not classifiable by occupation — F	-	-	-	-	-	20	-	-	-	-	-	-	-	-	-
— T	0.4	0.3	16	0.6	0.45	24	0.6	0.5	24	0.6	0.4	24	1	0.8	-
Y Armed forces — F	-	-	-	-	-	-	-	-	-	-	-	-	-	-	-
— T	-	-	-	-	-	-	-	-	-	-	-	-	-	-	-
Total — F	6	6	94	9	7	147	24	25	116	32	31	165	33	35	18
— T	34	25	538	47	33	746	52	42	666	75	53	781	78	61	80

Sources: As in Table 6.2.

Notes

1. On urban changes and services delivery, see various studies by Lebanese government agencies, listed in the References under Republique Libanaise.

2. Many studies have explored the contradictions of women's changing roles in Lebanon before, during and after the civil war, including their access to education and employment and the change in fertility patterns. For some of the earlier studies, see J. Chamie 1976; M. Chamie 1977; Dibs 1975; Hammoud 1976; Haddad 1978; Makhlouf 1979; Moughaizel 1979; Zurayk 1977, 1979; Richards 1980.

References

Abu-Nasr, J. 1979. 'Women's Employment in Lebanon'. *Al-Raida*, vol. 2, no. 9.

Al-Amin, R. 1979. *Al-Mara'a Wal Wathaef fil Qita'ain el 'am wal khass* (Women and Jobs in the Public and Private Sectors). UNESCO, the Seventh Conference for the Committee of the Rights of Lebanese Women, 6–7 March, Beirut.

Azzam, H., J. Abu-Nasr and I. Lorfing. 1985. 'An Overview of Arab Women in Population, Employment and Economic Development'. In J. Abu-Nasr, N. Khoury and H. Azzam, eds, *Women Employment and Development in the Arab World*, Studies in the Social Sciences, no. 41. Germany: Mouton Publishers, pp. 5–37.

Chamie, J. 1976. 'Religious Fertility Differentials in Lebanon'. Ph.D. dissertation, University of Michigan, Ann Arbor.

——— 1981. 'International Migration and Population Growth in the ECWA Countries'. *Proceedings of an ECWA Population Conference, Nicosia, Cyprus 11–16 May 1981, Volume 11*. Beirut: United Nations, Economic Commission for Western Asia, Population Division.

Chamie, M. 1977. 'Sexuality and Birth Control Decisions among Lebanese Couples'. *Signs: Women and National Development*, vol. 3, no. 1 (Autumn), pp. 294–312.

——— 1985. 'Labour Force Participation of Lebanese Women'. In J. Abu-Nasr, N. Khoury and M. Azzam, eds, *Women Employment and Development in the Arab World*, Studies in the Social Sciences, no. 41. Germany: Mouton Publishers, pp. 73–102.

Dibs, T. 1975. *Al-Mara'a a Wal Mihan al Hurra* (Women and the Liberal Professions). The Seventh Conference for Committee of the Rights of Lebanese Women, 6–7 March, Beirut. UNESCO.

Fa'our, Ali. 1981. 'Migration from South Lebanon with a Field Study of Forced Mass Migration'. In *Population Bulletin of ECWA*, No. 21. Beirut: ECWA, pp. 27–60.

Haddad, W. 1978. 'The Legal Provisions Governing the Status of Women in Some Arab Countries'. In *Population Bulletin of ECWA*, No. 14. Beirut: ECWA, pp. 26–46.

Hammoud, R. 1976. 'Nasseed al Inath fi Nitham al Ta'aleem fi Lubnan' (Women in the Lebanese Educational System). In *Majallet al Abbath al Tarbawiya* No 1. Beirut: School of Education, the Lebanese University, pp. 35–57.

Lorfing, I., and J. Abu Nasr. 1980a. 'The Female Industrial Workers and the Suburbs of Beirut in 1979'. In *Women and Work in Lebanon*, Monograph no. 1. Beirut: Institute for Women's Studies in the Arab World, Beirut University College.

—————— 1980b. 'Lebanese Women, Heads of Households'. In *Women and Work in Lebanon*. Monograph no. 1. Beirut: Institute for Women's Studies in the Arab World, Beirut University College.

Maalouf, Nayef and Khalil Abu Rjeily. 1987. *Al Wad'Al Tarbawi Fi Loubnan, Wagae' wa Mou'anat* (Educational Status of Lebanon, Facts and Problems). Beirut: Conseil pour la Recherche et le Developpement Pedagogique (CRDP).

Makhlouf, C. 1979. *Changing Veils*. London: Croom Helm.

Moughaizel, L. 1979. 'The Legal Status of Women among the Awlad'. *'Ali' Anthropological Quarterly*, vol. 40, no. 3.

Republique Libanaise, Conseil du Developpement et de la Reconstruction et Direction Generale de l'Urbanisme. 1984. *Analyses et Options*, Rapport de la Mission Franco-Libanaise d'étude et d'aménagement de la Région Métropolitaine de Beyrouth (December).

—————— 1986. *Region Métropolitaine de Beyrouth, Schema Directeur*. Beyrouth (June).

Republique Libanaise, Ministère du Plan, Direction Central de la Statistique. 1972. *Volume 1: Méthodes Analyses et Présentation des Résultats: L'Enquête par Sondage sur la Population Active au Liban, Novembre 1970. Volume 2: Tableaux et Résultats: L'Enquête par Sondage sur la Population Active au Liban, Novembre 1970*. Beyrouth: Direction Centrale de la Statistique.

Republique Libanaise, Office des Eaux de Beyrouth, BCEOM, TACE, CGE, SEURECA. 1984a. 'Volume 11: Données Urbaines et Besoins en Eau'. *Étude du Reseau de Distribution d'Eau Potable de la Ville de Beyrouth et ses Banlieues.*

—————— 1984b. 'Volume 11: Données Urbaines et Besoins en Eau, Annexe: L'Enquête et ses Résultats'. *Étude du Reseau de Distribution d'Eau Potable de la Ville de Beyrouth et ses Banlieues.*

Republique Libanaise, Office National de l'Emploi. 1983. 'La Profession Medicale au Liban'. *Serie Orientation Professionnelle*, No. 1. Sin il Fil, Liban: Imprimerie du CRDP.

Richards, Evelyne. 1980. 'The Employment Status of Women in Lebanon'. In *Women and Work in Lebanon*. Monograph no. 1. Beirut: Institute for Women's Studies in the Arab World, Beirut University College.

United Nations. 1988. *World Statistics in Brief, 11th Edition*. New York: UN.

United Nations, Economic Commission for Western Asia (UN ECWA). 1977. 'Employment and Development. ECWA Seminar on Population, Employment and Development (Amman).

—————— 1978. *The Population Framework: Data Collection, Demographic Analysis, Population and Development*. Beirut: UNECWA, Population Division.

—————— 1980. *Survey of Economic and Social Developments in the ECWA Region, 1980*. Beirut: ECWA.

—————— 1982. *Demographic and Related Socio-Economic Data Sheets for Countries of the Economic Commission for Western Asia, No. 3*. Baghdad: ECWA.

—————— 1985. *Survey of Economic and Social Developments in the ECWA Region, 1984*. Baghdad: ECWA.

—————— 1986. *Statistical Abstract of the Region of the Economic and Social Commission for*

Western Asia, 1975–1984 (9th issue). Baghdad: ECWA.

———— 1987. *Statistical Abstract of the Region of the Economic and Social Commission for Western Asia, 1976–1985* (10th issue). Baghdad: ECWA.

United Nations, Educational Bureau for the Arab States. 1980. 'Annexe Statistique (B) Tableaux et Indicateurs Socio-Economiques Relatifs aux Pays Arabes (1980–2000)'. UNEDBAS, Colloque Régional sur le Developpement Futur de l'Education dans les Pays Arabes, Beirut, 7–9 October.

———— 1988. *Kitab Marja'i Fi Al Tarbiya Al Sukkania, Al Jiz' Al Thaleth: Al Mourahaka* (Reference Book for Population Education, Part Three: Teen Ages), 2nd edn. Beirut: UN Funds for Population Activities.

Zurayk, H. 1977. 'The Effect of Education of Women and Urbanisation on Actual and Desired Fertility and on Fertility Control in Lebanon'. *Population Bulletin of ECWA*, No. 12. Beirut: ECWA.

———— 1979. 'The Changing Role of the Arab Women'. *Population Bulletin of ECWA*, No. 17. Beirut: ECWA, pp. 18–31.

7

Determinants of Female Labour-Force Participation in Jordan

Hussein Shakhatreh

Despite enjoying social and economic conditions well above those of many developing countries, Jordan is characterized by a very high birth rate and a very low female labour-force participation rate. This chapter reports on a quantitative study that focuses on the individual correlates of female labour-force participation in Jordan. The main objective of the study was to explore the nature and the strength of the main factors that influence female labour-force participation in Jordan so as to suggest policies to better integrate women into the workforce. The analysis used data obtained from the 1982–83 Manpower Survey in Jordan, which was conducted by the Department of Statistics based on a representative sample of 21,471 households. Of the 23,290 women in the sample, 18,657 were in the category 'ever married' and 4,633 in the category 'never married'. Bivariate and multivariate analyses were carried out for both single and married or ever married (divorced and widowed) Jordanian women, within the framework of a conceptual model that takes into account cultural, demographic and socio-economic variables.[1]

On Female Labour-Force Participation

Awareness of the importance of women's contributions to the development process, both as beneficiaries and as participants, has drawn increasing attention from scholars, planners and local and international organizations during the last two decades. These contributions can be thought of chiefly in economic and demographic terms, as well as in terms of benefits to the women themselves. With regard to economic contribution, the importance of women's employment would seem to be obvious. In countries where women's employment is already wide-spread, women are directly responsible for a major share of economic output, and, as earners, help raise many families out of poverty. In countries where the level of women's participation in the paid labour force is still low, they represent an under-utilized resource whose fuller utilization could go a long way toward raising output levels. Increases in education are also important because better educated women workers have much higher levels of productivity and earnings.

In population studies, it has become common to talk about the demographic contribution of raising women's status. Many authors have discussed how raising the status of women can contribute to the re-establishment of demographic balance at lower levels of both fertility and infant and child mortality. Women's status is commonly measured in terms of female educational attainment and women's share of paid employment (Buvinic 1976; Zurayk 1979). It is argued that more highly educated women, especially those who work outside the home, are likely to have fewer but healthier and better-educated children, which contrib-utes to the social development of the society and eases the burden of pressure on limited national resources (Standing 1978; UN 1985; Farooq and DeGraff 1988).[2] Thus, the World Population Plan of Action adopted at the 1974 World Population Conference in Bucharest insisted on the need for women to have equal opportunity in both education and employment so as to lower fertility and achieve development goals. The International Conference on Population, held in Mexico City in 1984, stressed in stronger terms the recommendation of the 1974 Conference to better integrate women as full participants in the process of develop-ment (UN 1987).

Many scholars consider woman's work to be one of the major factors raising women's social and economic status in society.[3] For example, Zurayk (1979), and in this volume, Moghadam (Chapter 2), consider female participation in the labour force to be the main indicator of the changing role of women in Middle Eastern societies. They assume that women who work outside the home gain economic independence that will have an impact on all aspects of their lives. Similarly, Standing (1978) asserts that the increase in female labour-force participation should enhance women's socio-economic independence and power in family decision-making processes. Moreover, the two indicators of women's status – education and labour-force participation[4] – interact with each other in a mutually beneficial way. Better-educated women are more likely to obtain satisfactory employment, and young women are more likely to remain in school if it is expected that they will bring in an income.

Determinants of female labour-force participation rates include several cultural, demographic and socio-economic factors. Social and cultural factors are expected to play a major part in determining women's labour-force status. However, there is a dearth of information on the cultural sphere and on attitudes towards female work. Therefore, using the available data, we try to explore the magnitude and the direction of the factors that affect women's decision to work. Women's work for pay outside the home is typically observed to rise with the process of socio-economic development. Similarly, the level of fertility falls as living standards rise. However, neither variable is necessarily related to economic variables in any close or rigid pattern, whether across societies or within a society across time.

Jordan has a high labour-force growth rate that exceeds its population growth, 6.0 per cent and 4.5 per cent respectively (World Bank 1986). Jordan has no official policy to curb the high fertility rate, the result of which is a relatively large population of young people. The high growth rate of the labour force means that Jordan faces a major problem of providing employment for new labour entrants, especially the educated ones. In the 1980s Jordan had a high unemployment rate, in the range of 8-9 per cent (Department of Statistics 1984), which was expected to become aggravated during the 1990s. Underemployment is another serious problem.

Jordan has a low crude labour-force participation rate (total labour force/total population) – 20 per cent in 1982 (Department of Statistics 1984). In 1980, among 159 countries, Jordan was ranked 158th in respect of the percentage of economically active population (Kurian 1984). The male crude labour-force participation (male labour force divided by the total male population) rate for 1982 is 34.6 per cent compared with 4.3 per cent female. The labour-force participation rate of those aged 15 years and above is 39.4 per cent. This relatively low proportion is due to the high ratio of young people to adults and the low female labour-force participation rate.

In 1982, female labour-force participation was 8.4 per cent of those women aged 15 years and above compared to 67.8 per cent for men in the same age group (see Table 7.1). Jordan was ranked in the bottom 10 of 144 countries with respect to the 1980 share of female labour in the total labour force (Kurian 1984). The share of the female labour force in the total labour force in 1982 in Jordan is about 10 per cent

Table 7.1   Some labour-force indicators for Jordan, 1952, 1961, 1979 and 1985

Years	1952	1961	1979	1985
Crude LFPR	24.2	24.1	21.3	20.0
Crude male LFPR	50.9	44.3	38.0	34.6
Crude female LFPR	2.2	3.0	3.3	4.3
LFPR males 15+	78.0	–	77.0	67.8
LFPR female 15+	3.1	–	7.5	8.4
% Female labour of total labour force	5.0	6.0	6.7	10.0

Note. It is worth mentioning here that there is uncertainty regarding the accuracy of female labour-force participation statistics in developing countries in general and in the Arab countries in particular (Anker 1983; Gerner-Adams 1979). According to Anker the inaccuracy is due to several reasons, which include: problems related to the interview setting, definition of female labour, and wording of questions. All of these lead to underestimation of female labour-force participation.

Sources: Department of Statistics, Jordan, *Population and Housing Census, 1961*, Vol. 2, 1962; Department of Statistics, Jordan, 1982–83 *Manpower Survey*, Results of First Round, 1984; ILO, *1985 Year Book of Labour Statistics*, Geneva, 1986; World Bank, *World Tables*, Vol. 2 (3rd edn), 1984.

(see Table 7.1) compared to 32 per cent in developing countries and 40 per cent in developed countries in 1980 (Farooq 1986). The female labour-force participation rate is among the lowest in the Arab world (see Moghadam, Chapter 2 in this volume).

Jordan has achieved an average annual increase of 5.8 per cent in its gross national product (GNP) during the last two decades (Cornelius 1988). In 1983–84 the female enrolment ratio in primary school was 99 per cent, and 78 per cent in secondary school (World Bank 1987). The female literacy rate was about 60 per cent, and female life expectancy was 65 years in 1983 (World Bank 1985). These socio-economic achievements raise questions about the low female labour-force participation rate in Jordan. Low female participation implies the exclusion of women from the process of development in Jordan. It is clear that, despite recent efforts to promote the role of women as a part of socio-economic development, earlier socio-economic development plans failed to integrate women into the process. Accordingly, almost half of the society is economically inactive. Jordan is entering a new era of socio-economic development and industrialization; it needs the participation of all its members so as to accelerate the process of development and transformation, and to give everybody in society the chance to share the gains of development. Moreover, there is a need to correct the distortion resulting from the unplanned high demand for academic training; this has created a surplus of professionals such as engineers and medical doctors while the country remains short of mid-level professionals, technicians and skilled workers. Planners should therefore take into consideration the need for full integration of women in the socio-economic development of the country. As Mernissi (1976) says:

> Development means, above all, the optimal utilization of the human and natural resources of a country. Any economic development in the Muslim countries which considers the utilization of 50 per cent of its human re-sources as secondary is a quixotic form of development that can only bring about illusory achievement.

Many people argue that the greater utilization of women's labour resources in countries that already face sharp unemployment among males might aggravate the issue of male unemployment (Durand 1975). Nevertheless, Standing (1978) argues against this assumption and indicates that increasing female labour-force participation may increase total employment by putting downward pressure on wage rates, thus leading employers to hire more workers. Moreover, unemployment and under-employment in Jordan have been aggravated by high military spending rather than allocation of resources towards productive investment and employment-creation.

The Importance of Cultural, Demographic and Socio-economic Factors

Most models used to analyse labour supply have been based on neo-classical economic theory. The neoclassical theory of labour supply, presented by Mincer (1962), derived from traditional utility maximization concepts. This theory implies that an individual maximizes his/her utility through a rational distribution of time between wage employment and leisure (Cain 1966; Bowen and Finegan 1969). Accordingly, the basic concept of the neoclassical theory of labour supply is that the wage rate determines the individual supply of labour, subject to constraints of time and budget (Killingsworth 1983; Standing 1978).

The original focus of neoclassical labour-supply theory on individual utility maximization has been modified to take into account the family as the unit of analysis, allowing for the possible interdependency of family members' decisions about labour supply. In other words, the individual's labour-supply decision should be studied within the context of the family, which is the unit that maximizes utility. In this new approach, female labour supply depends on other family income in addition to the woman's own wage. This new approach has been used by scholars such as Ashenfelter and Heckman (1974) and Killingsworth (1983) among others.

Some authors have argued that this theory of women's decisions about labour-force participation is unsuited to non-industrial societies. This is because it ignores women's non-market production of goods and services (Steel and Campbell 1982; Tovo 1984). This problem was recognized by Mincer (1962), Cain (1966) and Becker (1965). Becker introduced a theory of the allocation of time which tried to incorporate the concept of non-market work into the theory of labour supply. Nevertheless, the neoclassical theory of labour supply has been criticized by many sociologists and demographers as well as by some economists (Oppenheimer 1982; Leibenstein 1978). Oppenheimer's main criticisms of neoclassical labour-supply theory can be summarized in three points. First, she rejects 'the assumption of neoclassical economists that "tastes" are either invariant or vary randomly over time and among people at one point in time', so that they are normally relegated to the error term. Second, she criticizes the static nature of many micro-economic models. These models are based on the unrealistic assumption that individuals make most of their decisions simultaneously at the time of marriage, and never change them subsequently. Third, she challenges the 'monolithic character of the family which is presumed under the on-time utility-maximizing model'.

Oppenheimer (1982) offers what she calls a 'social demographic theory' to explain the increase in female labour-force participation and decrease in fertility in the United States. Oppenheimer contends that the change over time in the proportion of married women choosing to work is essentially a matter of changing tastes for paid employment. She also suggests that 'economic squeezes' are a major factor behind the change in tastes for paid employment. She defines 'economic squeeze' as an imbalance between life aspirations, the market cost of these aspirations, and the economic resources available to the household (other than the wife's income). This is very similar to the argument of Easterlin (1980) that the decline in fertility and increase in female employment during the 1960s and 1970s resulted from an effort by the younger generation to improve their standard of living in accordance with rising expectations and decreasing relative incomes for the young.

Oppenheimer's theoretical framework appears to be well-suited to explaining female labour-force participation in developing countries, including in the Middle East. It leaves room for cultural and social as well as economic factors. However, it is restricted to married women, while our concern is for all women. Moreover, despite Oppenheimer's claim that this theory takes into account social and cultural factors, the data she used to test her model do not contain any social and cultural factors. In other words, the model is tested by data that include only the usual economic-demographic variables.

In the present research, two empirical studies which explicitly include social and cultural variables in their models have been used to guide the analytical framework. These two studies are Anker and Knowles (1978), 'A Micro-Analysis of Female Labor Force Participation in Kenya', and Steel and Campbell (1982), 'Women's Employment and Development: A Conceptual Framework Applied to Ghana'. Both studies emphasize the importance of cultural, social and demographic as well as economic factors in influencing female labour supply. We will review the main ideas of both studies so as to provide guidance for the development of the framework for our own operational model.

Anker and Knowles (1978) provide a framework for the determinants of women's labour supply which we can classify under cultural, demographic and socio-economic factors. According to Anker and Knowles, cultural factors play an important role in shaping a woman's decisions regarding her participation in the workforce. To capture the effect of cultural factors on women's work in Kenya, binary variables for the wives of polygamous men, women whose husbands are living away, and Muslim women are used in the analysis. *A priori* expectations are that there is a positive relation between female participation in the work-force and the first two variables, and a negative one with the latter. Also, because of variations in labour-participation levels between rural and urban women, as well as factors affecting these levels, Anker and Knowles run separate analyses for each group.

With respect to demographic factors, Anker and Knowles consider six variables that are believed to influence women's labour-force partici-pation. These are: age, child-care burden, presence of women aged 15 years or above in the household, marital status, migration, and family size in adult consumer unit. They suggest that the correct measure of the child-care burden depends on the reference period used to refer to women's labour-force participation. If labour-force participation refers to a twelve-month period, the measure that is preferred is 'the number of children too young to take care of themselves'. However, if the measure of labour-force participation does not refer to the current time period, Anker and Knowles indicate that 'the measure of live births the woman has had would seem to be an appropriate measure of the child-care burden'.

Anker and Knowles list education, health factors and residence (social factors) as important elements that influence female labour-force participation. Because the relationship between education level and labour participation is likely to be nonlinear, a series of educational binary variables were used to study the effect of education on labour-force participation. They further argue that the expected earnings from work 'income potential' positively affect women's labour-force participation. Meanwhile, the need for income is an important factor in encouraging women to engage in work. They indicated that 'wage potential' is a function of the person's level of education. However, expected earnings may also be affected by certain macroeconomic conditions. These macroeconomic conditions include the overall employment rate, the average wages in the service sector, and the proportion of modern sector employment positions in the service sector. Thus three variables were used to measure these effects: the rate of unemployment in the modern sector, the average wage for modern sector employees, and the percentage of modern sector employment in the service sector.

Anker and Knowles indicate that the 'need for income' as perceived by the women depends on three major factors. They are: family income excluding the woman's contribution, the number of family members of various ages who live on the family's income, and the 'felt' need for material goods. The last factor is considered as a part of an individual's taste function (but is excluded from their analysis because of lack of data). Concerning the second point, they argue that the burden of household members is associated with their age. Thus, they convert family members into equivalent consumer units. For simplicity, individuals who are less than 15 years old are weighted as one-half of an adult.

Steel and Campbell (1982) stress the influence of cultural factors on female labour supply. They criticize the neoclassical female labour-supply models for their neglect of cultural and traditional norms. They state that 'less attention has been paid to sexism as it affects supply through socio-cultural traditions and demand through discrimination'. This emphasis on cultural values does not reduce the importance of the demographic and socio-economic factors on female labour force: 'Female labor supply is affected by social norms, education, fertility, etc., as well as by the market wage and family income.'

Under the cultural determinants of labour supply, four points have been stressed by Steel and Campbell (1982):

1. *Religion* They argue that 'Islamic prohibitions against female contact with men outside the family impose a heavy social cost on women who nevertheless decide to seek market employment, and their choice of occupations is sharply restricted.'

2. *Norms* Social norms regarding women's 'proper' place (for example, in the home) have negative effects on women's decisions to join the workforce.

3. *Attitudes* Women's attitudes toward the acceptability of market employment have a significant effect on female labour supply.

4. *Discrimination* They also stress labour market segregation, which may result in a higher unemployment rate, and lower wages for women compared to men.

Both studies encompass the three main groups of factors which affect female labour-force participation: cultural, demographic and socio-economic. However, Anker and Knowles's framework is more comprehensive and detailed. In addition, they applied multivariate analysis techniques, using regression analysis, while Steel and Campbell used contingency table techniques. The analysis of the present study draws from the Anker and Knowles framework to study the determinants of female labour-force participation in Jordan.

The Conceptual Model for Analysing Female Labour Supply

Labour supply refers to both participation, that is, the decision to work or seek employment, and hours of work. In the present study, only participation was studied.[5] In the 1982–83 Manpower Survey of households, 23,290 Jordanian women aged between 15 and 59 years, who were not students at the time of the survey, and who were related directly to the household head (as daughters or wives) or were themselves household heads, represented the population. Two models were designed to test the strength of variables that determine the labour-force participation of 'never-married' and 'ever-married' Jordanian women. These were designated the 'single women's conceptual model' and the 'married women's conceptual model'. The variables were grouped under three categories: cultural factors, demographic factors and socio-economic factors. Major contributions to this study included the use of religion as a proxy for social factors and the category of single women who were still living with their parents. To the best of our knowledge, no such multivariate study had been previously carried out in Jordan.

Cultural factors

Uthoff and Pernia (1986) suggest including indices of norms and of religious and ethnic characteristics to measure the effect of cultural factors in any analysis of female labour-force participation. The data used here did not include any variables to measure directly norms and attitudes toward women's work. With regard to the index of ethnicity, there was not much variation in ethnicity (over 98 per cent of Jordan's population are Arabs), so this variable will not be considered.

The only index that could be used as proxy for cultural factors in these data is religion. Islam is the dominant religion in the country, and 95 per cent of the population is Muslim, with the remainder mostly Christian. Muslim women in Jordan have a lower participation rate (7.4 per cent) than Christian women (26.5 per cent).

Demographic factors

Demographic factors include age, family size, child-care burden, marital status, and presence in the household of other adult women (15 years of age or above). The relation between female labour-force participation and age is curvilinear. For married women, age is an important factor that affects their labour-force participation. In most studies the expectation is that younger married women are less likely to be in the labour force than older women, since they are at the peak of their childbearing years (Standing and Sheehan 1978; Mohan 1986). In the present study, the expectation was different because of the continuity of childbearing up until the late age of fecundity. Age is dealt with here as a categorical variable with seven age categories.

The family size in equivalent adult units is an element in determining the household's need for the woman's wage. Anker and Knowles state that 'the more household members, the more the need for income must be ceteris paribus'. Since individual consumption is a function of age, household members are converted into equivalent consumer units. To do this, we will use a scale deployed by Standing (1978). According to this scale, all those household members over the age of 15 are assumed to count as an adult and to take a unit value. Thus, the members of the household will be weighted as follows:

$$
\begin{array}{ll}
0{-}4 & = 0.4 \\
5{-}9 & = 0.6 \\
10{-}14 & = 0.8 \\
15{+} & = 1.0
\end{array}
$$

Unlike Anker and Knowles, in this study we consider family size to have a negative effect on female labour-force participation, since the greater the number of household members, the greater the responsibility of the woman for household duties. In other words, the greater the family size, the less likely it is that the woman in the household will be in the workforce.

The presence of children is expected to have a negative impact on married women's labour-force participation, particularly in urban areas. However, there may be a nonlinear relationship, such that in a larger family other children take care of younger children, making it easier for the mother to leave the home. To measure the effect of child-care burden on women's work, a series of dummy variables for the presence of children of different groups is incorporated in the model. Each dummy variable takes the value of 1 if the child is classified in the category, and 0 otherwise. The *a priori* expectation is that the presence of young children (5 years of age or less) has a negative impact on female labour-force participation. The presence of older children is expected to be neutral.

Marital status is used as a control variable in the 'ever-married' woman model, with the expectation that currently married women have lower labour-force participation than women separated from their spouses by death or divorce. The latter are assumed to be more responsible for their families and their own expenses. A binary variable is incorporated in the model, with the value of 1 assigned to those who are currently married and 0 to those who are divorced or widowed. In addition, marital status has three categories in the pooled model, with participation rates expected to be much lower for currently married women than for those women without spouses.

Socio-economic factors

Socio-economic factors play an important role in determining female labour-force participation. Five variables under this category are included in the models: respondent's residence, education, available income (family income excluding the contribution of the respondent), regional unemployment rate, and regional average wage.

Place of residence is included as a control variable with the expectation that female labour-force participation is higher in the urban areas than in the rural areas. The reasons are: (1) urban residents have a less conservative environment regarding sex roles; (2) urban areas have greater job opportunities, especially for women. It is worth mentioning here that the Jordanian Department of Statistics defines urban population as those living in locations of 5,000 people or more. However, according to this definition, there is some exaggeration in the degree of urbanization, since some villages have grown to above 5,000 people. Mazur (1979) indicated that, except for the three largest cities, most Jordanian towns are medium-sized and still quite rural-oriented.

In this study, a new classification is therefore adopted. This definition differentiates among three groups of population. The first group includes the population of the three largest cities in the country (metropolitan population). The second group includes towns that have more than 10,000 and fewer than 100,000 people (town population). The third group includes the remaining localities (rural population). The residence variable is a trichotomous variable: denoted as 1 if the woman resides in a metropolitan area; 2 if the woman resides in a town; and 3 if the woman resides in a rural area.

Education is seen by many economists as a proxy measure for a woman's opportunity of income or her possibility of being employed. Sociologists also consider education as a function of modernization and a factor behind female employment. In our model a categorical variable with five categories is used to capture the effect of respondents' years of education. The five categories are: illiterate, 1–6 years, 7–9 years, 10–12 years and 13 years of education and above. These categories allow for nonlinear effects of different levels of education on labour-force participation. In particular, it is expected that the impact of secondary (10–12 years) and higher education (13+ years) on women's labour-force participation in Jordan will be much greater than that of lower levels of education. This is because educational credentials are very important for gaining access to jobs and because more specialized training at the post-secondary level is often tied to specific employment offers or obligations.

Family income reflects the family's need for income as seen by the woman. Family income is usually used to determine the household's need for the woman's wage. Tovo (1984) uses the term 'available income' to measure the income available to the household without considering the woman's earnings. This expression will be used in our analysis. Thus, a measure of the household need for income is derived by:

Available income = Total income – Respondent's income

In this study, total income represents the household monthly income from all sources, including the respondent's monthly income. The *a priori* expectation is that the available income will have a negative effect on women's work in Jordan, especially for married women. To the extent that single women work in order to achieve personal fulfilment rather than to contribute to the family, they will be less affected by the level of family income.

Regional unemployment rate and regional average wage variables indicate local job-market conditions. Unemployment rate is another factor that might affect women's labour-force participation. Two contradictory hypotheses describe the effect of unemployment rates: the first is the 'discouraged worker effect', and the second, the 'add factor effect'. The first hypothesis suggests that the unemployment rate has a negative effect on female labour-force participation. The second hypothesis sees a positive effect. This hypothesis implies that reduced aggregate demand lowers the income of other family members; hence, other family members will look for a chance to work and so increase the possibility of participating in the labour force. In this study, our expectation is that unemployment rate will have a negative effect on women's labour-force participation.

The average wage level for employed females in a locality is expected to have a positive effect on women's labour-force participation. The standardized average wage is calculated for each of the five regions of Jordan by regressing the natural logarithm of wages for each employed woman in the sample on her human capital characteristics (age and education), personal characteristics (religion, residence and marital status) and regional dummies. The estimated coefficients on the regional dummies represent region-specific intercept terms of the wage function. They control for variations in the composition of the female workforce across regions.

Single Women's Conceptual Model

'Single woman' is defined here as a woman who has never married. In Jordanian society, such women typically live with their parents, and it is the responsibility of their fathers to meet their expenses. However, the labour-force participation of this group is much higher than for women as a whole (34.6 per cent of single women compared to 10.5 per cent of the study sample). Most Jordanian women who are economically active – 65.2 per cent – are single. Thus, we contend that it is important to analyse the factors that affect the labour-force participation of this group of women within a separate model.

Except for child-care burden and the presence of adult women aged 15 years or more,[6] all the variables that were specified above and are included in the married women's model are also included in the single women's model. In addition, the education of single women's fathers and mothers is added to this model. We will now discuss the variables that we think may impact upon single women's decisions differently from those of married women.

We believe that cultural factors will have weaker effects on single women's labour-force participation than on that of married women. This is partly because single women are concentrated among the youngest age groups. Usually, the young age groups are more educated than those in the older groups, who are almost all married. Single women, since they are younger, may have more liberal views toward women's work and other aspects of life. In other words, they are less constrained by conservative views.

The father's and mother's level of education are believed to have an important effect on their daughter's labour-force participation, since it affects their attitudes toward sex roles. Thus the father's and mother's level of education will be a factor only in the single women's model.

The 'need for income' may have more of a positive impact on single women's work, because it is less of an embarrassment for the father to let his daughter work than his wife. In addition, the chances of finding a job is higher for the daughter than for her mother, since it is assumed that she has a higher level of education than her mother. Moreover, women's contribution to the family income has become increasingly important, because of the changes in economic conditions and the increase in the cost of living. Even the concept of a single-wage-earner family is less acceptable among persons of the younger generation. Many young men prefer to marry a working woman rather than a non-working woman so she can help meet the future expenses of the family.

Available income variable will be employed in the model as a continuous variable. Also, unlike respondent's education, we take parental level of education as continuous variables. This conceptual framework suggests that the single woman's decision to work is affected largely by her mother's and father's education, in addition to the other cultural, demographic and socio-economic variables of the individuals themselves or their households and communities. All these variables are exogenous variables.

Hypotheses

1. Cultural factors strongly affect women's decisions concerning participation in the workforce.

2. Single women are less affected by cultural factors than married women.

3. The presence of young children affects 'ever-married' women's labour-force participation.

4. Family size, in equivalent adult consumer units, has a negative effect on women's decision to work.

5. Respondent's years of education have a positive effect on women's labour-force participation, especially at the highest levels of education.

6. Family income (excluding respondent's contribution) has a negative effect on female labour-force participation, especially for married women.

7. The presence of other women aged 15 and above in the household affects positively 'ever-married' women's participation in the workforce.

8. The unemployment rate has a negative – discouraging – effect on women's decision to work.

9. The father's and mother's education have a positive effect on single women's labour-force participation.

Analysis of Findings

As mentioned above, the study used multivariate logit regression to examine the effects of the factors that affect women's labour-force participation. The analysis was carried out for single women and 'ever-married' women separately. In addition, analysis was done for a pooled model which includes all women in the study sample, with the inclusion of marital status as a control variable.

In general, the findings supported our hypotheses concerning the effects of cultural, demographic, social and economic factors on female labour-force participation. In all three of the models, respondents' religion, which stands for cultural and attitudinal factors, was found to have a very significant effect on women's decision to join the workforce. This finding is in contrast to that of Anker and Knowles (1978), who found that Islam had an insignificant effect on women's labour-force participation in Kenya. However, the effect of religion appeared much stronger for 'never-married' women than for 'ever-married' women. This is the opposite of what was hypothesized.

Our study confirmed the inverse relationship between fertility and female labour-force participation in Jordan. The presence of young children appears to affect 'ever-married' women's labour-force participation negatively. Women who have had children, regardless of number or age, are less likely to be in the labour force than those who remain childless. In addition, the results showed that the presence of pre-school children between 2 and 5 years has a significant negative effect on women's labour-force participation. Finally, the presence of other women aged 15 and above living in the household was found to have a particularly strong positive relation to 'ever-married' women's labour-force participation. Each of these results is consistent with our hypotheses about the depressive effect of child-care and housework burdens on work outside the home.

Marital status was found to have a very strong effect on female labour-force participation. The results from the pooled model showed that single women and previously married women have significantly higher participation than currently married women. Furthermore, single women have higher participation rates than previously married women, controlling for other variables in the model. These results are consistent with our hypotheses.

A respondent's residence was found to have a significant effect on her decision to join the workforce. In all three models, residence in rural areas proved to have a strong negative effect on women's labour-force participation. Conversely, urban residence had a significantly positive influence in all three models. Residence in metropolitan areas had a positive effect on single women's labour participation compared to that of town areas, but no significant effect (and a negative sign) on 'ever-married' women's decision to work. However, the magnitude of each of these effects was rather modest, which suggests relatively little differentiation in Jordan between rural and urban areas.

Of all the factors considered in the three models, education was found to have the most significant influence on female labour-force participation. In all cases, women with some education have a significantly greater likelihood of being in the workforce than do illiterate women. However, the results showed that the respondent's years of education start to have an important positive effect chiefly in secondary education and above. The participation rates of women with fewer than 10 years of schooling are quite low – between 2.0 and 7.1 per cent – while those with 10–12 years have a participation rate of 25.8 per cent, and those with more than 12 years have participation rates of 69-77 per cent. In contrast to women with secondary or higher education, single women and 'ever-married' women with low levels of education or no education have very low rates of labour-force participation. In particular, college and higher education has the most significant influence on female labour-force participation. A respondent's mother's and father's education also had a significant effect in explaining levels of single women's labour-force participation, independent of the respondent's own level of education.

The results regarding the hypotheses about economic variables were mixed. Family available income was found to have a significant negative influence on participation in the labour force, but only for 'ever-married' women. It was also found to have an effect in the pooled model, which is dominated by 'ever-married' women, but especially in the single women's labour-force-participation model. Indeed, the coefficient on income in the single women's model is positive. This suggests that the decision of single women to participate is not affected by the economic needs or resources of the household but rather is determined by the individual woman. Finally, regional unemployment rate is found to have no significant relation to women's participation in the workforce.

Policy Implications

The study discussed in this chapter showed that there are many factors that affect female labour-force participation in Jordan. Cultural and educational factors are found to have the greatest influence on Jordanian women's presence in the workforce. Other demographic and economic factors are also found to affect women's participation. In this section, we discuss some of the implications of these findings for labour-market and other policies in Jordan and make a number of concrete policy recommendations.

Concern about low female labour-force participation rates in Jordan has been expressed by many scholars, women's organizations and government officials. This low rate of participation exists in spite of the labour law that grants equal opportunities to women and men. Many seminars have been held in Jordan during the last few years to discuss the promotion of women's roles in the social and economic development process. Taking into consideration the findings of this study, the following policy measures might be useful in promoting female participation in the workforce:

1. An extensive media campaign, concentrating on the importance of women's roles in the process of socio-economic development as beneficiaries and as contributors, should be developed. This is directed both at men – to make them more sympathetic and respectful toward women – and at women, to help raise their self-esteem. This might encourage women to be more aware of the positive role that they can play during their lives to strengthen themselves, their families and their society.

2. Women should participate more directly in the decision-making process and play a role in the making of regulations and laws, especially those that have a direct impact on their status and affairs. As a minimum, this should include special hearings designed to find out the opinions of women on proposed legislation.

3. Moreover, effort should be made to bring cultural traditions of the dominant society into line with Islam, as properly interpreted. In particular, a number of traditions which are based on a misinterpretation of Islam have hampered women from being active members in our society. The government should work together with Islamic scholars to promote the idea that a woman can be a worker and at the same time a good Muslim.

4. Women should be encouraged to join women's and labour organizations which might give them better chances to participate in different activities and to increase their vocational aspirations.

5. Educational opportunities, especially secondary education and beyond, should be made available to all women. In addition, women (and their parents) should be encouraged through the media to expand their education beyond the primary stage and not to be content with a low level of education, given the importance of secondary and post-secondary education in promoting women's work.

6. Vocational education should be promoted among women. This kind of education should give women better opportunities of being employed.

7. Child-care centres should be made available to provide services at

a reasonable cost for working women so as to make it unnecessary for them to quit their jobs to care for their children. In addition, Jordanian housewives should be encouraged to take in other women's children for paid in-home child care, since this at the same time creates a job for one woman and frees other women for regular jobs.

8. An intensive campaign should be carried out to promote family-planning practice among married women in order to control their fertility. This would help them to remain at work, since we find that childbearing has a significant negative effect on women's labour-force participation. To date, Jordan has no official policy regarding family planning.

9. We call for greater enforcement of the existing Jordanian labour laws concerning equal rights of women and men for jobs and wages, and the issuing of new laws to further guarantee women's equal access to remunerative employment. This would include a crackdown on certain institutions that still discriminate between men and women in job selection, or that dismiss women from work when they get married. Regulations should be designed to facilitate the re-entry into work of those women who quit work to bear children and subsequently assume child-care responsibility.

10. A system of part-time employment should be adopted and encouraged to make it easier for those women who have children and housework responsibilities and who cannot take full-time employment but would nevertheless like to work.

11. A more complete system of compiling data regarding women's work and characteristics should be worked out.

12. Programmes need to be developed that will create employment opportunities for both sexes, but particularly for women. These will help reduce the high unemployment rate, which averages about 23 per cent among women.

Further Research

Several areas need further research to be carried out in order to provide a better picture of the conditions that influence Jordanian women's decisions to join the workforce. To begin with, data on people's attitudes towards women working need to be collected, along with a variety of other sociological or psychological variables. Second, more information should be collected about job characteristics and the degree of compatibility between work roles and women's other roles. This would include information about distance travelled to work, type of child care utilized by those women with children, and the reasons given by those not employed for not working.

Another area which requires further investigation is the interaction of labour-force participation and demographic behaviour. Our study aim was to explore factors that affect women's labour-force participation and their magnitudes, utilizing labour-force survey data. These data were not designed explicitly to study the determinants of female labour-force participation, and are even less appropriate for the study of fertility patterns. Moreover, they only give a cross-sectional 'snapshot' with no information of how patterns of labour-force participation and child-bearing change over the life cycle. Therefore, a follow-up study is needed that will simultaneously collect fertility histories and work histories for each woman in the household.

Further analysis of the causal links in the model is needed so as to decide the total effect of each predictor on women's labour-force participation. This kind of path analysis was beyond the scope of the present study. It would involve modelling each of the important predictor variables, which are themselves influenced by other variables in the model. For example, religion, residence and parental education help predict respondents' education and marital status. Thus, these variables can have both direct and indirect effects on female labour-force participation.

Notes

1. For a full exposition of the methodology and the conceptual models, see H. Shakhatreh, *The Determinants of Female Labour-Force Participation in Jordan*, unpublished Ph.D. dissertation, Department of Population Planning and International Health, University of Michigan, 1990.

2. While women's education is one of the strongest and most consistent predictors of lower risk of infant and child mortality (Cochrane et al. 1980), the health implications of women's work outside the home are much less clear cut. The positive effect of increased income may be cancelled by the negative effect of neglect of children. According to Leslie (1989), any negative effects are most likely to be observed for very low-income women in nuclear families who lack adequate assistance in taking care of their children.

3. There is no consensus among scholars regarding the definition and the indicators of women's status. In addition, there is disagreement on the factors that suppress the opportunities for women and the way to improve and enhance women's status (Curtin 1982; Mason 1984 and 1986). Curtin states that 'theoretically, women's status has been defined as the degree of women's access to (and control over) material resources (including food, income, land and other forms

of wealth) and to social resources (including knowledge, power and prestige) within the family, in the community and society at large.' Mason (1986) has documented several indicators of female status commonly used in the literature. These indicators can be grouped into three categories: demographic, kinship-family, and economic indicators. The demographic indicators include female age at marriage, average husband–wife age difference, and parents' preferences for male children. The kinship–family indicators are exemplified by, among others, *purdah* (female seclusion), female property inheritance, patrilocal post-marital residence, arranged marriage, male feeding priority, and egalitarianism of the husband–wife relationship. Finally, female education and female labour-force participation are the two most commonly used as economic indicators of female status in relation with fertility behaviour.

4. According to Curtin (1982) there are limitations to the use of women's levels of education and labour-force-participation rates as indicators of women's status. He states that 'in societies where alternative sources of childcare are almost universally available to mothers through the extended family, labour-force participation of mothers may not be a sexist issue. Likewise, in societies with a high percentage of illiterates, measures of status based on education assign different ranking only to those few who are literate. The illiterate majority is given one low status ranking, when in fact these persons have different rankings relative to each other.'

5. Most workers in Jordan are subject to a single choice between working and not working. They do not have control over the hours worked, although the standard workday varies among firms, especially between the public and private sectors. What is more, the system of temporary or part-time work is not generally available, especially in the modern sector. Although some (5.9 per cent of the total female labour force) work for their own or for family businesses, and therefore may have flexible hours, for most working women in Jordan the hours worked do not represent a relevant decision variable. A further consideration is that wages in Jordan are usually paid on a monthly basis and are not based on the hourly rate. An exception is the wages of those who work in the agricultural or informal sector, which are sometimes paid on a daily basis. Otherwise, workers in Jordan are 'rationed' with regard to their labour because of the rigid limits on the length of the working day. We therefore limit the analysis to female labour-force participation as a dependent variable in our two models.

6. Child-care variable is only applicable for current or previously married women. Because single women in Jordan, as in other Middle Eastern countries, are not allowed to have premarital sexual relations, no children are expected for single women. Therefore the presence in the household of adult women who are expected to take care of children is not applicable to single women.

References

Anker, R. 1983. 'Female Labour Force Participation in Developing Countries: A Critique of Current Definitions and Data Collection Methods'. *International Labour Review*, vol. 122, no. 6 (November–December).

Anker, R. and J. Knowles. 1978. 'A Micro Analysis of Female Labour Force

Participation in Kenya'. Population and Labour Policies Programme, Working Paper No. 116. Geneva: ILO.

Ashenfelter and Heckman. 1974. 'The Estimation of Income and Substitution Effects in a Model of Family Labor Supply'. *Econometrica*, vol. 42, no. 1, pp. 73–85.

Becker, G. 1965. 'A Theory of Allocation of Time'. *Economic Journal,* vol. 75, no. 229, pp. 493–517.

Bowen, W. and T.A. Finegan. 1969. *The Economics of Labor Force Participation.* Princeton, NJ: Princeton University Press.

Buvinic, M. 1976. *Women and World Development: An Annotated Bibliography.* Washington DC: Overseas Development Council.

Cain, G. G. 1966. *Married Women in the Labor Force: An Economic Analysis.* Chicago: University of Chicago Press.

Cochrane, S., D. O'Hara and J. Leslie. 1980. *The Effects of Education on Health: A Background Study for World Development Report.* Washington DC: World Bank.

Cornelius, D. 1988. 'Raising Women's Status and Persistent High Fertility: The Case of Jordan'. Paper presented at the Annual Meetings of Population Association of America, New Orleans, 22 April.

Curtin, L. 1982. *Status of Women: A Comparative Analysis of Twenty Developing Countries.* Washington DC: Population Reference Bureau.

Department of Statistics, Jordan. 1962. *Population and Housing Census, Vol. 2.*

——— 1984. *Labor Force Survey 1982–1983: Results of Round 1.*

Durand, J. 1975. 'The Labor Force in Economic Development and Demographic Transition'. In L. Tabah, ed., *Population Growth and Economic Development in the Third World*, Volume 1. Dollhain, Belgium: International Union for the Scientific Study of Population, pp. 47–78.

Easterlin, R. 1980. *Birth and Fortune: The Impact of Numbers on Personal Welfare.* New York: Basic Book Publishers.

Farooq, G. and D. S. DeGraff. 1988. 'Fertility and Development: An Introduction to Theory, Empirical Research and Policy Issues'. Background paper for Training and Population, Human Resources and Development, No. 7. Geneva: ILO.

Gerner-Adams, D.J. 1979. 'The Changing Status of Islamic Women in the Arab World'. *Arab Studies Quarterly*, vol. 1, no. 4.

ILO. 1986. *Yearbook of Labour Statistics 1985.* Geneva: ILO.

Killingsworth, M. R. 1983. *Labor Supply.* New York: Cambridge University Press.

Kurian, G. T. 1984. *The New Book of World Rankings.* New York: Facts on File.

Leibenstein, H. 1978. *General X-efficiency Theory and Economic Development.* New York: Oxford University Press.

Leslie, J. 1989. 'Women's Work and Child Nutrition in the Third World'. In J. Leslie and M. Paolisso, eds, *Women, Work, Child Welfare in the Third World.* Boulder, CO: Westview Press.

Mason, K. 1986. 'The Status of Women: Conceptual and Methodological Issues in Demographic Studies'. *Sociological Forum*, vol. 1, no. 2.

——— 1984. *The Status of Women: A Review of its Relationships to Fertility and Mortality.* New York: The Rockefeller Foundation.

Mazur, M. P. 1979. *Economic Development in Jordan.* Boulder, CO: Westview Press.

Mernissi, F. 1976. 'The Moslem World: Women Excluded from Development'. In

I. Tinker and M. Bramsen, eds, *Women and World Development*. Washington DC: Overseas Development Council.

Mincer, J. 1962. 'Labor Force Participation of Married Women'. In H.G. Lewis, ed., *Aspects of Labor Economics*. Princeton, NJ: Princeton University Press, pp. 63–195.

Ministry of Planning, Jordan. 1986. *Five Year Plan for Economic and Social Development 1986-90*. Amman: MOP.

Mohan, R. 1986. *Work, Wages, and Welfare in a Developing Metropolis: Consequence of Growth in Bogota, Columbia*. Published for the World Bank, New York: Oxford University Press.

Oppenheimer, V. K. 1982. *Work and the Family: A Study in Social Demography*. New York: Academic Press.

Shakhatreh, H. 1990. *The Determinants of Female Labour-Force Participation in Jordan*. Unpublished Ph.D. dissertation, Department of Population Planning and International Health, University of Michigan.

Standing, G. 1978. *Labour-Force Participation and Development*. Geneva: ILO.

Steel, W. F. and C. Campbell. 1982. 'Women's Employment and Development: A Conceptual Framework Applied to Ghana'. In E.G. Bay, ed., *Women and Work in Africa*. Boulder, CO: Westview Press.

The Economist Intelligence Unit (EIU). 1989. *Jordan: Country Profile*. London: EIU.

Tovo, M. 1984. 'The Determinants of Female Labor Force Participation'. Unpublished Ph.D. dissertation, Vanderbilt University, Nashville, Tennessee.

United Nations (DIESA). 1985. *Women's Employment and Fertility: A Comparative Analysis of World Fertility Survey Results for 38 Developing Countries*. New York: UN, Population Studies No. 96.

——— 1987. *Fertility Behavior in the Context of Development: Evidence from the World Fertility Survey*. New York: Population Studies No. 100.

Uthoff, A. and E. M. Pernia. 1986. *An Introduction to Human Resources Planning in Developing Countries*. Background paper for Training in Population, Human Resources and Development, No. 2. Geneva: ILO.

World Bank. 1983. *World Tables*, Volume 2, 3rd edn. Washington DC: World Bank.

——— 1985. *World Development Report*. New York: Oxford University Press.

——— 1986. *Jordan: Issues of Employment and Labor Market Imbalances, Volumes 1 and 2* (for official use only). Washington DC.

——— 1987. *World Development Report*. New York: Oxford University Press.

Zurayk, H. 1979. 'The Changing Role of Arab Women'. *Population Bulletin of the United Nations, ECWA*, No. 17.

8

Measuring Female Labour Force with Emphasis on Egypt

Richard Anker and Martha Anker

Introduction

Official statistics on the female labour force in developing countries, and the Arab region in particular, embody large underestimates (for example, Anker 1994; UNDP 1993; Anker, Khan and Gupta 1988). Such inaccurate data negatively affect development planning and women's status (see, for example, Dixon-Mueller and Anker 1988 for a full discussion of these effects).

Egyptian labour-force data are no exception. The 1991 Egyptian census found a crude female labour-force participation rate of 6.2. Furthermore, until 1982, Egyptian national labour-force surveys and population censuses consistently found that only about 5 per cent of Egyptian women were in the labour force, even though casual observation and in-depth studies of farm families found otherwise; for example, earlier studies found that approximately 25 per cent of all labour inputs in cultivation and a higher percentage of work activities with animals were provided by women. In contrast, the 1983 Egyptian national labour-force survey found that women comprised about 20 per cent of the agricultural labour force and that the crude female activity rate was approximately 12 per cent. As we shall see below, even these higher rates reported in Egyptian national labour-force surveys since 1983 still greatly undercount female labour-force activity according to data from the ILO/CAPMAS Labour Force Methods Test which is reported on in the present chapter.

Since information on labour-force participation is based on survey interviews, improving the information on female labour-force participation requires improving the survey techniques for collecting such information. Four factors which have been identified in the literature as being particularly important sources of inaccuracy in labour-force measurement are:

(i)   Ambiguous, biased and poorly understood labour-market concepts and definitions.

(ii) Poorly constructed and ambiguous questionnaires.

(iii) Biases and preconceived impressions of interviewers, especially male interviewers.

(iv) Biases and lack of knowledge of (mostly male) proxy-respondents.

Other factors of importance in particular surveys or censuses include: the length of the reference period (a longer reference period helps to identify women who work only part of the year); the minimum amount of work-time required for a person to be included in the labour force (a relatively high minimum work-time for unpaid family workers causes many women who work on a family farm or in a family enterprise to be excluded from the measured labour force); the time of the year when a survey/census is conducted (surveys conducted in slack season cause women who work seasonally to be excluded from the measured labour force).

The effects of these factors are culturally specific and thus vary from country to country. It is therefore important to examine how well the female labour force is measured in each country and to experiment with ways of improving the data collection in each country (for example, questionnaire design, organization of data collection, and so on). Unfortunately there is little hard statistical evidence on which factors are important in causing female labour-force activity to be under-reported (as most of the statements and available evidence in the research literature on this are impressionistic). For this reason, methodological surveys were designed (Anker 1983) and carried out in India (Anker, Khan and Gupta 1987; 1988) and in Egypt (Anker and Anker 1989; Anker 1990).[1] These methodological surveys involved the use of a controlled experimental design where replicate (and therefore comparable) samples of households were asked to provide information on the labour-force activity of female household members. In order to be in a position to observe statistically how the reporting of female labour-force activity varies according to the use of different questionnaire designs (typical worded questionnaire/activity schedule), interviewers (male/female), respondents

150

Figure 8.1 Schematic representation of study design for one sample village from ILO/CAPMAS Egyptian Methods Test survey using three treatment factors (interviewer type, questionnaire type, respondent type)

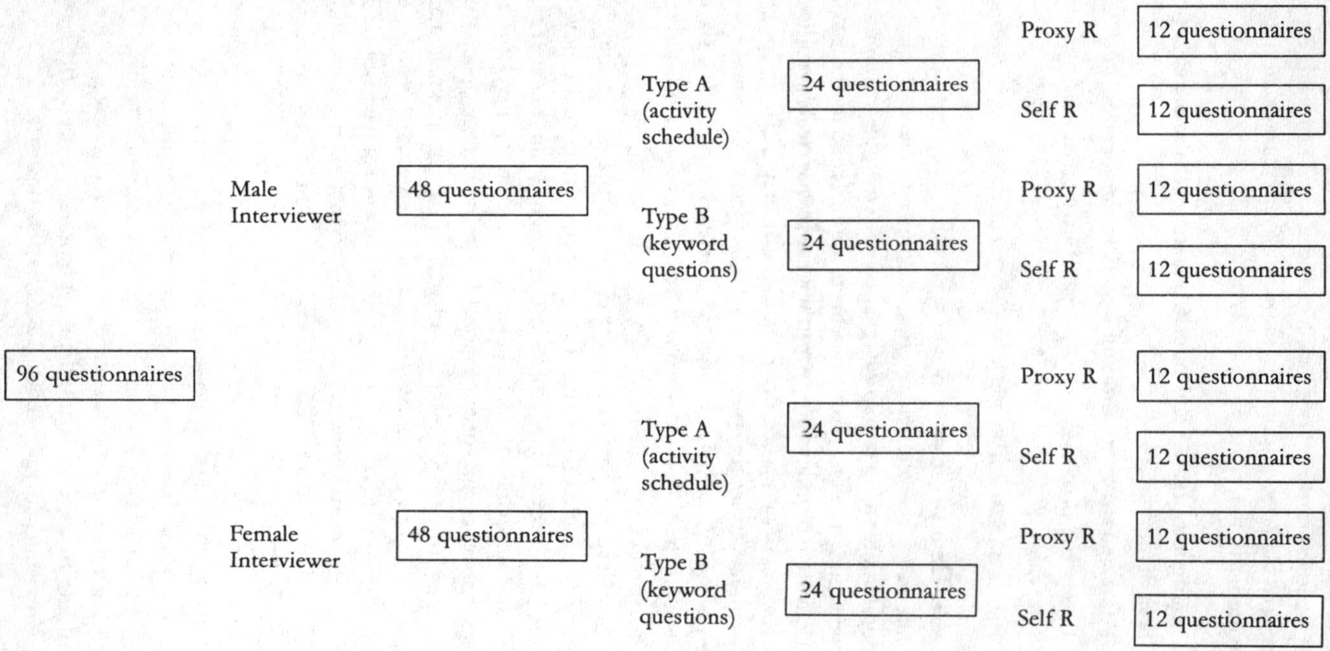

(self-respondent female/male proxy-respondent) and labour-force definitions (activities included in labour force; minimum amount of work-
time required; length of reference period), each of these four factors was
built into the study design of these methods test surveys.

Methods Tests

A methods test allows statistical organizations and researchers to establish statistically whether or not different types of respondents or different
interviewing conditions affect responses in their country. They can
provide useful insights into how best to present, ask and phrase
questions. A methods test is a controlled experiment which is designed
to provide statistical evidence on how various questionnaire types and
field-work techniques affect responses and thus the measurement of
information. For example, it is possible to find out whether proxy-
respondents provide different responses as compared to self-respondents, male respondents as compared to female respondents, interviews
when others are present as compared to private interviews, postal or
telephone interview as compared to personal interview, and so on. This
is important information for a national statistical organization because
decisions to change field operations or questionnaire design cannot be
taken lightly or be based on impressionistic observations and un-
substantiated opinions. For this reason, methodological surveys are
recommended as an important tool in improving data collection.

Four major issues were studied in the ILO/CAPMAS Egyptian
Methods Test. Each of these issues has received considerable attention
in the scientific literature and each is discussed in the next section.

1. What type of questionnaire provides the most accurate data on female
   labour-force activity? In particular, does a simplified activity schedule
   or a keyword-based questionnaire provide more accurate data?
2. Does the sex of the interviewer have an effect on the reporting of
   the female labour-force activity rate?
3. Do proxy-respondents (i.e. persons who answer for someone else)
   provide different responses on female labour-force activity as
   compared to self-respondents? Does the presence of other persons
   during the interview affect responses?
4. Does the effect of the above three treatment variables on the
   reporting of female labour-force activity vary according to how the
   labour force is defined?

In order to investigate such *measurement* issues, methods tests frequently use a balanced multi-stage sample design. The ILO/CAPMAS Egyptian Methods Test compared results of two questionnaire types, with each questionnaire type randomly assigned to households. To enable comparison of results obtained by male and female interviewers, one half of the interviews were done by male interviewers and the other half by female interviewers. To enable comparison of responses provided by self-respondents and proxy-respondents, half of the interviews were answered by self-respondents, and the other half by proxy-respondents. And finally, to observe how results differ according to the labour-force definition being used, four different definitions were developed and used in the analysis.

In addition to the main treatment factors – which were built into the sample design – the effect of several secondary factors not built into the sample design were also examined. Among the secondary factors studied in the ILO/CAPMAS Methods Test are two groups of *non-behavioural* factors:

(i) Relationship of the respondent to the woman on whom labour-force data were collected (e.g. mother-in-law, spouse, etc.).
(ii) Characteristics of the interview environment (e.g. presence of other persons, respondent's difficulty in understanding questions).

The study design of a methods test may differ from country to country. For example, the ILO/CAPMAS Egyptian Methods Test sample was fully balanced with respect to the first three treatment factors listed above, while the ILO/ORG Indian Methods Test sample was not balanced with regard to sex of interviewer and self-respondent/proxy-respondent status of respondent, because cultural and social norms in India frequently prevented male interviewers from interviewing female self-respondents. For this reason, male interviewers in the Indian study were allowed to interview any responsible adult household member (as is the usual practice in most countries for census and large surveys). In Egypt, male interviewers experienced no difficulty interviewing women.

Figure 8.1 shows schematically what a balanced sample design would look like for one sample village where 96 interviews are done, and three treatment factors (questionnaire type, interviewer type, and respondent type) are built in. This is, in fact, the study design used in the ILO/CAPMAS Egyptian Methods Test. The total sample size in the Egyptian study worked out to be approximately 1,100 consisting of approximately 96 households in each of twelve sample villages.[2]

It is important for readers to realize that a methods test does not provide a direct indication of which results are closer to reality; rather, test results indicate how reporting of labour-force activity differs according to the treatment factors, and not which responses are more accurate. It is common to use the simple assumption that the higher the rate reported the more accurate the data – believing that respondents are unlikely to report events which have not occurred. Although use of such an assumption is debatable, as it is possible to be over-reported as well as under-reported, we feel that it is a reasonable assumption for investigating female labour-force activity.[3]

Factors Affecting Accuracy of Female Labour-Force Data

Survey questionnaires as means of collecting labour-force data

Questionnaires rely on fixed and structured formats, where interviewers read out questions from a printed questionnaire. Labour-force questionnaires typically rely on questions containing keywords or phrases, such as 'main activity', 'secondary activity', 'work', 'economic', 'pay or profit', that are embedded in questions. There is evidence that respondents often misunderstand typical labour-force questions, often including wage and salary and business-related activities and excluding relevant farm and other unpaid family-related activities (Anker, Khan, Gupta 1988; Anker and Anker 1989).

The ILO/ORG Methods Test in India and the ILO/CAPMAS Methods Test in Egypt used two types of questionnaires: (a) a keyword questionnaire which included a nested set of keyword questions that began with a very general question on 'main activity' and became progressively more specific, with follow-up keyword questions on 'secondary activity', 'work', 'help on a family farm or business', 'helping family by caring for livestock, processing food for storage, cooking for hired labourers, gathering fuel, sewing clothes'; and (b) an activity schedule that included a list of fifteen or so specific and important economic activities. (This specific activity list differed somewhat in the India and Egypt Methods Tests in order to take into consideration national differences.) As discussed below, results from both Methods Tests indicated a large under-reporting of female labour-force activity when only some of the keyword questions were asked; this was especially so when a broad definition of the labour force was used.

Activity/time-use questionnaire

An activity/time-use questionnaire uses a predetermined list of common labour-force activities. Each respondent is asked which of these pre-determined activities listed on the questionnaire form they performed.

For each activity performed, additional information is then collected (for example, whether a wage or a salary was received, whether products were sold by a family enterprise, the amount of time an activity was performed in the past week and in the past season). Taken together, this information provides a basis for determining whether or not a woman was in the labour force according to different definitions (e.g. for different reference periods, such as past week, past season, past year).

The form used in the Egyptian Methods Test survey differs from more typical activity/time-use questionnaires in two major respects. First, the Egyptian list of activities is considerably shorter partly because greater use is made of generic activity categories such as 'farming for family', 'animal husbandry', 'any other job'. Second, activities not considered to be labour-force activities (for example, child care, cleaning), even according to a comprehensive labour-force definition (see below), are excluded.

Keyword questionnaire

As discussed above, labour-force surveys typically employ what we have called 'keyword' questions – that is, questions that are based mainly on a key word or phrase which is embedded within a longer question. Typical keywords or phrases employed are 'work', 'main activity', 'economic activity' and 'pay or profit'. Since a great deal of labour-force activity frequently goes unreported in response to keyword questions, it is often recommended to ask a series of follow-up keyword questions (or follow-up activity list).

The keyword questionnaire used in the ILO/CAPMAS Methods Test uses this approach, with specific follow-up questions on labour-force activity. It is, in essence, a 'nested' questionnaire: with each additional question a new questionnaire can be considered to have been completed. This nested design serves a very useful purpose for a methods test: it allows us to ascertain how many additional women are identified as labour-force participants with each additional keyword question, and consequently how many keyword questions are required to obtain a reasonably accurate estimate of the female labour force. Just as with the activity schedule, additional information is collected on employment status, whether any products were sold by a family enterprise, and time taken (hours/minutes per day in days when done; number of days done in past week and in past three-month season) for each activity performed.

This questionnaire begins with two typical, simple keyword questions:

B1. What was your (her) main activity in the past 12 months?
B2. What was your (her) next most important activity in the past 12 months?

For women, it is important to ask about secondary activities, since even a fully employed woman is often reported to be a 'housewife'. Such a response to keyword questions on 'main occupation' and 'work' is hardly surprising, especially since the main role or activity of many employed women, in terms of time, is household-related. The low female labour-force participation rate recorded in the 1976 Egyptian census as well as in the Egyptian national labour-force surveys – where the keywords used were 'main occupation' – is undoubtedly due partly to use of these keywords. Taken together, questions B1 and B2 comprise a typical keyword questionnaire where respondents are asked about main activity and next most important activity.

Respondents were then asked another typical keyword question – this time using the keyword 'work':

B3. Apart from ... have you (she) worked in the past 12 months for earnings?

Taken together, questions B1 to B3 form another typical version of a keyword questionnaire. Particularly interesting for us is the extent to which responses from questions B2 and B3 help to increase the reported level of female labour-force activity.

Respondents were then asked four fairly specific keyword questions (B4–B8). Questions B4 and B5 ask about work for family or self (such as grain trade, making baskets, rugs, sweets, and so on) in constant and nonconstant places respectively. B6 asks about work on a family farm and B7 about work inside the home in the so-called putting-out system. Question B8 is very specific, consisting of a series of eight subquestions on the performance of eight important activities (for example, making baskets, keeping poultry, doing animal husbandry, gathering fuel, making cow-dung cakes, fetching water) which respondents frequently do not consider to be labour-force activities and thus often neglect to mention in response to keyword questions such as B1 to B7. Question B8 is in essence similar to a shortened version of the activity schedule but this time in sentence form.

Finally, questions B9 and B10 ask about any other activity for income and any other important activity in terms of time in order to capture important activities not already mentioned in response to questions B1 to B8.

Labour-force definitions

The difficulty faced by respondents in answering general 'keyword' questions becomes obvious when one stops to consider the ambiguities involved in the internationally accepted definition of labour-force activity – that is, what words such as 'work', 'job', 'main activity', 'main occupation', and so on, are *supposed* to mean.

Internationally accepted definitions of labour-force activity rely on an 'economic' concept as defined by the United Nations system of national income account statistics (SNA); for example:

> *All production of primary products* should, in principal, be included in gross output (in national income), whether for own account consumption, for barter or for sale for money. It is also desirable to include in gross outputs: (i) the output of producers of other commodities, which are consumed in their household and which they also produce for the market and (ii) *the processing of primary commodities by the producers of these items* in order to make such goods as butter, cheese, flour, wine, oil, cloth or furniture for their own use *though they may not sell any of these manufactures.* (UN 1968)

Under these circumstances of ambiguous and poorly understood concepts, we feel there is a need for *several* labour-force measures that indicate the type (for example, paid, not paid) and level (for example, part-time, full time or number of hours) of labour-force activity based on different definitions of what comprises 'economic activity'.

A number of important purposes are also served by having several labour-force definitions. First, different definitions provide information on different aspects of the labour market. And, as planning needs are varied and multi-dimensional, measures of the labour force also should be varied in order to assist in planning. Second, because of inherent ambiguities in defining the labour force, it is in our opinion not possible to have one 'correct' labour-force definition. By using several definitions, it becomes possible for data users to be clear about what is being measured by each labour-force definition. Third, also due to ambiguities in labour-force concepts, it is likely that the broader and more encompassing the labour-force definition, the greater will be the inaccuracy with which it is measured.

For these reasons, four labour-force definitions were developed and used in earlier publications (see Anker 1983; Anker, Khan, Gupta 1987; 1988): paid labour force, market labour force, standard (internationally accepted) labour force and extended labour force. These definitions, which provide information on different aspects of the labour market and national income, are defined as follows from narrowest to broadest:

(i) *Paid labour force* (persons in wage or salary employment for which they are paid in cash or in kind).

This definition corresponds fairly closely to the employment status category of 'employees' currently in use. It was proposed in the background documents prepared for the Thirteenth International Conference of Labour Statisticians (ILO 1982) and by Boserup (1975). Data on the 'paid labour force' provides planners with information on people who have 'jobs', often live in an urban area, sometimes belong to a trade union, are sometimes politically vocal, and usually have wage or salary income as their only source of income. These are persons (in addition to the unemployed, of course) for whom planners are most likely to feel they must create a sufficient number of jobs.

(ii) *Market-oriented labour force* (persons in 'paid labour force' plus persons engaged in an activity on a family farm or in a family enterprise or business that sells some or all of its products or services).

The following are included in the market labour force: employers; own-account workers; unpaid family workers; and members of producers' co-operatives – but only those who are involved in enterprises where sales and/or monetary transactions occur. The 'market-oriented labour force' covers persons engaged in the money economy and therefore persons who are directly affected by government policies such as subsidization, price setting and marketing.

(iii) *Standard labour force* (persons engaged in activities whose products or services should be included in the national income accounts statistics (SNA) according to United Nations recommendations).

This definition of the labour force corresponds to what we consider to be the recommendation of the Thirteenth International Conference of Labour Statisticians (ILO 1982). Given the difficulty of interpreting and following these international recommendations in rural areas of a country such as Egypt where subsistence production is important, our definition may differ slightly from that of others. However, by being

very specific as to which activities we include, our definition is unam-
biguous. Our 'standard labour force' includes persons engaged in the
production of economic goods and services, irrespective of whether
these goods or services are sold. Thus certain important anomalies in
current measurement practices are eliminated. For example, all activities
associated with primary products – such as food 'production' and food
'processing', including animal tending and milking; threshing in the home
compound; processing and preparing food for preservation and storage;
and unpaid gathering of food or fruit – are considered labour-force
activities here, whether or not market-related exchanges occur.

(iv) *Extended labour force* (in addition to persons in the 'standard labour
force', the 'extended labour force' includes persons engaged in activities
not included in the most recent United Nations recommendations on
the SNA, but which none the less contribute to meeting their family's
basic needs for goods and services, which are generally purchased in
developed countries). The 'extended labour force' includes activities such
as gathering and preparing fuel (for example, gathering sticks and wood,
preparing cow-dung cakes). Water-fetching might also be included in
countries where long distances have to be travelled, but was not included as an 'extended labour force' activity in the ILO/CAPMAS
Egyptian Methods Test.

The basic rationale underlying the concept of the extended labour
force is the usefulness of having data on the satisfaction of basic needs
which is comparable across cultural and development levels and of
broadening the definition of 'economic' activity beyond the often
arbitrary distinctions made in the United Nations system of national
income accounts statistics. There is also the possibility that future SNA
statistics may be extended to include all non-monetary subsistence
activities, and it would be useful to have a time series of comparable
labour-force data.

Respondents

Most respondents to labour-force surveys are 'heads of household' who
provide information for all household members. Some analysts believe
that this may cause female labour-force activity to be under-reported.
First, since the household head is usually assumed to be male, female
labour force would be under-reported if male respondents believe that
women should be housewives and that the reporting of female labour-

force activity in the household would negatively affect their family's status (for example, Pittin 1982; Dixon 1982; UN 1980). Second, the head of household may not be knowledgeable on the labour-force activities of other household members.

Also, the presence of other persons during an interview may affect responses, as most interviews in Third World countries occur in the presence of other persons besides the respondent and interviewer (for example, 97 and 89 per cent of interviews took place with someone else present in the Indian and Egyptian Methods Tests, respectively). The respondent may be reluctant to provide sensitive or personal information and this may include female labour-force activity in a country like India or Egypt.

Interviewers

Interviewers in Third World countries are usually male. This fact would help cause an underestimation in female labour-force activity if the preconceived notion of many men that women do not, and should not, 'work' affects the way in which they ask questions and record answers. As with the gender of respondents, there is little statistical evidence available on whether the interviewer's gender affects female labour-force estimates. This is important information for survey organizations and likely to be culture- and country-specific.

Results

This section presents some illustrative results from the ILO/CAPMAS Egyptian Methods Test survey. For some detailed results, readers are referred to an earlier paper by the authors (Anker and Anker 1989).

Presence of others during interview and interviewers' assessment of quality of data

Interviewers can provide useful information on the quality of each individual interview. In the present experiment, interviewers were asked to assess the quality of the interview in several ways. First, to indicate whether (and what type of) other persons were present during the interview. Second, to give their impression of the extent to which the presence of other persons affected responses. Third, to assess the extent to which the respondent had difficulty in understanding the labour-

Table 8.1 Presence of other persons at the Methods Test interview by gender of interviewer, respondent type and questionnaire type (%)

Type of other person(s) present	Male investigator		Female investigator		Type of respondent		Type of interviewer		Activity schedule questionnaire	Keyword schedule questionnaire	Total
	Self-R (females only)	Proxy-R	Self-R (females only)	Proxy-R	Self-R	Proxy-R	Male I	Female I			
	(1)	(2)	(3)	(4)	(5)	(6)	(7)	(8)	(9)	(10)	(11)
None	15.6	11.2	9.1	10.0	12.4	10.6	13.4	9.5[b]	11.1	11.9	11.5
Mother-in-law/mother	8.6	6.6	7.1	5.4	7.9	6.0	7.6	6.3	8.9	5.1[b]	6.9
Spouse	37.1	41.5	38.7	41.9	37.9	41.7	39.3	40.3	38.4	41.1	39.8
Other adult male	34.8	31.0	44.7	41.9	39.7	36.3	32.9	43.3[a]	37.4	38.6	38.0
Other adult female	28.9	29.8	57.7	52.7	43.2	40.9	29.4	56.3[a]	39.4	44.6	42.1
Children	37.9	33.7	50.6	47.3	44.2	40.3	35.8	56.8	40.2	44.3	42.3
Total No.	256	258	253	241	509	499	514	494	495	513	1008

Notes: [a] Differences (e.g. between columns 1 and 2; 3 and 4; 5 and 6; 7 and 8; 9 and 10) significant at .01 level based on chi-square test. [b] Differences (e.g. between columns 1 and 2; 3 and 4; 5 and 6; 7 and 8; 9 and 10) significant at .05 level based on chi-square test

Source: ILO/CAPMAS Methods Test survey.

force questions being asked, and to assess the degree of difficulty the respondent had in providing time-use information.

Presence of other persons during interview

Interviews in rural Egypt (as in other rural areas of the world) are 'events' that attract attention and so rarely take place privately. Persons other than the interviewer and respondent were present in 89 per cent of sample interviews in the ILO/CAPMAS Methods Test.

Information was collected in the ILO/CAPMAS Methods Test on whether or not five different types of other persons were present during the interview: mother-in-law or mother; spouse; another adult male; another adult female; children. These categories are not mutually exclusive, and persons of several different categories may have been present during the same interview. For this reason, the column percentages in Table 8.1 add up to over 100 per cent. In approximately 40 per cent of interviews, a spouse, an adult male other than the spouse, another adult female and/or a child was present. Obviously, it is quite common for several types of other persons to have been present during the interview.

Since the presence of other persons can influence a respondent's answers, it is also important to check whether this occurred. According to interviewers, other persons often affected the respondent's answers (in approximately 37 per cent of interviews) – although this was felt to have a major effect in only about 4 per cent of the interviews (Table 8.2).

Tables 8.1 and 8.2 provide data on the effect (according to interviewers) other persons' presence had on responses, tabulated by our three main experimental factors of questionnaire type, respondent type and interviewer type. There were no significant differences between self-respondents and proxy-respondents in which types of other persons were present during the interview. However, according to the impressions of interviewers, the answers of self-respondents were significantly more likely to have been affected by other persons than were proxy-respondents.

Female investigators were much more likely than male investigators to have other persons present during the interview, especially other adult males, other adult females and children (and this situation was not sensitive to whether or not there was a self-respondent or proxy-respondent involved). However, interviewers' impressions of the

Table 8.2 Interviewers' assessment of the effect of other persons' presence in Methods Test on responses, tabulated by questionnaire type, interviewer type and respondent type (%)

Presence of other persons and effect on responses	Questionnaire type		Sex of interviewer		Type of respondent		Total
	Activity questionnaire (1)	Keyword questionnaire (2)	Male (3)	Female (4)	Self (5)	Proxy (6)	(7)
No other person present	11.4	11.9	13.6	9.7	12.6	10.8	11.7
No answer provided and no effect	28.0	30.3	28.4	30.0	26.0	32.5	29.2
No answer provided and minor effect	17.6	15.9	15.4	18.1	18.8	14.6	16.7
Answer provided and no effect	24.8	20.4	20.9	24.2	21.6	23.5	22.5
Answer provided and minor effect	15.5	16.8	17.2	15.2	16.2	16.2	16.2
Answer provided and major effect	2.7	4.7	4.5	2.9	5.0	2.4	3.7
Total N	483	511	507	487	501	493	994
% (some effect)	35.8	37.4	37.1	36.2	40.0	33.2	36.6

Source: ILO/CAPMAS Methods Test survey.

influence other persons had on the answers were not significantly different for male and female interviewers.

Finally, for questionnaire type, the only significant difference regarding the presence of other persons between the activity schedule and key-word questionnaire was that for some chance reason there were significantly more mothers/mothers-in-law present when the activity schedule was used. However, this did not have a differential effect on responses, according to the impressions of interviewers.

Interviewers' assessment of respondents' difficulty in understanding labour-force questions

According to the impressions of interviewers, almost 60 per cent of respondents had at least some difficulty in answering the labour-force questions and approximately 25 per cent of respondents had considerable or great difficulty in answering these questions. Clearly our interviewers felt that labour-force data are not easy to collect. What we do not know, of course, is whether such an indication of difficulty is typical of the difficulty of interviewing in rural Egypt or is specific to labour-force questions. When we investigated whether respondents' supposed difficulty related to our main study factors, the following was found. First, there were no significant differences between the keyword questions and the activity schedule in their ability to be understood by respondents. Second, self-respondents and proxy-respondents did not differ significantly in their ability to understand labour-force questions, nor was there a significant difference between male and female respondents. Third, male interviewers reported that they experienced significantly more difficulty than female interviewers; interestingly, however, there was no interaction between the sex of the interviewer and the sex of the respondent, since neither male nor female interviewers reported significantly greater difficulty when the respondent was male than when the respondent was female.

Interviewers' assessment of respondents' difficulty in providing time-use data

Interviewers also provided data on their assessment of the ease or difficulty each respondent had in providing information on time use. Three categories were precoded: no difficulty; could only provide reasonable answers after probing; had difficulty even after probing.

Table 8.3 Comparison of activity rates for nineteen activities and four labour-force definitions (for the past year) for keyword questions and activity schedule as reported by self-respondents and proxy-respondents

| Activity/labour force | Activity rates for key word questions by question and respondent type | | | | | | | | | | Activity schedule | |
| | B1 | | B1 to B2 | | B1 to B3 | | B1 to B8 | | B1 to B10 | | | |
	S	P	S	P	S	P	S	P	S	P	S	P
1 Farming for family	7.9	9.4	15.7	14.8	16.1	15.2	19.5	17.2	19.5	17.6	16.7	16.4
2 Farming for others	4.9	3.1	7.1	4.3	7.1	5.1	7.1	5.5	7.9	5.5	12.8	8.8
3 Animal husbandry	1.9	3.5	6.4	7.4	8.2	9.0	32.6	32.0	33.0	32.0	30.7	31.2
4 Poultry caring	1.1	0.8	4.9	5.9	7.1	7.8	57.3	59.4	57.3	59.4	60.2	59.2
5 Sewing, knitting	0.8	0.0	3.4	4.3	3.8	4.3	7.5	6.3	7.5	6.3	8.4	8.0
6 Making carpets, etc.	0.0	0.0	0.0	0.0	0.0	0.0	0.0	0.4	0.0	0.4	0.0	0.0
7 House construction	0.0	0.0	0.0	0.4	0.0	0.8	0.0	0.8	0.0	0.8	5.2	2.8
8 Vegetable trade	0.4	0.8	0.8	1.2	0.8	0.4	1.9	1.2	1.9	1.2	1.6	1.2
9 Petty trade	0.0	0.8	0.4	0.0	0.8	1.2	0.8	1.2	0.8	1.2	0.8	0.8
10 Non-agricultural wage	1.1	0.0	1.1	0.0	1.1	0.0	1.1	0.0	1.1	0.0	1.2	0.4
11 Government service	2.6	1.6	3.0	1.6	3.0	1.6	3.4	1.6	3.4	1.6	2.8	0.8
12 Professional	0.0	0.0	0.0	0.0	0.0	0.0	0.0	0.0	0.0	0.0	0.0	0.0
13 Other cash earning	0.4	0.4	1.1	1.6	1.5	1.6	2.3	2.7	2.3	2.7	2.4	0.8
14 Gathering fuel	0.0	0.0	0.0	0.4	0.0	0.4	52.1	44.1	52.1	44.1	46.6	44.4
15 Making dung cakes	0.0	0.0	0.4	0.0	0.0	0.4	27.7	26.6	27.7	26.6	25.1	22.4
16 Processing food	0.4	0.0	0.8	0.0	0.8	0.0	48.3	47.7	48.3	47.7	45.4	43.2
17 Fetching water	0.8	0.0	4.9	7.0	5.6	7.8	47.2	42.2	47.2	42.2	52.2	49.6
18 Grinding grain	0.4	0.0	0.8	0.8	1.5	1.2	52.8	50.8	52.8	50.8	64.9	59.2
19 Other activity	0.4	0.4	1.1	1.2	3.0	2.7	3.0	2.7	4.9	5.5	14.3	17.2

Notes: No minimum work-time constraint is used, since data on time was not collected for the past one year. All comparisons for each of the nineteen separate activities between responses of self-respondents and proxy-respondents were insignificant at the .05 level using a two-tailed t test.

S = self-respondent; P = proxy-respondent

Source: ILO/CAPMAS Methods Test survey.

According to interviewers, almost half the respondents experienced some difficulty in providing time-use data, but in almost all instances this difficulty could be resolved by probing. Indeed, according to interviewers, only about 4 per cent of respondents continued to have difficulty with providing time-use data even after probing.

Self-respondents and proxy-respondents did not have significantly differing degrees of difficulty in providing time-use information, nor was there significantly differing degrees of difficulty for male and female respondents. However, male interviewers did tend to report significantly higher levels of difficulty than female interviewers. This result is in keeping with the answers to the question on the difficulty of understanding the labour-force questions discussed above, where male interviewers reported significantly higher levels of difficulty than did female interviewers. It is not clear whether these two results represent differences in perception between male and female interviewers, or a real difference in the ability of respondents to understand and answer these questions when they were posed by male interviewers as opposed to female interviewers.

Respondent type

Information on female labour-force activity was randomly collected for equal numbers of female self-respondents and (most male) proxy-respondents. The interest in this section is whether or not self-respondents and proxy-respondents reported different female activity rates, and in particular whether mostly male proxy-respondents under-reported female labour-force activity.

When we look at each of our nineteen separate activities, we observe similar reporting by self-respondents and proxy-respondents – although there is a clear tendency for self-respondents to report insignificantly higher rates (see Table 8.3). This tendency becomes statistically significant when aggregated across activities for the paid labour force and the market labour force (see Table 8.4); in addition, these same significant differences are found for both keyword questions and the activity schedule.

This tendency for proxy-respondents to under-report also occurs for hours worked; proxy-respondents report fewer hours worked as compared to self-respondents (see Table 8.5).

In short, there is a significant difference in rural Egypt between the reporting of female labour-force activity by female self-respondents as

ILO LF

B1	21.7	19.5	19.5	21.7	15.7	15.6	20.2	19.1	16.5	16.4
B1 to B2	41.2	38.3	37.9	41.2	29.6	23.8	39.0	35.9	29.6	26.2
B1 to B3	43.4	40.6	40.2	43.4	31.8	25.4	41.6	38.7	32.6	28.1
B1 to B8	85.8	84.4	84.0	84.6	53.9	49.6	79.0	75.8	57.3	52.0
B1 to B10	85.8	84.4	84.0	84.6	54.3	49.6	79.0	75.8	57.7	52.3
Activity schedule	91.6	88.8	88.4	91.6	52.6	47.2	82.4	81.7	58.2	48.4[b]

Extended LF

B1	21.7	19.5	19.5	21.7	15.7	15.6	20.2	19.1	16.5	16.4
B1 to B2	41.6	38.7	38.3	41.6	29.6	24.2	39.3	36.3	29.6	26.6
B1 to B3	43.8	41.0	40.6	43.8	31.8	25.8	41.9	39.1	32.6	28.5
B1 to B8	88.0	85.5	85.2	86.1	56.2	52.3	80.1	77.3	61.0	55.1
B1 to B10	88.0	85.5	85.2	86.1	56.6	52.3	80.1	77.3	61.4	55.5
Activity schedule	92.0	90.0	89.6	92.0	57.8	50.0	82.5	83.6	62.9	50.8[a]

Notes: [a] Difference between responses of self-respondents and proxy-respondents significant at .01 level using two-tailed t test.
[b] Difference between responses of self-respondents and proxy-respondents significant at .05 level using two-tailed t test.
[c] Information on work-time was not collected for last year.

Source: ILO/CAPMAS Methods Test survey.

Table 8.4 Comparison of activities reported by self-respondents and proxy-respondents for four aggregate labour-force definitions for past week, past season and past year reference periods

Labour force measure /question type	Last year No minimum time[c]		Last 3 months No minimum time		At least 130 hours in last 3 months		Last week No minimum time		At least 10 hours in last week	
	Self R	Proxy R	Self R	Proxy R	Self R	Proxy R	Self R	Proxy R	Self R	Proxy R
Paid LF										
B1	9.7	5.1[b]	9.7	5.1[b]	9.4	4.3[b]	9.4	5.1	9.0	4.7
B1 to B2	12.7	6.6[b]	12.7	6.6[b]	11.6	5.5[b]	12.4	6.3[b]	11.2	5.9[b]
B1 to B3	12.7	7.7[b]	12.7	7.4[b]	12.0	6.3[b]	12.4	7.0[b]	11.6	6.6[b]
B1 to B8	13.5	8.2	13.5	8.2	12.0	6.6[b]	12.7	7.8	11.6	7.0
B1 to B10	14.2	8.2[b]	14.2	8.2[b]	12.7	6.6[b]	13.5	7.8[b]	12.4	7.0[b]
Activity schedule	18.7	10.8[b]	18.3	10.4	13.5	8.0[b]	17.1	8.8[a]	15.1	8.0[b]
Market LF										
B1	18.7	16.8	18.4	16.8	14.2	13.7	17.2	16.8	15.0	14.5
B1 to B2	31.1	25.8	30.3	25.4	24.7	19.1	29.2	25.0	24.3	21.1
B1 to B3	32.6	27.3	31.8	27.0	26.2	19.9	31.1	26.6	26.2	21.9
B1 to B8	40.8	31.6[b]	39.7	31.3[b]	28.8	22.7	37.5	30.9	29.2	26.6
B1 to B10	41.2	32.0[b]	40.1	31.6[b]	29.6	22.7	37.8	31.3	30.0	27.0
Activity schedule	46.6	36.0[b]	43.8	34.8[b]	29.4	24.0	45.4	33.6[a]	34.3	25.6[b]

168

ILO LF							
B1	26.9	26.4	26.7	(103)	21.7	20.9	21.3	(108)
B1 to B2	24.4	23.3	23.9	(196)	20.0	17.8	19.0	(207)
B1 to B3	24.8	23.8	24.4	(210)	20.9	18.2	19.6	(219)
B1 to B8	24.6	24.8	24.7	(405)	20.6	19.0	19.8	(441)
B1 to B10	24.8	24.9	24.8	(405)	20.8	19.0	19.9	(441)
Activity schedule	26.8	20.9[a]	23.8	(411)	20.3	17.0[b]	18.7	(451)
Extended LF							
B1	26.9	26.4	26.7	(103)	21.7	20.9	21.3	(108)
B1 to B2	24.2	23.2	23.8	(198)	19.9	17.8	18.9	(209)
B1 to B3	24.6	23.7	24.2	(212)	20.7	18.2	19.5	(221)
B1 to B8	27.3	27.9	27.6	(412)	22.6	21.2	22.0	(448)
B1 to B10	27.6	28.0	27.8	(412)	22.9	21.4	22.1	(448)
Activity schedule	29.6	23.6[a]	26.6	(416)	22.5	18.8[b]	20.7	(455)

Notes: [a] Difference between self-respondents and proxy-respondents significant at .01 level using two-tailed t test. [b] Difference between self-respondents and proxy-respondents significant at .05 level using two-tailed t test.

Source: LO/CAPMAS Methods Test survey.

Table 8.5 Comparison of results for number of hours worked by women in the labour force for self-respondents and proxy-respondents for past week and past season reference periods

Labour force measure/ question type	Mean number of hours worked last week				Mean number of weekly hours worked last season			
	Self R	Proxy R	Total	N	Self R	Proxy R	Total	N
Paid LF								
B1	35.1	29.9	33.3	(38)	29.9	25.4	28.4	(39)
B1 to B2	32.7	31.8	32.4	(49)	28.6	24.9	27.4	(51)
B1 to B3	33.2	33.7	33.3	(51)	29.2	24.2	27.4	(53)
B1 to B8	32.2	31.2	31.8	(54)	27.6	22.7	25.8	(57)
B1 to B10	31.4	31.2	31.3	(56)	27.2	22.7	25.6	(59)
Activity schedule	30.0	28.7	29.6	(65)	22.6	20.5	21.9	(72)
Market LF								
B1	29.2	28.0	28.6	(89)	23.9	22.5	23.2	(92)
B1 to B2	27.4	27.6	27.5	(142)	23.3	21.8	22.7	(146)
B1 to B3	27.1	28.2	27.6	(151)	23.7	21.9	22.9	(154)
B1 to B8	26.3	29.9	27.9	(179)	22.4	24.1	23.2	(186)
B1 to B10	26.5	29.8	28.0	(181)	22.7	23.8	23.3	(188)
Activity schedule	27.3	25.2	26.4	(198)	20.9	15.5	20.3	(197)

compared to mostly male proxy-respondents. In rural Egypt, proxy-respondents under-reported the existence of female activity in the paid labour force (especially wage and salary work in, for example, agriculture) and the amount of time spent in unpaid family work. On the other hand, these differences are small in comparison with those observed by questionnaire type and labour-force definition, as is discussed in the next section.

These results differ from those found in the Indian Methods Test where there were no differences between self-respondents and proxy-respondents. Clearly the reporting of female labour-force activity is culture-specific. This helps re-emphasize the usefulness of methods tests.

Questionnaire type and labour-force definition

The ILO/CAPMAS Methods Test used two questionnaire types (keyword questionnaire and activity/time-use questionnaire) in the field test and four labour-force definitions in the analysis (paid, market, standard, extended labour forces).

Table 8.6 compares results from the keyword questionnaire with results from the activity schedule regarding performance of 19 activities during the past year (irrespective of the amount of time spent in each activity). Column 1 presents activity rates based on the activity schedule, while column 2 presents activity rates based on the complete keyword questionnaire consisting of questions B1 to B10. Column 3 indicates the keyword questions for which the activity rate from the cumulative keyword questions is significantly lower at the .05 level than the rate from the activity schedule.

As in the ILO/ORG Indian Methods Test, activity rates from these two questionnaire types are quite similar when a 'sufficient' number of keyword questions are asked – with the number of questions required related to the type of activity performed and the specificity of the keyword questions asked. Thus, activity rates based on keyword question B1 alone are generally very much lower than those based on the activity schedule, and these differences are statistically significant for all activities except grocery selling/petty trading, other cash earning, and non-agricultural wage or salary employment. Asking the next keyword question on 'next most important activity' helps identify two additional activities: farming for family and vegetable/fruit selling. Of the remaining keyword questions, only B8 (which asks separately and specifically about eight different activities) causes reported activity rates to be similar

Table 8.6 Comparison of activity rates (for past year) for nineteen activities based on responses to keyword questions and activity schedule

Activity	Activity rate based on activity schedule (performed at all during past year) (1)	Activity rate for completed keyword questionnaire B1 to B10 (performed at all during past year) (2)	Keyword questions for which activity rate based on keyword questions is significantly lower than activity rate based on activity schedule (3)
1. Farming for family	16.6	18.5	B1
2. Farming for others	10.8	6.7	B1 to B10
3. Animal husbandry	30.9	32.5	B1 to B7
4. Poultry keeping	59.7	58.3	B1 to B7
5. Sewing, knitting	8.2	6.9	B1 to B7
6. Making carpets, etc.	0.0	0.2	–
7. House construction	4.0	0.4	B1 to B10
8. Vegetable trade	1.4	1.5	B1
9. Petty trade	0.8	1.0	–
10. Non-agricultural wage	0.8	0.6	–
11. Government service	1.8	2.5	–
12. Professional	0.0	0.0	–
13. Other cash earning	1.6	2.5	–
14. Gathering fuel	45.5	48.2	B1 to B7
15. Making dung cakes	23.8	27.2	B1 to B7
16. Processing food	44.3	48.0	B1 to B10
17. Fetching water	50.9	44.7	B1 to B10
18. Grinding grain	62.1	51.8	B1 to B10
19. Other activity	15.8	5.2	B1 to B10

Notes: – Implies that there are no significant differences between results when B1 is asked as compared to results based on the activity schedule.

N is equal to 501 for the activity schedule and 523 for the keyword questions.

Source: ILO/CAPMAS Methods Test Survey.

Table 8.7 Comparison of results for four aggregate labour-force definitions based on keyword questions and activities schedule for past year, past season and past week reference periods

Reference period	Labour force definition	Activity rate (no/time constraint) Activity schedule	Keyword questions B1 to B10	Activity rate (minimum 10 hours per week time constraint) Activity schedule	Keyword questions B1 to B10	Keyword questions for which activity rate is significantly lower than activity rate based on keyword questions[a] (no minimum time constraint)	Minimum time constraint (10 hours last week or 130 hours last season)
(1)	(2)	(3)	(4)	(5)	(6)	(7)	(8)
Past year	Paid	14.8	11.3	na	na	B1 to B7[b]	B1
	Market	41.3	36.7	na	na	B1 to B7	na
	Standard	90.2	85.1	na	na	B1 to B10	na
	Extended	91.0	86.8	na	na	B1 to B10	na
Past season	Paid	14.4	11.3	10.8	9.8	B1 to B6[b]	B1
	Market	39.3	35.9	26.7	26.2	B1 to B9[b]	B1 to B7
	Standard	90.0	84.3	49.9	52.0	B1 to B10	B1 to B7
	Extended	90.8	85.7	53.9	54.5	B1 to B10	B1 to B7
Past week	Paid	13.0	10.7	11.6	9.8	B1	B1
	Market	39.5	34.6	29.0	28.5	B1 to B7	B1 to B5
	Standard	82.0	77.4	53.3	55.1	B1 to B7	B1 to B7
	Extended	83.0	78.8	56.9	58.5	B1 to B7	B1 to B7

Notes: [a] Significance is at .05 level based on a two-tailed t test. [b] The increase in labour-force activity rate that would arise from including the results from the next keyword question is less than 1 percentage point; when the next additional keyword questionnaire is counted, the difference between the activity questionnaire and the cumulative keyword questions is no longer significant.
na Not applicable as data on time was not collected for past one-year reference period.
N Is equal to 501 for activity schedule and 523 for keyword questions.

Sources: ILO/CAPMAS Methods Test Survey.

(that is, insignificantly different) to those obtained using the activity schedule for six specifically mentioned activities. These results reinforce our *a priori* hypothesis that general keyword questions can be sufficient for obtaining data on women's participation in obvious labour-force activities such as non-agricultural wage and salary employment, petty trading and own farm activity (although surprisingly this was not so for agricultural wage labour). Other 'less obvious' labour-force activities, however (even including some which involve monetary transactions such as animal husbandry and poultry-keeping), require special mention.

We now turn our attention to a comparison of activity schedule and keyword question results for our four aggregate labour-force measures: paid, market, standard and extended labour forces. Table 8.7 presents reported activity rates based on our two questionnaire types (columns 3 and 4 for rates when no minimum work-time constraint applies and columns 5 and 6 for rates when a 10-hours-per-week and 130-hours-per-season minimum work-time criterion apply). In columns 7 and 8 an indication is given of the keyword questions for which reported rates for the activity schedule significantly exceed reported rates for the keyword questions.

The number of keyword questions which need to be asked to obtain similar results (that is, not significantly different) to those obtained using the activity schedule is a function of the narrowness of the labour-force definition and the length of the reference period. Thus, for example, for the paid labour force, only B1 ('main activity') and B2 ('next most important activity') had to be asked in order to obtain an activity rate not significantly different from results based on the activity schedule when the reference period is the past week, and eight keyword questions had to be asked when the reference period was the past year. For the reporting of market, standard and extended labour forces, it was necessary to ask the very specific keyword question B8 to get results which are not significantly different from those of the activity schedule.

It is very important to note that the differences in activity rates between questionnaire types discussed above are greatly reduced when a minimum work-time criterion (columns 5, 6 and 8) is applied. Thus, in contrast to results when no work-time criterion is applied (columns 3, 4 and 7), the paid labour force is fully measured by the first two general keyword questions for the past season as well as past week reference periods; and the standard and extended labour forces are fully measured when B8, which mentions specific labour-force activities, is asked.

Some general implications of these results include the following. First, the activity schedule format is significantly better than the keyword question format in identifying the performance of less obvious labour-force activities which are included in the standard and extended labour forces. At the same time, the activity schedule format is not superior when one takes into consideration how much time women spend in labour-force activities in the standard and extended labour forces (that is, when 10 hours in the past week or 130 hours in the past season minimum time criteria are used).

Second, if keyword questions are used, they should specifically mention particular activities in order to ensure identification of many non-wage, non-agricultural labour-force activities. The use of keyword questions and phrases such as 'main activity', 'next most important activity' and 'work for earnings' are not good for identifying many labour-force activities.

Third, it appears that inclusion of specific keyword questions in a questionnaire (which is somewhat akin to including a short activity list) can have a major effect on responses to earlier keyword questions on 'main activity' and 'next most important activity'. Note that reported activity rates from the ILO/CAPMAS Methods Test survey for the paid, market and standard labour forces far exceed those obtained in Egypt's population censuses and national labour-force surveys, even when only one or two general keyword questions (B1 and B2) were asked. It appears that the inclusion of additional questions in the questionnaire helps 'educate' interviewers to what should be considered labour-force activities.

Summary and Conclusion

This chapter has been concerned with the chronic underestimation of female labour-force participation in developing countries and the Arab World and Egypt in particular. Discussion has focused on reasons for this under-reporting on population censuses and labour-force surveys, the usefulness of methods tests for investigating these issues, and results from the ILO/CAPMAS Methods Test survey for Egypt. This discussion indicates that much of the underestimation of the size of the female labour force for rural Egypt can be eliminated by giving proper attention to how the labour force is defined and how information on labour-force activity is collected.

Notes

1. Readers are also referred to somewhat similar methodological surveys conducted in South America (Argentina and Paraguay) by Catalina Wainerman (Wainerman 1992).

2. Readers should note that the ILO/CAPMAS Egyptian Methods Test collected labour-force information for only *one* adult woman in each sample household, regardless of the number of adult women in the household. Two especially designed tables were used to select randomly the women on whom labour-force information was to be collected. These tables and the selection procedures used are described in Anker, Khan and Gupta 1988. This procedure resulted in a sample which under-represents women who lived in large households. There were two important reasons for collecting information on only one woman per household, which in our opinion outweighed this disadvantage. First, we felt it would be inappropriate to use the same questionnaire more than once in a sample household as answers on the second (or third, or fourth, etc.) interview in the household would in all probability have been affected by exposure to previous interviews. Second, we wanted to have as wide a distribution of households as possible within our limited sample, and we felt that restricting the number of interviews in a household to one would help in this respect.

3. This assumption was used in the ILO/ORG Indian Methods Test and the ILO/CAPMAS Egyptian Methods Test, as well as in other methods tests (see, e.g., Woltman et al. 1980, for a methods test study in the United States on the reporting of crime).

References

Anker, R. 1994. 'Measuring Women's Participation in the African Labour Force'. In A. Adepoju and C. Oppong, eds, *Gender, Work and Population in Sub-Saharan Africa*. London: Currey.

———— 1990. 'Methodological Considerations in Measuring Women's Labour-Force Activity in Developing Countries: The Case of Egypt'. In *Research in Human Capital and Development*, Vol. 6. JAI Press.

———— 1983. 'Female Labour Force Participation in Developing Countries: A Critique of Current Definitions and Data Collection Methods'. *International Labour Review*, vol. 122, no. 6 (November–December).

Anker, R., and M. Anker. 1989. 'Improving the Measurement of Women's Participation in the Egyptian Labour Force: Results of a Methodological Survey'. *ILO Population and Labour Policies Working Paper No. 163*, Geneva: ILO.

Anker, R., M.E. Khan and R.B. Gupta. 1987. 'Biases in Measuring the Labour Force: Results of a Methods Test Survey in Uttar Pradesh, India'. *International Labour Review*, vol. 126, no. 2 (March–April).

———— 1988. *Women's Participation in the Labour Force: A Methods Test in India for Improving its Measurement*. Women, Work and Development Series No. 16, Geneva: ILO.

Boserup, E. 1975. 'Employment of Women in Developing Countries'. In L. Tabah, ed., *Population Growth and Economic Development in the Third World*. Liège: Ordina.

Dixon, R. 1982. 'Women in Agriculture: Counting the Labour Force in Developing Countries'. *Population and Development Review*, vol. 8, no. 3, pp. 539–66.

Dixon-Mueller, R. and R. Anker. 1988. *Assessing Women's Contributions to Development*. Population, Human Resources and Development Planning Training Paper, No. 6. Geneva: ILO.

ILO. 1982. Thirteenth International Conference on Labour Statisticians, Amended Draft Resolution Concerning Statistics of the Economically Active Population, Employment, Unemployment and Underemployment (mimeo). Geneva.

Pittin, R. 1982. *Documentation of Women's Work in Nigeria: Problems and Solutions*. Working Paper No. 125. Geneva: ILO.

UNDP. 1993. *Human Development Report*. New York: Oxford University Press.

United Nations (UN). 1968. 'A System of National Accounts'. *Studies in Methods*, Series F, No. 2, Rev. 3. New York: United Nations.

——— 1980. *Sex Based Stereotypes, Sex Biases and National Data Systems*. New York, doc. ST/ESA/STAT/99.

Wainerman, C. 1992. 'Improving the Accounting of Women Workers in Population Censuses: Lessons from Latin America'. *ILO Population and Labour Policies Working Paper No. 178*. Geneva: ILO.

Woltman, H.F., et al. 1980. 'A Comparison of Three Mixed-Mode Interviewing Procedures in National Crime Survey'. *Journal of American Statistical Association*, vol. 75, no. 371, pp. 534–43.

Annex:

Human Development Indicators
for the Arab Region

Compiled by Valentine M. Moghadam

Table A1 Human development index, Arab countries

	Life expectancy at birth (years) 1990	Adult literacy rate (%) 1990	Mean years of schooling 1990	Literacy rate index	Mean years index	Educational attainment	Real GDP per capita (PPP$) 1989	Adjusted real GDP	Human development index	GNP rank minus HDI rank
Algeria	65.1	57.4	2.6	0.49	0.20	1.17	3,088	3,088	0.533	−37
Egypt	60.3	48.4	2.8	0.37	0.22	0.97	1,934	1,934	0.385	−2
Iraq	65.0	59.7	4.8	0.51	0.39	1.41	3,510	3,510	0.589	−39
Jordan	66.9	80.1	5.0	0.77	0.40	1.93	2,415	2,415	0.586	−13
Lebanon	66.1	80.1	4.4	0.77	0.35	1.88	2,250	2,250	0.561	6
Libyan Arab Jamahiriya	61.8	63.8	3.4	0.56	0.27	1.40	7,250	4,927	0.659	−38
Morocco	62.0	49.5	2.8	0.39	0.22	1.00	2,298	2,298	0.429	−9
Oman	65.9	35.0	0.9	0.21	0.06	0.48	10,573	4,997	0.598	−45
Saudi Arabia	64.5	62.4	3.7	0.55	0.30	1.39	10,330	4,994	0.687	−34
Syrian Arab Republic	66.1	64.5	4.2	0.57	0.33	1.48	4,348	4,348	0.665	17
Tunisia	66.7	65.3	2.1	0.58	0.16	1.33	3,329	3,329	0.582	−10
United Arab Emirates	70.5	55.5	5.1	0.46	0.41	1.32	23,798	5,079	0.740	−45
Yemen	51.5	38.6	0.8	0.25	0.06	0.56	1,560	1,560	0.232	−24

Source: UNDP, *Human Development Report 1992*, pp. 127–8.

179

Table A2 Profile of human development, Arab countries

	Life expectancy at birth (years)		Population with access to			Daily calorie supply (as % of requirements)	Adult literacy rate (%)	Combined primary & secondary enrolment ratio	GNP per capita (US$)	Real GDP per capita (PPP$)
	Total	Female	health services (%)	safe water (%)	sanitation (%)					
	1990	1990	1987–89	1988–90	1988–90	1988	1990	1988–89	1989	1989
Algeria	65.1	66.1	90	71	51	112	57	79	2,230	3,088
Egypt	60.3	61.5	–	89	65	127	48	89	640	1,934
Iraq	65.0	66.1	89	92	71	125	60	75	–	–
Jordan	66.9	68.8	97	99	–	118	80	–	1,640	2,415
Lebanon	66.1	68.0	–	93	–	125	80	92	–	–
Libyan Arab Jamahiriya	61.8	63.7	–	94	–	144	64	–	5,310	–
Morocco	62.0	63.7	74	61	58	114	50	50	880	2,298
Oman	65.9	67.8	91	47	41	–	–	79	5,220	10,573
Saudi Arabia	64.5	66.5	97	94	–	118	62	63	6,020	10,330
Syrian Arab Republic	66.1	68.1	76	76	–	127	65	85	980	4,348
Tunisia	66.7	67.5	91	68	45	122	65	79	1,260	3,329
United Arab Emirates	70.5	73.5	90	–	–	151	–	91	18,430	23,798
Yemen	51.5	52.0	35	46	–	95	39	58	650	–

Source: UNDP, *Human Development Report 1992*, pp. 130–31.

180

Table A3 Trends in human development, Arab countries

	Life expectancy at birth (years)		Under-five mortality rate (per 1,000 live births)		Population with access to safe water (%)		Adult daily calorie supply (as % of requirements)		Adult literacy rate (%)		Combined primary & secondary enrolment ratio		Real GDP per capita (PPP$)	
	1960	1990	1960	1990	1975–80	1988–90	1965	1988	1970	1990	1970	1988–89	1960	1989
Algeria	47.0	65.1	270	98	77	71	72	112	25	57	46	79	1,300	3,088
Egypt	46.1	60.3	301	85	75	89	97	127	35	48	55	89	500	1,934
Iraq	48.5	65.0	222	86	66	92	89	125	34	60	49	75	–	–
Jordan	46.9	66.9	217	52	–	–	93	118	47	80	–	–	1,120	2,415
Lebanon	59.6	66.1	91	56	–	94	99	125	69	80	77	92	–	–
Libyan Arab Jamahiriya	46.7	61.8	269	112	87	–	83	144	37	64	–	–	–	–
Morocco	46.7	62.0	265	112	–	–	92	114	22	50	32	50	540	2,298
Oman	40.1	65.9	378	49	–	–	–	–	–	–	25	79	2,040	10,573
Saudi Arabia	44.4	64.5	292	91	64	94	79	118	9	62	31	63	3,640	10,330
Syrian Arab Republic	49.7	66.1	217	59	–	–	89	127	40	65	61	85	1,230	4,348
Tunisia	48.3	66.7	254	62	35	68	94	122	31	65	64	79	850	3,329
United Arab Emirates	53.0	70.5	239	30	–	–	–	–	–	–	63	91	–	–
Yemen	36.5	51.5	–	–	–	–	81	95	8	39	–	–	–	–

Source: UNDP, *Human Development Report 1992*, pp. 130–31.

Table A4 Human capital formation, Arab countries

	Adult literacy rate (% 15+)			Mean years of schooling (25+)			Scientists and technicians (per 1,000 people)	R & D scientists and technicians (per 10,000 people)	Tertiary graduates (as % of corresponding age group)	Science graduates (as % of total graduates)
	Total 1990	Male 1990	Female 1990	Total 1990	Male 1990	Female 1990	1985–89	1985–89	1986–88	1986–88
Algeria	57	70	46	2.6	4.4	0.8	–	–	2.2	42
Egypt	48	63	34	2.8	3.9	1.6	–	5.4	3.8	22
Iraq	60	70	49	4.8	5.7	3.9	3.6	–	–	–
Jordan	80	89	70	5.0	6.0	4.0	–	1.1	5.6	28
Lebanon	80	88	73	4.4	5.3	3.5	–	0.7	2.9	26
Libyan Arab Jamahiriya	64	75	50	3.4	5.5	1.3	11.6	5.7	–	–
Morocco	50	61	38	2.8	4.1	1.5	–	–	1.1	26
Oman	–	–	–	0.9	1.4	0.3	6.6	–	–	–
Saudi Arabia	62	73	48	3.7	5.9	1.5	–	–	2.5	13
Syrian Arab Republic	65	78	51	4.2	5.2	3.1	3.6	–	4.0	41
Tunisia	65	74	56	2.1	3.0	1.2	1.4	–	0.9	44
United Arab Emirates	–	–	–	5.1	5.1	5.2	–	–	1.7	11
Yemen	39	53	26	0.8	1.3	0.2	0.2	–	0.2	11

Source: UNDP, *Human Development Report 1992*, pp. 136–7.

Table A5 Female–male gaps, Arab countries[a]

	Life expectancy 1990	Population 1990	Literacy 1970	Literacy 1990	Mean years of schooling 1990	Primary enrolment 1960	Primary enrolment 1988–89	Secondary enrolment 1988–89	Tertiary enrolment 1988–89	Labour force 1988–90	Parliament 1990
Algeria	103	100	28	65	18	67	85	77	44	5	2
Egypt	104	97	40	54	42	65	79	78	52	12	2
Iraq	103	96	36	71	69	38	87	65	63	6	12
Jordan	106	95	45	79	66	63	–	–	–	11	–
Lebanon	106	106	73	83	66	94	–	72	58	37	–
Libyan Arab Jamahiriya	106	91	22	67	23	26	90	–	37	10	–
Morocco	106	100	29	62	36	40	69	71	58	26	–
Oman	106	91	–	–	22	–	95	71	71	9	–
Saudi Arabia	106	84	13	66	26	–	75	74	73	8	–
Syrian Arab Republic	106	98	33	65	60	44	92	71	72	18	9
Tunisia	103	98	39	76	41	49	90	80	65	15	4
United Arab Emirates	106	48	29	–	101	–	100	117	–	7	–
Yemen	101	108	15	49	18	–	–	40	111	15	3

Note: [a] Females as a percentage of males. All figures are expressed in relation to the male average, which is indexed to equal 100. The smaller the figure the bigger the gap, the closer the figure to 100 the smaller the gap, and a figure above 100 indicates that the female average is higher than the male.

Source: UNDP, *Human Development Report 1992*, pp. 144–5.

Table A6 Education flows, Arab countries

| | Apparent primary intake rate (%) | | Primary enrolment ratio (net) | | Primary repeaters (as % of primary enrolment) | Completing primary level (%) | Transition to second level (%) | Secondary enrolment ratio (gross) | | Secondary repeaters (as % of secondary enrolment) | Tertiary enrolment ratio | |
| | Total | Female | Total | Female | | | | Total | Female | | Total | Female |
	1988	1988	1988–89	1989–89	1988	1988	1988	1988–89	1988–89	1988	1988–89	1988–89
Algeria	92	87	88	81	7	38	82	61	53	13	11	6
Egypt	87	79	–	–	3	95	–	81	71	–	20	13
Iraq	91	87	84	78	19	58	56	47	37	32	14	11
Jordan	–	–	–	–	6	84	91	–	–	8	–	–
Lebanon	–	–	–	–	–	–	–	67	56	–	28	20
Libyan Arab Jamahiriya	–	–	–	–	–	–	–	–	–	–	10	6
Morocco	64	53	55	45	15	63	61	36	30	17	11	8
Oman	95	93	83	81	11	91	86	48	40	11	4	3
Saudi Arabia	73	70	56	48	13	90	–	46	39	–	12	10
Syrian Arab Republic	100	100	97	93	7	88	72	54	45	13	20	17
Tunisia	95	93	95	90	21	79	43	44	39	17	8	6
United Arab Emirates	100	100	100	100	5	94	94	64	69	10	9	15
Yemen	–	–	–	–	–	74	–	21	12	–	2	2

Source: UNDP, *Human Development Report 1992*, pp. 154–5.

Table A7 Education imbalances, Arab countries

	Primary pupil–teacher ratio 1988	Secondary technical enrolment (as % of total secondary) 1987–88	Tertiary science enrolment (as % of tertiary) 1987–88	Third-level students abroad (as % of those home) 1987–88	Education (as % of GNP) 1960	Education (as % of GNP) 1989	Education (as % of total public expenditure) 1989	Higher education (as % of all levels) 1988	Radios (per 1,000 people) 1988–89	TVs (per 1,000 people) 1988–89	Daily newspaper circulation (per 1,000 people) 1988–89
Algeria	28	4.9	14	6.6	5.6	9.4	27.0	–	232	73	21
Egypt	30	21.8	38	1.5	4.1	6.8	–	29.8	322	98	38
Iraq	23	13.7	33	3.3	5.8	3.7	–	20.6	202	68	–
Jordan	18	8.0	–	41.4	3.0	5.9	–	32.0	252	77	53
Lebanon	–	–	45	21.3	–	–	16.8	–	834	327	97
Libyan Arab Jamahiriya	–	–	–	6.7	2.8	10.1	20.8	–	224	91	–
Morocco	26	1.4	59	13.9	3.1	7.3	25.5	–	209	70	–
Oman	27	5.1	34	–	–	3.7	12.4	13.4	645	762	45
Saudi Arabia	16	1.9	34	5.7	3.2	7.6	16.2	–	280	277	–
Syrian Arab Republic	26	6.9	31	8.8	2.0	4.1	13.1	24.0	248	59	15
Tunisia	30	13.3	31	24.5	3.3	6.3	14.8	16.8	188	75	–
United Arab Emirates	18	0.8	46	24.8	–	2.1	14.9	–	322	109	200
Yemen	–	–	12	33.2	–	6.1	21.3	3.9	74	38	16

Source: UNDP, *Human Development Report 1992*, pp. 156–7.

Table A8 Employment, Arab countries

	Labour force (as % of total population) 1990–92	Women in labour force (as % of total labour force) 1990–92	Percentage of labour force in — Agriculture 1965	1990–92	Industry 1965	1990–92	Services 1965	1990–92	Social security benefits expenditure (as % of GDP) 1985–90	Earnings per employee annual growth rate (%) 1970–80	1980–90
Algeria	23.6	4.4	57.0	18.0	17.0	33.0	26.0	49.0	–	–1.0	–
Egypt	31.0	21.0	55.0	42.0	15.0	21.0	30.0	37.0	1.1	4.1	–2.1
Iraq	24.2	5.8	50.0	14.0	20.0	19.0	30.0	67.0	–	–	–
Jordan	23.1	9.9	37.0	10.2	26.0	25.6	37.0	64.2	0.0	–	–1.1
Lebanon	30.1	27.2	29.0	14.3	24.0	27.4	47.0	58.4	1.2	–	–
Libyan Arab Jamahiriya	23.7	8.7	41.0	18.1	21.0	28.9	38.0	53.0	–	–	–
Morocco	33.0	26.0	61.0	45.6	15.0	25.0	24.0	29.4	1.5	–	–3.6
Oman	28.1	8.1	62.0	50.0	15.0	21.8	23.0	28.6	–	–	–
Saudi Arabia	29.1	7.1	68.0	48.5	11.0	14.4	21.0	37.2	–	–	–
Syrian Arab Republic	28.0	18.0	52.0	22.0	20.0	29.0	28.0	48.0	–	2.8	–5.5
Tunisia	29.8	21.0	49.0	26.0	21.0	34.0	29.0	40.0	3.6	4.2	–0.8
United Arab Emirates	49.8	6.2	21.0	4.5	32.0	38.0	47.0	57.3	–	–	–
Yemen	24.7	13.1	72.8	62.5	8.2	11.0	18.7	26.4	–	–	–

Source: UNDP, *Human Development Report 1994*, pp. 162–3.

186

Table A9 Wealth, poverty and social investment, Arab countries

	Real GDP per (PPP$) 1989	GNP per capita Total (US$) 1989	Income share of lowest 40% of households (%) 1980–88	Ratio of highest 20% to lowest 20% 1980–88	Population below poverty line Total (%) 1980–89	Population below poverty line Rural (%) 1980–89	Public expenditure on education (as % of GNP) 1989	Public expenditure on health (as % of GNP) 1987
Algeria	3,088	2,230	–	–	23	25	9.4	5.4
Egypt	1,934	640	–	–	23	25	6.8	1.1
Iraq	–	–	–	–	–	30	3.7	0.8
Jordan	2,415	1,640	–	–	15	17	5.9	2.7
Lebanon	–	–	–	–	–	15	–	–
Libyan Arab Jamahiriya	–	5,310	–	–	?	–	10.1	3.2
Morocco	2,298	880	17.1	4.0	37	45	7.3	1.0
Oman	10,573	5,220	–	–	–	6	3.7	2.2
Saudi Arabia	10,330	6,020	–	–	–	–	7.6	3.6
Syrian Arab Republic	4,348	980	–	–	–	54	4.1	0.4
Tunisia	3,329	1,260	16.3	7.8	18	15	6.3	2.2
United Arab Emirates	23,798	18,430	–	–	–	–	2.1	1.0
Yemen	–	650	–	–	–	30	6.1	1.5

Source: UNDP, *Human Development Report 1994*.

Table A10 Military expenditure and resource use imbalances, Arab countries

	Military expenditure (as % of total)		Military expenditure (as % of combined education and health expenditure)	Average annual arms imports (1989)		Armed forces	
				US$ millions	As % of national imports	Per teacher	Per physician
	1960	1990	1990	(1988–92)	1991	1990	1990
Algeria	2.1	1.9	11	199	2.6	0.5	12
Egypt	5.5	4.5	52	659	8.4	0.9	7
Iraq	8.7	23.0	271	993	–	5.7	105
Jordan	16.7	11.0	138	73	2.9	2.0	24
Lebanon	–	3.5	–	13	0.5	0.5	7
Libyan Arab Jamahiriya	1.2	7.4	71	140	2.8	1.1	15
Morocco	2.0	4.3	72	103	1.5	1.1	39
Oman	–	15.8	293	94	3.0	1.9	21
Saudi Arabia	5.7	19.8	151	1,738	6.8	0.4	4
Syrian Arab Republic	7.9	9.2	373	524	17.4	2.7	47
Tunisia	2.2	2.9	31	14	0.3	0.5	10
United Arab Emirates	–	5.4	44	413	3.0	2.1	15
Yemen	–	14.1	197	50	–	1.0	31

Source: UNDP, *Human Development Report 1994*, pp. 170–71.

Table A11 Urban crowding, Arab countries

	Urban population (as % of total)			Urban population annual growth rate (%)		Population in largest city (as % of urban)	Major city with highest population density		Population in cities of over 1 million (as % of urban)	Persons per habitable room	Houses without electricity (%)
							City	Population per km2			
	1960	1989	2000	1960–90	1990–2000	1980		1980–88	1990	1980–85	1980
Algeria	30	52	60	4.7	4.3	12	Algiers	7,930	23	2.8	–
Egypt	38	47	54	3.1	3.6	39	Cairo	29,393	52	–	54
Iraq	43	71	75	5.2	3.9	–	Baghdad	5,384	29	–	–
Jordan	43	68	74	4.5	4.2	37	Amman	11,104	38	–	–
Lebanon	40	84	87	3.8	2.5	–	–	–	–	–	–
Libyan Arab Jamahiriya	23	70	76	8.1	4.5	64	–	–	65	1.8	28
Morocco	29	48	55	4.3	3.8	26	Casablanca	12,133	36	2.4	–
Oman	4	11	15	7.5	7.5	–	–	–	–	–	–
Saudi Arabia	30	77	82	7.6	4.5	18	–	–	29	–	–
Syrian Arab Republic	37	50	56	4.5	4.6	33	–	–	60	–	–
Tunisia	36	54	59	3.6	2.7	30	–	–	37	3.1	66
United Arab Emirates	40	78	78	12.5	2.1	–	–	–	–	–	–
Yemen	9	29	37	5.8	6.2	33	–	–	–	–	–

Source: UNDP, *Human Development Report 1992*, pp. 168–9.

Table A12 Demographic change, Arab countries

	Estimated population (millions)			Annual population growth rate (%)		Ratio of population growth rate 1985–90 to 1955–60	Fertility rate 1990	Ratio of fertility rate 1990 to 1960	Contraceptive prevalence rate (%) 1985–89	Crude birth rate 1990	Crude death rate 1990	Population density (per 1,000 ha) 1990
	1960	1990	2000	1960–90	1990–2000							
Algeria	10.8	25.0	32.9	2.8	2.8	128	5.1	70	–	35	8	106
Egypt	25.9	52.4	64.2	2.4	2.0	100	4.3	61	38	33	10	543
Iraq	6.8	18.9	26.3	3.4	3.4	118	6.2	85	–	42	7	436
Jordan	1.7	4.0	5.6	2.9	3.3	103	5.8	76	26	39	6	439
Lebanon	1.9	2.7	3.3	1.3	2.1	9	3.6	57	–	31	8	2,899
Libyan Arab Jamahiriya	1.3	4.5	6.5	4.1	3.6	101	6.8	95	–	44	9	26
Morocco	11.6	25.1	31.6	2.6	2.3	94	4.5	63	36	34	9	563
Oman	0.5	1.5	2.2	3.7	3.8	182	7.1	99	–	44	7	69
Saudi Arabia	4.1	14.1	20.7	4.2	3.9	157	7.1	99	–	42	7	66
Syrian Arab Republic	4.6	12.5	17.8	3.4	3.6	130	6.5	89	20	44	6	679
Tunisia	4.2	8.2	9.9	2.2	2.0	133	3.7	53	50	29	7	526
United Arab Emirates	0.1	1.6	2.0	10.0	2.1	120	4.6	66	–	22	4	190
Yemen	5.2	11.7	16.6	2.7	3.6	171	7.5	100	–	52	15	199

Source UNDP, *Human Development Report 1992*, pp. 170–71.

Table A13 Aggregates of human development indicators, Arab states compared with Latin America and the Caribbean

	Arab States	Latin America and the Caribbean
Profile of human development		
Life expectancy		
total	62.1	67.4
female	63.6	70.2
Access to health services	76	75
Access to safe water	74	79
Access to sanitation	–	65
Calorie supply (% of requirement)	116	116
Adult literacy rate	58	84
Primary and secondary enrolment	73	84
GNP per capita	1,887	1,962
Real GDP per capita	3,593	4,514
Trends in human development		
Life expectancy		
1960	46.7	56.0
1990	62.1	67.4
Under-five mortality		
1960	271	157
1990	101	70
Access to safe water		
1975–80	–	60
1988–90	74	79
Calorie supply		
1965	92	100
1988	116	116
Adult literacy rate		
1970	34	73
1990	58	84
Primary and secondary enrolment		
1970	50	68
1988–89	73	84
Real GDP per capita		
1960	1,007	1,761
1989	3,321	4,514
Human capital formation		
Adult literacy rate		
total	58	84
male	70	86
female	46	83

Table A13   (continued)

	Arab States	Latin America and the Caribbean
Mean years of schooling		
total	3.0	5.2
male	4.1	5.3
female	1.8	5.1
Scientists and technicians	13.7	29.6
R & D scientists	–	4.1
Tertiary graduates	2.3	2.5
Science graduates	28	29
Health profile		
Access to health services	76	75
Access to safe water	74	79
Access to sanitation	–	65
Maternal mortality	320	210
People per doctor	3,720	1,230
People per nurse	960	1,020
Nurses per doctor	4.2	1.3
Public health expenditure		
1960	0.9	1.4
1987	2.1	1.8
Food production per capita	101	103
Agricultural production	12	10
Daily calories per capita	2,894	2,734
Daily calories as % of requirement	116	116
Education flows		
Primary enrolment		
total	80	87
female	71	83
Primary repeaters	9	14
Primary completers	85	47
Transition to second level	60	79
Secondary enrolment		
total	52	50
female	44	49
Secondary repeaters	21	8
Tertiary enrolment		
total	13	17
female	9	16

Table A13   (continued)

	Arab States	Latin America and the Caribbean
Education imbalances		
Primary pupil–teacher ratio	28	27
Secondary technical enrolment	15.0	16.5
Tertiary science enrolment	36	34
Tertiary students abroad	6.2	1.0
Education expenditure		
1960 (as % of GNP)	3.5	2.1
1989 (as % of GNP)	5.9	4.2
As % of total expenditure	19.1	17.9
Higher education expenditure	–	19.2
Employment		
Labour force	30.4	39.7
Women in labour force	17.4	31.8
Labour force in agriculture		
1965	63.0	44.0
1986–89	33.0	25.4
Labour force in industry		
1965	13.9	20.9
1986–89	24.0	25.0
Labour force in services		
1965	23.1	35.1
1986–89	43.0	49.9

Source: UNDP, *Human Development Report 1992,* pp. 176, 178.

Select Bibliography

Abu Nasr, Julinda, Nabil F. Khoury and Henry T. Azzam, eds. 1985. *Women, Employment, and Development in the Arab World*. Berlin, New York, Amsterdam: Mouton Publishers.

Adams, Michael, ed. 1988. *The Middle East*. New York and Oxford: Facts-on-File.

Al-Qudsi, Sulayman, Ragui Assaad and Radwan Shaban. 1993. 'Labor Markets in the Arab Countries: A Survey'. Prepared for the Initiative to Encourage Economic Research in the Middle East and North Africa, First Annual Conference on Development Economics, Cairo, 4–6 June.

Anker, Richard and Catherine Hein, eds. 1986. *Sex Inequalities in Urban Employment in the Third World*. London: Macmillan Press for the ILO.

Arab Council for Childhood and Development. 1989. *The State of the Child in the Arab World*.

Beck, Lois and Nikki R. Keddie. 1978. *Women in the Muslim World*. Cambridge, MA: Harvard University Press.

Berquist, Charles, ed. 1984. *Labor in the Capitalist World-Economy*. Beverly Hills, CA: Sage.

Blumberg, Rae Lesser. *Making the Case for the Gender Variable*. Washington DC: AID Office for Women in Development.

Centre d'Études et de Recherches Démographiques (CERED). 1989a. *Éducation et Changements Démographiques au Maroc*. Rabat: Direction de la Statistique.

——— 1989b. *Femmes et Condition Feminine au Maroc*. Rabat: Direction de la Statistique.

Chamari, Alya Chérif. 1991. *La Femme et La Loi en Tunisie*. Casablanca: Editions le Fennec for UNU/WIDER.

Charles, Maria. 1992. 'Cross-National Variation in Occupational Sex Segregation'. *American Sociological Review*, vol. 57, no. 4 (August), pp. 483–502.

Clark, Roger, Thomas Ramsbey and Emily Stier Adler. 1991. 'Culture, Gender, and Labor Force Participation: A Cross-National Study'. *Gender & Society*, vol. 5, no. 1 (March), pp. 47–66.

DeLancey, Virginia and Elweya Elwy. 1990. *Women in Agricultural Development: Rural Women and the Changing Socio-Economic Conditions in the Near East*. Rome: FAO.

Dixon, R. 1982. 'Women in Agriculture: Counting the Labour Force in Developing Countries'. *Population and Development Review*, vol. 8, no. 3, pp. 539–66.

Doan, Rebecca Miles. 1992. 'Class Differentiation and the Informal Sector in Amman, Jordan'. *International Journal of Middle East Studies*, vol. 24, no. 1 (February), pp. 27–38.

Doumato, Eleanor A. 1992. 'Gender, Monarchy, and National Identity in Saudi Arabia'. *British Journal of Middle Eastern Studies*, vol. 19, no. 1, pp. 31–47.

El-Sanabary, Nagat. 1993. 'The Middle East and North Africa'. In Elizabeth M. King and Anne M. Hill, eds. *Women's Education in Developing Countries: Barriers, Benefits, and Policies*. Baltimore: Johns Hopkins University Press for the World Bank, pp. 136–74.

Farsoun, Samih, ed. 1985. *Arab Society: Continuity and Change*. London: Croom Helm.

Fergany, Nader. 1994. *Urban Women, Work and Poverty Alleviation in Egypt*. Cairo: Almishkat Center for Research and Training (for the ILO and UNDP).

Fernea, Elizabeth, ed. 1985. *Women and the Family in the Middle East*. Austin, TX: University of Texas Press.

Hammam, Mona. 1986. 'Capitalist Development, Family Division of Labor, and Migration in the Middle East'. In Eleanor Leacock and Helen Safa, eds, *Women Work: Development and the Division of Labor by Gender*. Massachusetts: Bergin & Garvey Publishers, pp. 158–73.

Harik, Iliya and Denis J. Sullivan, eds. *Privatization and Liberalization in the Middle East*. Bloomington, IN: Indiana University Press.

Hatem, Mervat. 1983. 'Women and Work in the Middle East: The Regional Impact of Migration to the Oil Producing States'. Paper presented to the conference on Women and Work in the Third World, Berkeley, CA: University of California, April.

Hijab, Nadia. 1988. *Womanpower: The Arab Debate on Women at Work*. Cambridge: Cambridge University Press.

ILO. *Yearbook of Labour Statistics* (various years). Geneva: ILO.

Joekes, Susan. 1982. 'Female-led Industrialisation. Women's Jobs in Third World Export Manufacturing: The Case of the Moroccan Clothing Industry'. Sussex: IDS Research Reports.

—— 1985. 'Working for Lipstick? Male and Female Labour in the Clothing Industry in Morocco'. In Haleh Afshar, ed., *Women, Work and Ideology in the Third World*. London: Tavistock, pp. 183–212.

Khoury, Nabil F. and Kailas C. Doctor, eds. 1991. *Education and Employment Issues of Women in Development in the Middle East*. Nicosia: Imprinta Publishers.

Lewin-Epstein, Noah and Moshe Semyonov. 1992. 'Modernization and Subordination: Arab Women in the Israeli Labor Force'. *European Sociological Review*, vol. 8, pp. 38–51.

Longva, Anh Nga. 1993. 'Kuwaiti Women at a Crossroads: Privileged Development and the Constraints of Ethnic Stratification'. *International Journal of Middle East Studies*, vol. 25, no. 3 (August), pp. 443–56.

Mehra, Rekha, David Bruns, Paul Carlson, Geeta Rao Gupta and Margaret Lycette. 1992. *Engendering Development in Asia and the Near East: A Sourcebook*. Washington DC: International Center for Research on Women.

Mernissi, F. 1981. *Developpement Capitaliste et Perceptions des Femmes dans la Société Arabo-Musulmane: Une Illustration des Paysannes du Gharb, Maroc*. Étude de récherche préparée pour le Séminaire Régional Tripartite du BIT pour l'Afrique, La place des Femmes dans le Developpement Rural, Dakar, Sénégal, 15–19 June.

———— 1987. *Beyond the Veil: Male–Female Dynamics in Modern Muslim Society*. Indiana: Indiana University Press.

The Middle East and North Africa 1990. 1989. (36th edn) London: Europa Publishers.

Moghadam, Valentine M. 1993. *Modernizing Women: Gender and Social Change in the Middle East*. Boulder, CO: Lynne Rienner Publishers.

———— ed. 1994. *Gender and National Identity: Women and Politics in Muslim Societies*. London: Zed Books.

Niblock, Tim and Emma Murphy, eds. 1993. *Economic and Political Liberalization in the Middle East*. London: British Academic Press.

Oppenheimer, V. K. 1982. *Work and the Family: A Study in Social Demography*. New York: Academic Press.

R'chid, Abderrazak Moulay. 1991. *La Femme et La Loi au Maroc*. Casablanca: Éditions le Fennec for UNU/WIDER.

Richards, Alan, and John Waterbury. 1990. *A Political Economy of the Middle East: State, Class and Economic Development*. Boulder, CO: Westview Press.

Saadi, Nouredine. 1991. *La Femme et La Loi en Algérie*. Casablanca: Editions le Fennec for UNU/WIDER.

Shami, Seteney, et al. 1990. *Women in Arab Society: Work Patterns and Gender Relations in Egypt, Jordan and Sudan*. Providence and Paris: Berg/UNESCO.

Shannon, Thomas Richard. 1989. *An Introduction to the World-System Perspective*. Boulder, CO: Westview Press.

Shorter, F. and H. Zurayk, eds. 1985. *Population Factors in Development Planning in the Middle East*. New York: The Population Council.

Standing, Guy. 1978. *Labour Force Participation and Development*. Geneva: ILO.

Tinker, Irene, ed. 1990. *Persistent Inequalities: Women and World Development*. New York: Oxford University Press.

Turchi, Boone A., Mary T. Mulhern and Jacqueline J. Mahal. 1991. *Women's Income, Fertility and Development Policy*. GENESYS Special Studies No. 4. Washington DC. Prepared for the US AID conference on Women, Economic Growth and Demographic Change in Asia, the Near East and Eastern Europe, 14–15 May.

United Nations (UN). 1991. *The World's Women: Trends and Statistics 1970–1990*. New York: United Nations.

UNDP. *Human Development Report* (various years from 1990). New York: Oxford University Press.

UN/ESCWA. 1994a. *Arab Women in ESCWA Member States*. New York: United Nations.

———— 1994b. 'Executive Summary: Participation of Women in Manufacturing: Patterns, Determinants and Future Trends Regional Analysis, ESCWA Region'. Amman: ESCWA and UNIDO.

Ward, Kathryn, ed. 1990. *Women Workers and Global Restructuring*. Ithaca, NY: ILR Press.

Watson, Helen. 1992. *Women in the City of the Dead*. London: Hurst & Co.

About the Contributors

Martha Anker is a senior statistician at the World Health Organization in Geneva. She has an M.A. in mathematics from the University of Michigan and has written numerous journal and technical articles on health statistics and demography. She is currently involved in the development of new methodologies for evaluating health status and health services.

Richard Anker is head of the Labour Market Analysis and Information Unit at the International Labour Office in Geneva. He has a Ph.D. in Economics with a specialization in demography from the University of Michigan. He is the author of a number of books and journal articles on a wide range of topics including women and development, labour-force measurement and survey techniques, poverty monitoring, fertility and economic-demographic models.

Samih Boustani is a regular data-base consultant to UNESCO, ESCWA and the ILO, currently based in Paris. He was previously a senior statistician with the Programs Division of the Council for Development and Reconstruction in Lebanon.

Salma Galal is a community development expert with experience in diverse fields pertaining to health, women, children and communication, and is based in Cairo. She has a Ph.D. in medical sociology from the University of Hanover in Germany.

Nabil F. Khoury is a senior economist at the International Labour Organization. He is presently the Director of the ILO Multidisciplinary

Advisory Team for Arab States. He has a Ph.D. in Economics from the Sorbonne in Paris. He is the author/editor of a number of books in labour economics and human resources development.

Helen Lackner is a sociologist with specialization in rural women's development programmes, agricultural extension and participatory research, based in London. She worked as a consultant to FAO, UN, World Bank and the ILO. She has an M.Sc. in the sociology of developing countries from the London School of Economics.

Valentine M. Moghadam has been with UNU/WIDER in Helsinki since 1990 as Senior Research Fellow and coordinator of the research programme on women and development. Born in Iran, she studied in Canada and the United States, earning a doctorate in sociology in 1986. She is the author of *Modernizing Women: Gender and Social Change in the Middle East* and many journal articles, and has edited several books.

Nada Mufarrej is an economist with specialization in applied macroeconomics. She is currently with the Council for Development and Reconstruction in Lebanon, involved in monitoring World Bank projects.

Hussein Shakhatreh is a senior demographer and statistician at the Ministry of Planning in Amman, Jordan. He is presently the Director of the Department of Human Resources Planning. He has a Ph.D. in population planning from the University of Michigan.

Huda C. Zurayk is a senior associate at the Population Council Regional Office for West Asia and North Africa in Cairo. She is presently visiting professor at the American University of Beirut. She has a Ph.D. in biostatistics from the Johns Hopkins University.

Fadia Saadeh is a senior demographer at the World Bank in Washington DC. She worked as a lecturer at the American University in Beirut. She has a Ph.D. in population dynamics from Johns Hopkins University.

Index